CLASSIC

HIKES

of the

WORLD

CLASSIC
HIKES
of the
WORLD

23 Breathtaking Treks

With detailed routes and
maps for expeditions on
six continents

PETER POTTERFIELD

W. W. NORTON & COMPANY
NEW YORK · LONDON

First Edition

For information about permission to reproduce selections from this book, write to
Permissions, W. W. Norton & Company, Inc., 500 Fifth Avenue, New York, NY 10110

The text of this book is composed in Adobe Caslon, with Univers Condensed and Knockout
Production manager: Diane O'Connor
Book design: BTDNYC
Cover photograph by Peter Potterfield in Buckskin Gulch, Utah

LIBRARY OF CONGRESS CATALOGING-IN-PUBLICATION DATA

Potterfield, Peter.
   Classic hikes of the world : 23 breathtaking treks with detailed routes and maps for
expeditions on six continents / Peter Potterfield ; with photographs by the author.—1st ed.
      p. cm.
   Includes index.
   ISBN 0-393-05796-8 (hardcover)
   1. Hiking—Guidebooks. I. Title.
   GV199.5.P68 2005
   796.51—dc22

                                                                    2004026046

W. W. Norton & Company, Inc., 500 Fifth Avenue, New York, N.Y. 10110
www.wwnorton.com

W. W. Norton & Company Ltd., 10 Coptic Street, London WC1A 1PU

4 5 6 7 8 9 0

For my wife, Anne

Into the Grand Canyon via the South Kaibab trail. PHOTO BY JIM NELSON.

CONTENTS

Acknowledgments 8

Introduction 9

One: North America 12

JOHN MUIR TRAIL
Southern California, United States 14

GRAND CANYON
Northern Arizona, United States 26

CHESLER PARK
Southern Utah, United States 38

MAROON BELLS CIRCUIT
South-central Colorado, United States 46

BUCKSKIN GULCH
Southern Utah, United States 54

THE WONDERLAND TRAIL
Washington, United States 62

DIABLO LAKE TO LAKE CHELAN
Washington, United States 74

WHITE MOUNTAIN TRAVERSE
New Hampshire, United States 82

McGONAGALL PASS
Alaska, United States 90

WEST COAST TRAIL
British Columbia, Canada 100

THE ROCKWALL TRAIL
Yoho and Kootenay National Parks
Alberta and British Columbia, Canada 108

Two: South America 114

FITZ ROY GRAND TOUR
Argentine Patagonia 116

TORRES DEL PAINE CIRCUIT
Chilean Patagonia 124

Three: Europe 132

KUNGSLEDEN
Lapland, Arctic Sweden 134

TOUR DE LA VANOISE GLACIERS
French Alps, France 142

WEST HIGHLAND WAY
Scotland, United Kingdom 150

Four: Africa 158

MOUNT KILIMANJARO
Tanzania, East Africa 160

Five: Asia 168

BALTORO GLACIER TO K2 BASE CAMP
Baltistan, Pakistan 170

EVEREST BASE CAMP TREK
Nepal Himalaya 178

ROYAL TREK
Annapurna Region, Nepal 188

Six: Pacific 196

KALALAU TRAIL
Kauai, Hawaii, United States 198

ROUTEBURN TRACK
South Island, New Zealand 204

Seven: Antarctic Region 212

SHACKLETON CROSSING
South Georgia Island, South Atlantic Ocean 214

INDEX 222

ACKNOWLEDGMENTS

I am in debt to my editor, John Barstow, for his patience, skill, and foolproof instincts, and to Helen Whybrow, who suggested I was the right guy for the book. Of the many people who helped me complete this project, some truly went above and beyond the call of duty, or even friendship: Alberto del Castillo, Ann Obenchain, James Martin, Jim Nelson, Bob Farrington, Todd Burleson, Gordon Janow, Eric Simonson, Annika Benjes, Pia Harjemo, Putte Eby, Yvonne Niva, Birgitta Jansson, Simone Flight, Kirstie Bedford, Lucy Powell, Brad Monaghan, Chris Birt, Jackie Davidson, Candy Aluli, Laura Beemer, Emele Cox, Mike Gauthier, Kelly Bush, R. J. Secor, Colin Simpson, Johanna Campbell, Charles Corfield, Brian Okonek, Colby Coombs, Mike Wood, Daryl Miller, Jiban Ghimire, Lakpa Rita Sherpa, Bill Davis, Dave Hahn, Matthew Swait, Gigi de Young, Coral Darby, Greg Mortenson, Nazir Sabir, Ashraf Aman, Allen Carbert, Ed Viesturs, David Schiefelbein, Burns Petersen, Monica Campbell-Hoppe, Richard J. Bailey, Tina Norris, Elaine Goldsmith, Judy Armstrong, Judith Tewson, Roger Hostin, Martin Fuhrer, Jake Norton, Pat O'Hara, Keith Gunnar, and Eugene Toomey.

Breakfast on the slickrock of Canyonlands. PHOTO BY PETER POTTERFIELD.

INTRODUCTION

I am awakened at Dingboche by a sound drifting in from the edges of consciousness, soothing and exotic, but not identifiable. As sleep fades, my oxygen-starved brain grinds on toward lucidity, and finally recognition: yak bells. The mellow, muted peeling of the bells rings out as the shaggy beasts forage among the sparse vegetation near our tents. At more than fourteen thousand feet above sea level, I think, the wooly creatures that carry our loads will find precious little to eat here. But the bells are a gentle wake-up call in a strange land, and a reminder I am deep within an outrageous landscape and a profoundly different culture.

Lying inside the tent among the billowy folds of nylon and down, I relish the warmth, and the moment. Ahead is another day of wonder in the heart of the Himalaya. Dingboche is a cluster of sturdily built stone houses and walled fields stretching along a narrow valley. The village manages to be austere yet idyllic at the same time. It's high and open, but protected within its ring of hills. This part of Nepal, the Khumbu, is named for the glacier that tumbles down the flanks of nearby Mount Everest—Sagarmatha to the locals—and it lies near the heart of the ancestral home of the Sherpa people. There is a low bustle of activity in the village, and the laughter of children carries on the wind to our cluster of tents.

We've been here a few days already, acclimating to the higher elevations beyond, and will spend a few more days yet. After other journeys in more obscure parts of the range, this time I'm off to Everest, in the congenial company of a small band of climbers and scientists and Sherpa. Everest base camp is just two or three days' walk up the valley and on to the moraine. But the pace of life in the Himalaya is measured, and patience a virtue for the pilgrim, especially here, where altitude slows progress.

For acclimatization I wander among the windswept, treeless slopes above the village. High on the hill above our camp are two big spooky stupas, ancient, weathered, and wild. Prayer flags, bleached and ragged from the elements, whip around in the wind, snapping and popping, sending their supplications skyward. The Buddha's eyes, a familiar religious icon, are painted on the gray flanks of the structures in an eerie indigo pigment, faded and wind blasted. The old stupas seem ineffably mystical, yet somehow satisfying. They remind me of a promise made to myself, a promise to spend time in the places that remain wild, to see the beauty of a natural world.

My first backcountry forays were made decades ago, in the early 1970s, to places much closer to home. Into the mountains of Shenandoah National Park, the hills of western Massachusetts, and soon into the bigger wildernesses of the Rockies and the Sierra, I trudged in heavy hiking boots under the backbreaking load of my bulging Co-op Cruiser external-frame pack. I loved it from the beginning, despite the self-inflicted agonies that resulted from my rookie decisions on what to carry and how to go. One could live comfortably, I learned with real amazement, in the wilderness, and see wonders, and feel free. An overnight backpack could put me back in touch with the sun and moon and stars, and the earthy, uplifting challenges of moving on foot through the wilderness, on trail and off. If there's been a surprise these past thirty years, it's that I enjoy backcountry travel now more than I ever have.

Classic Hikes of the World is the result of an adult lifetime spent loving wilderness travel. I'm pretty good at it by now, and can move through the backcountry with lighter loads but greater comfort than ever. And I've gotten better at figuring out where to go. When I realized early on that there were more great wilderness places than one could see in a lifetime, I understood the need to prioritize. The hikes in this volume reflect that awareness of limited opportunity. These are the routes I think bring the greatest returns on time and effort and expense—at least so far. I'm still looking.

People ask me: What are your favorite hikes? I used to struggle with a reply until I realized the truth: They are all my favorites. How does one compare, say, flying to Las Vegas, driving for five hours to the Grand Canyon, and spending four days in the embrace of that wonder with, say, driving to Mount Rainier to spend four days on the wild north side? Can one rate a trip to exotic Kathmandu followed by two weeks in the Khumbu district ahead, or behind, a journey to Argentina and a glorious week roaming the hills east of Fitz Roy? I don't see how.

What I can see, however, is that getting out in any of these wild places, whether close to home or far away, is one of the best things we can do with the time we are given. I'm no wilderness snob, either. If you can't do one of these hikes, do one of the local favorites near your place. But I have worked to make this book not just a collection of appealing destinations, but a utilitarian one, because I've learned from long experience that good information can make any wilderness excursion more fun. But reliable information can be hard to come by.

When I first heard word-of-mouth reports from international travelers of Kungsleden, the 250-mile (400 km) route through the wilds of Arctic Sweden, I was intrigued. But I was also stopped cold. All my attempts to find out what it was, much less how to do it, were frustrated. The few cryptic references I found to Kungsleden were all in Swedish, and so were not much help. I finally just packed up and went to take a look, and that's how I learned where it is and what it's like and the best way to do it. For Kungsleden and the other routes I've done, *Classic Hikes of the World* offers the benefit of that experience.

The difficulties I faced learning the practical realities of hiking Kungsleden—or New Zealand's incomparable Routeburn Track, or the trek to Everest base camp, or the magical length of Buckskin Gulch—colored the way I approached the descriptions in each chapter. I hoped to achieve just a couple of things: to share my enthusiasm for these wonderful hikes and to provide practical and useful information about how to go about doing them. It was my intention that any fit hiker could do most of the routes in *Classic Hikes of the World* with nothing more than the information in this book and a good topographic map.

HOW TO USE THIS BOOK

While the hiking routes described in *Classic Hikes of the World* have tremendous variety of terrain and character, each chapter in the book has uniform elements that make it easy to compare one hike to another.

Each write up begins with a short, **bold-faced block** of pertinent information. This, at a glance, provides a thumbnail overview for each hike: distance, average number of days required to complete the route, a subjective rating of the physical effort required and psychological challenge encountered, and, finally, the best location from which to stage for the route.

The number of days recommended for each hike represents a range that reflects the likely time spent on the trail. The low end of the range is the number of days usually required by a fit hiker moving reasonably fast; the high end of the range is what's required for a hiker of average fitness taking time to relish the experience.

Physical challenge is presented on a scale of 1 to 5. Hikes at the low end of the scale, such as the Routeburn Track, are there because the time spent on the trail each day is less than six hours, and elevation gain, trail condition, and other factors are moderate. Hikes at the high end of the scale, such as the hike along the Na Pali Coast on the Kalalau Trail, are rated high because of long days, typically problematic weather conditions due to heat and or rain, and extremely difficult trail conditions. Other hikes, such as the trek to Mount Everest base camp, are rated difficult because even though the stages might not be much longer than those on the Routeburn, the effects of altitude raise the level of difficulty dramatically.

The rating for psychological challenge, also on a scale of 1 to 5, reflects the more subtle aspects of a given hike that nonetheless can have a significant impact on one's experience. For instance, hiking in New Zealand is relaxing and enjoyable. There are no carnivorous animals to worry about, the track is well marked, eliminating route-finding anxieties, and huts encountered daily offer shelter and company. For these reasons, the Routeburn deserves as low a rating for psychological challenge as it is high for appeal. Hiking from Wonder Lake to McGonagall Pass, on the other hand, comes with unusual elements, such as dangerous river crossings and unpredictable grizzly bears. These features add stress and uncertainty, which calls for the highest rating for psychological challenge. The trek to K2 base camp can be extremely trying to one's psyche: Frightening roads, cultural disorientation, frequently exacerbated by altitude sickness, can weigh on one's spirit far beyond whatever physical efforts are required to get there.

Staging is meant to offer a helpful suggestion, based on my experience, on the best place to prepare for the route in question. Some are obvious: Moab, Utah, is best for Chesler Park; Kiruna, Sweden, the best choice for Kungsleden. In some cases, I've provided a choice: for the Maroon Bells Circuit, tony Aspen is easiest, and closest, but many people find less expensive Glenwood Springs to be more comfortable; for Buckskin Gulch, you can set up in either Kanab, Utah, or Page, Arizona; they are nearly equidistant from the trailhead.

Beyond the informative copy block, the hike descriptions have additional common elements:

Each chapter begins with a brief overview of the hike, noting its appeal and unique features, along with some historical notes. Then comes a more thorough discussion of logistics and strategy that helps provide a feel for how to get where you need to go, where to buy what you need in the way of food or fuel, where to start a given route, and how to incorporate available variations, if any, into your plans. Every hike has its own unique circumstances; some are complicated, some are not. For the Grand Canyon, is it best to walk rim to rim and take a shuttle van back, or hike rim to rim to rim? For Vancouver Island's West Coast Trail, how do you get to the trailhead way out there on a remote coast, and how do you get back from the opposite end? For the Tour de la Vanoise Glaciers, how best do you get to the starting point at Pralognan, and where do you stay along the route? These kinds of practical considerations of transport, supply, and accommodation are discussed in this section.

Following logistics is a section on the **hazards**, if any, one might expect to encounter, and how to prepare yourself. Another short section follows providing information on the best **time of year** to do the route, which can be more complicated than you might expect. For instance, it may be that July and August have statistically the best weather for a hike of Mount Rainier's Wonderland Trail. But that, predictably, is also when the Rainier backcountry sees its heaviest use, so one faces increased competition for campsites and hiking

Near the end of his 62-mile (100 km) solo journey through the Arctic of northern Sweden, the author encountered Swedish photographer Pär Axelstjerna, who took this portrait near Kebnekaise.

permits. For those reasons, hiking in early or late season may turn out to be the smart choice.

Finally comes the heart of the book: the **route description**. Rather than a cryptic or abbreviated note on where the route goes, these route descriptions are meant to be useful, advising you in some detail on the correct route, potential trouble spots, recommended camps, detours around predictable obstacles, and particularly strenuous or potentially dangerous trail sections.

Each chapter concludes with practical information to plan for the hike: current address, telephone number, and Web information for the appropriate management agency or permit issuer, and, where applicable, guide services, shuttle services, resupply points, and other appropriate service providers.

But the really important information on how best to use this book is simply to do it. Use it as a practical guide or as an inspiration. Take a walk in the wilderness. See the quality of light in the evening, get your heart rate up on the steep sections, feel the wind against your face. Look out over that canyon, or that mountain, or that coastline, and remember again how a landscape with nothing in it but the earth can revitalize you.

One

NORTH AMERICA

JOHN MUIR TRAIL
Sierra Nevada

*Southern California,
United States*

DISTANCE: **220 miles (354 km) one-way**
TIME: **18–24 days**
PHYSICAL CHALLENGE: **1 2 3 4 5**
PSYCHOLOGICAL CHALLENGE: **1 2 3 4 5**
STAGING: **Lone Pine, or Yosemite National Park, California**

W hile the John Muir Trail officially runs for 210 miles (338 km) from the summit of Mount Whitney to Happy Isles in Yosemite Valley, it's really a 222-mile (357 km) route when you figure the mileage from Whitney to the nearest trailhead. This legendary trail travels through what many consider the most inspiring terrain available to backpackers in North America. In the long course of its winding route, the trail flanks granite peaks over 13,000 and even 14,000 feet (4,000–4,300 m) high, skirts mountain lakes large and small, traverses high, rugged basins, and passes over verdant meadows and through forested valleys. The trail travels the length of three national parks, one national monument, and two wilderness areas.

Much of the trail's appeal lies in the weather. Once you've been there, it's hard to think about the Sierra in summer without the memory of blue skies and bright sunshine, day after day. Even though the occasional thunderstorm can be inconvenient, even unnerving, it won't last long enough to present real problems. This combination of frequently perfect weather, high altitude, and scenic backcountry makes the allure of the Muir Trail patently irresistible to wilderness travelers.

The route is long, but not difficult. Big elevation days and a few potentially dangerous river crossings don't change the fact the trail in general is reasonable and without route-finding problems. The great length, however, makes it problematic for hikers to take sufficient time and organize the logistics to do the whole thing in one go. The alternative is to

PRECEDING SPREAD: *Grand Canyon North Rim.* PHOTO BY JAMES MARTIN.

RIGHT: *The Minarets from Lake Ediza.* PHOTO BY JAMES MARTIN.

experience the JMT in sections, or to visit it via loop trips. For that, you need to know where to get on and where to get off.

While many are drawn to the JMT, the country through which it meanders is so vast that one doesn't feel the pressure of crowds. One week in late June, I was camped at Palisade Lakes, a famously scenic spot, for two days. A few hikers walked by, but that was all. To my amazement, no other party made camp. Even in Yosemite's Tuolumne Meadows, by moving our camp above Cathedral Pass to the flanks of Tressider Peak, we not only got a better view of Cathedral Peak but left everyone else below. If you stick to the route, you're definitely going to meet people coming the other way, but the hike along the Muir Trail also provides opportunity for solitude.

The trail, appropriately, bears the name of wilderness lover John Muir, who founded the Sierra Club in 1892. Muir lobbied for the route because he believed the more people who went to the Sierra, the more would grow to love the mountains and the safer the Sierra would be from human exploitation. Though he died before it was built, Muir's efforts resulted in the California legislature's appropriation in 1915 of the money necessary to start work. Parts of the trail were finished within years, but it was not until 1938—the centennial of Muir's birth—that the final portions were built over Mather and Forester Passes, finally connecting Yosemite with Mount Whitney by trail.

Quieter, less scenic sections separate spectacular climaxes along the route. Personal favorites will differ, but it's hard to argue about highlights such as the Whitney group. Even if you don't hike up to the top of the highest mountain in the contiguous 48 states, this is a staggering mountain environment. Sprawling Rae Lakes, lined up one after the other in their golden meadow, are well worth the effort it takes to get there. My personal favorite is the area beneath the dramatic Palisades Peaks, from Mather Pass to Evolu-

tion Basin. Farther north, Thousand Island Lake and the Tuolumne high country stand out, while at the conclusion of the route in Yosemite Valley, classic waterfalls apply the finishing touch.

LOGISTICS & STRATEGY

Whether you're planning a through-hike or a five- to eight-day excursion, a wilderness permit is required. For the Whitney region (Lone Pine Lake to Crabtree Meadows), you need a permit even if you're only day hiking. At the Yosemite end, permits are obtained through the Yosemite Association, which grants them up to 24 weeks in advance. At the Mount Whitney end, you'll need to apply to the private contractor working with Inyo National Forest. In 2003, this office opened for permits on February 15 for the following season, but this is a new system, so expect changes.

The best access to the southern end of the JMT is without question via Whitney Portal, out of Lone Pine, a fact that puts this permit in high demand. Apply early so you can avoid having to use alternatives approaches, such as New Army Pass or Kearsarge Pass, from the east, or the much longer routes from the west. *All* the entrances to the southern end of the Muir Trail from the east have strenuous first days; it's just the nature of the beast. Working up out of the Owens Valley to the crest of the Sierra is hot, dry work. Options from the west aren't really practical, with perhaps one exception: You can drive from Fresno to the Cedar Grove trailhead, and from there hike up Bubb's Creek to access Vidette Meadow. That approach requires about a day and a half, so it's a reasonable way in, but you miss the Whitney group.

Whitney Portal, then, is the best option, so consider obtaining the permit part of the challenge of doing the JMT, and be diligent. Once you've got your permit, you're ready to go. There are great opportunities for side trips, or

Painted Lady at Upper Rae Lakes. PHOTO BY JAMES MARTIN.

even cross-country travel. Using various entrances and exits to the trail and sections of Steve Roper's off-trail high route, the Muir Trail can be a key component of many exceptional Sierra adventures.

You are free to camp in most places on the route as long as you camp 100 feet (30 m) from a trail or any stream. There are areas where camping is prohibited, such as that near Mount Whitney and around scenic Shadow Lake, but not as many as you would think. Just where you camp will be influenced by multiple factors, not the least of which is the location of bear boxes.

Bears are a big problem on the JMT, and throughout the Sierra. In many areas, bear-resistant food containers are required, and hefty fines are levied on those who don't comply. The containers keep the bears from becoming even

OPPOSITE: FAR LEFT: *Approaching the southern end of the John Muir Trail from the east, through classic Eastern Sierra flora and fauna.* PHOTO BY PETER POTTERFIELD.

NEAR LEFT: *Polemonium (sky pilot) growing in a protected niche at 13,000 feet (3,962 m) on Mount Whitney.* PHOTO BY JAMES MARTIN.

more habituated to robbing hikers. Bear boxes—big metal boxes like those found in campgrounds at Yosemite, fixed in place onto a concrete slab—are a fairly recent development. They are totally bombproof, and you can fit all your food and toiletries easily. You'll grow to like them, even to the point where their presence becomes a persuasive argument to camp in a well-used spot with boxes, rather than seek out a place with more solitude but no boxes.

Back in the days when counter-balanced food bags hung high in trees were the recommended anti-bear measure, I was camped in Lyell Canyon when ten days worth of food (delicious stuff, purchased carefully in San Francisco) was devoured in a few minutes by a bear. Fortunately I could hike out to Tuolumne Meadows and buy more food, even if it didn't compare to what I lost. Imagine the pickle you would be in if all your food was eaten a week from a resupply point.

How to replenish your food along the route is a major consideration. While the exceptionally athletic backpacker might complete the trail is as little as ten or twelve days without a resupply, most through-hikers will take about twice that long. Three weeks allows for a few rest days to savor the best camps, but it means about two resupply stops.

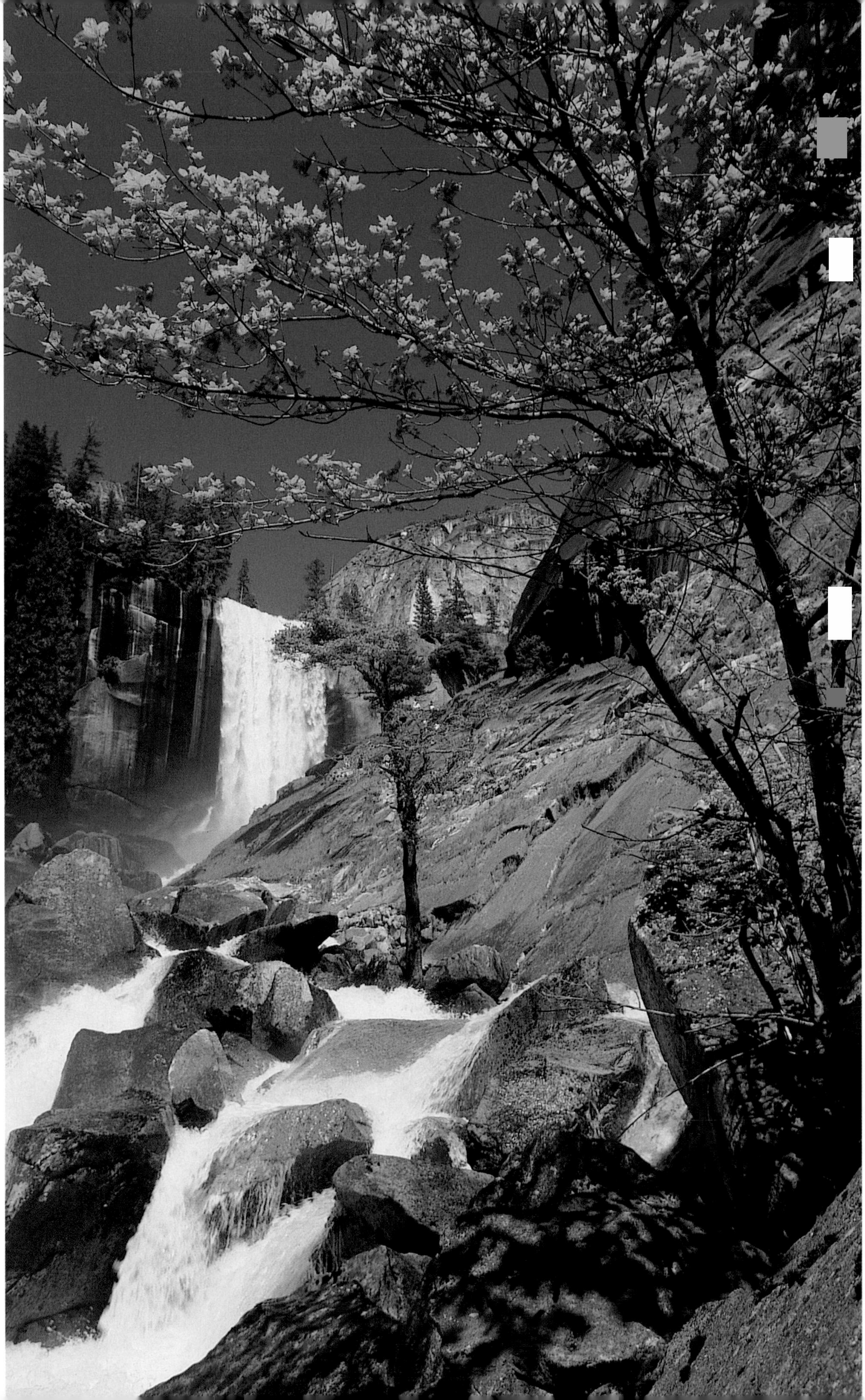

Getting on and off the JMT is no easy matter: Most of the approaches from the east are steep, hot, and strenuous, while those from the west are gentler but too long to be practical. The potential resupply points right on the trail are:

• **Tuolumne Meadows,** 24 miles (39 km) from Yosemite Valley and 196 (316 km) from Whitney Portal, where there's a well-stocked store and post office that will hold your package.
• **Reds Meadow Resort,** 163 miles (262 km) from Whitney Portal, 57 miles (92 km) from Yosemite. The store here will hold a package for you for a small fee, but you have to drop it off; they won't accept one that comes in the mail.
• **Muir Trail Ranch,** at the Florence Lake Trail, about 110 miles (177 km) from either terminus. A few miles off the JMT takes you to this resort that will hold a package for a fee.
• **The Vermillion Valley Resort,** at the Lake Edison Trail, 88 miles (142 km) from Yosemite, 140 (255 km) from Whitney Portal. A ferry ride across Lake Edison, or a 5-mile hike, takes you to this hiker-friendly resort that will hold a package for a fee.

Those limited opportunities mean you're probably going to have to hike out to replenish your stores at least once. Assuming south-to-north travel, the best opportunity is probably going to be via Bishop Pass to the town of Bishop. At 85 miles (137 km) from Whitney Portal, follow the 12-mile (19 km) Bishop Pass Trail through Dusy Basin and down to South Lake, where you can call a trailhead shuttle company to pick you up or have friends meet you with supplies. New enterprises, such as one llama packing service that meets you on the trail, deserve investigation.

For resupply, other recommended exits off the trail include, from the south:

• **Kearsarge Pass,** 42 miles (68 km) from Whitney Portal
• **Bishop Pass,** 85 miles (137 km) from Whitney Portal
• **Mammoth Pass from Crater Meadow,** where there are two short routes that can get you to Mammoth Lakes, California, at 156 and 157 miles (251 and 253 km) from Whitney Portal
• **Devils Postpile,** 162 miles (261 km) from Whitney Portal, where a short route leads to a road and from there to Mammoth Mountain Resort or to Mammoth Lakes, California

An efficient way for fit hikers to crank the trail with just one real resupply stop requires only that you be able to carry

seven to ten days' worth of food and can complete the route in 20 days. Start at Tuolumne Meadows (or stash the first half of your food there and hike up from the Muir Trail start in Yosemite Valley with just a few days' worth). From Tuolumne, hike south, reaching hiker friendly Vermillion Valley Resort on Lake Edison in seven to ten days. Pick up the second half of your food there and hike down to Whitney Portal in another seven to ten days.

Resupply points can also serve as exit and entry points you can use to hike the JMT in sections. There are dozens of options allowing access to short, scenic sections of the trail; two of the more popular ones are:

• **Tuolumne Meadows to Mammoth Lakes:** Pick up the JMT at the Tuolumne Meadows store on CA 120, hike south through Lyell Canyon, over Donohue Pass, and past Thousand Island Lake about 30 miles (48 km) to the intersection with the Shadow Lake Trail. From there hike out to Agnew Meadows or the Devils Postpile Road, and then out via shuttle bus to Mammoth Mountain Ski Area or the town Mammoth Lakes.
• **Kearsarge Pass to Bishop Pass:** Hike over Kearsarge Pass (a high, relatively short access to the trail) to the JMT, then north past Charlotte Lake to Rae Lakes and the Upper Basin, on to Palisade Lakes, into Le Conte Canyon, then to Dusy Basin and out via Bishop Pass to the trailhead at South Lake. This is a great week-long trip, with 8 miles (13 km) from the trailhead for Kearsage Pass at Onion Valley to the JMT, 43 miles (69 km) on the JMT, and 12 miles (19 km) out to South Lake via Bishop Pass.

Another good way to sample parts of the JMT is to do loop hikes that join the JMT for some of their length. When doing these loop hikes you'll rack up more mileage getting to the JMT than hiking on it, but that's okay because you still get to see the country. One of the better ones is the Rae Lakes Loop, which starts from the west side, above Fresno, California. Start at the Cedar Grove trailhead in Kings Canyon National Park, hike up Bubb's Creek to Vidette Meadow, up to Rae Lakes, and return via Paradise Valley. This is a great 43-mile (69 km) trip with very little backtracking.

HAZARDS

Bears are troublesome and potentially dangerous. Some campgrounds have sturdy bear boxes in which to store food, in others a bear-resistant food container is required. Hikers should expect that bear-resistant containers might soon be required all along the trail.

Consistent good weather makes sunburn and dehydration potential problems, so wear a really big hat and use a hydration system.

OPPOSITE: *Vernal Falls and the Merced River, near the northern end of the John Muir Trail.* PHOTO BY GORDON WILTSIE.

SEASON

Summer in the Sierra is usually gloriously sunny, with only thunderstorms or weak systems to cloud the blue skies. July to September is generally considered the best time to hike the JMT, but the season will vary depending on the previous winter's snowfall. Snow in the passes is the issue. Expect to be hiking on snow at the higher passes in July and sometimes even in August. Hiking into October is often feasible, as snow usually doesn't fall until the end of the month, but by then you're pressing your luck.

ROUTE

The trailhead at Whitney Portal is 13 steep road miles (21 km) west of the small town of Lone Pine, California. You can get to Lone Pine via Los Angeles, but the best access is through Reno, Nevada. From there, it is a four- to five-hour drive down US Highway 395 to Lone Pine.

At the end of the Whitney Portal Road is a campground, parking lots, restrooms, water source, and a store that rents bear-resistant food containers. The trail starts next to the store at 8,360 feet (2,550 m) and begins its ascent toward the Sierra Crest. Lone Pine Creek, at 3 miles (5 km), may be the first water; the last reliable water is at

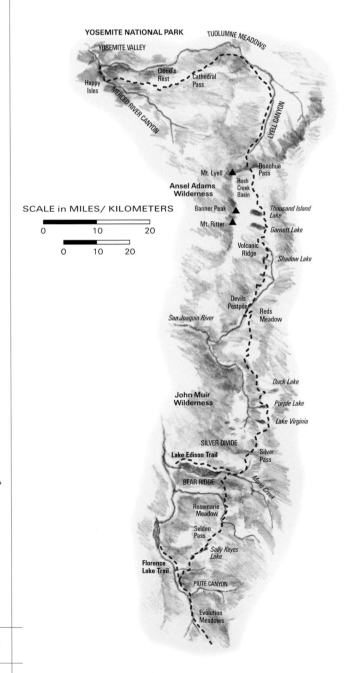

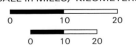

Looking toward Mount Tyndall from below Forester Pass in Sequoia National Park. PHOTO BY JAMES MARTIN.

Trail Camp, at 12,000 feet (3,660 m), 6 miles (9½ km) from the start. Switchbacks work up the final steep, 600 feet (180 m) to Trail Crest, the true gateway to the High Sierra. The view here takes in the Great Western Divide, and Hitchcock Lakes below, which may still have ice in August. The Whitney Portal Trail descends steeply to intersect the John Muir Trail 11 miles (18 km) from the trailhead. From the intersection, you have two choices: the JMT goes up and right 2 miles (3 km) to the summit of Mount Whitney at 14,495 feet (4,419 km), or down and left 208 miles (335 km) to Yosemite Valley.

Going north, the JMT heads down through wild and awesome Hitchcock Basin to Hitchcock and Guitar Lakes. The little tarn west of Consolation Lake is the last legal spot to camp (there's no camping at Guitar or Hitchcock), otherwise you have to go all the way to Crabtree Meadows (ranger station), at 6 miles (9½ km) from the JMT trail intersection, a very nice camp in a large meadow.

Crabtree to Forester Pass is mellow travel on a high plateau split by a major north-south fault. From Crabtree, the JMT winds past Sandy Meadow and Wallace Creek, and up onto the Bighorn Plateau, one of the neat places on this stretch of trail, with views over to the Kaweahs. Tyndall Creek Camp (ranger station), 11 miles (18 km) from Crabtree, makes a good campsite.

As you travel from the Bighorn up to Forester Pass, 5 miles (8 km) from Tyndall Creek, you'll find yourself entering rugged country. The basin on the south side of the pass is austere, rocky, and wild. The cool thing up here is looking at the peaks of the Kings Kern Divide—Jordan, Geneva, Ericsson, and Junction—as you cross the divide itself, and the great uprising of the Whitney group to the south. In the meantime, you're passing other near-14,000-foot (4,300 m) peaks, such as Williamson, Barnard, and Tyndall. This is some of the highest country in the Sierra, and this stretch of trail is wild and ultrascenic.

Dusy Basin nestles below Bishop Pass, a day off the John Muir Trail, and a popular resupply route for through-hikers. PHOTO BY PETER POTTERFIELD.

When you cross Forester Pass—at 13,120 feet (4,000 m) the highest point on the entire route—you leave Sequoia and enter Kings Canyon National Park. North of Forester the trail covers several miles of high, treeless basin until you drop down to 11,000 feet (3,350 m), where there's a couple of little sites you can nestle in to if you want to camp. But most people keep going down into the forest, to Center Basin Cutoff and some decent camps about 4 miles (6 km) from Forester Pass. The 5 miles (8 km) from Center Basin Cutoff to Vidette Meadow is open and pleasant in late season, but mosquito hell in June and July.

After Vidette Meadow comes the long, dry 3-mile (5 km) hump up to Glen Pass at 11,980 feet (3,652 km). From the pass, above Charlotte Lake (ranger station), you can look down to Charlotte Dome and the panorama of the Great Western Divide. The view is dominated by Mount Brewer, to the south, standing on its own. Continue on the JMT 5 miles (8 km) from Vidette Meadow and you arrive at Rae Lakes (ranger station), one of the jewels of the Sierra: open forest and meadow dotted with beautiful lakes and unique rocky peaks, such as Fin Dome. The lakes follow in succession for several miles until you get to the turnoff for Baxter Pass, another one of the exit/entrance points to the JMT, but one you don't want to consider as it's very strenuous.

A word about access: Between Baxter Pass and Whitney Portal, Kearsarge Pass is by far the easiest. Shepherd Pass is long, and perhaps the hardest of the popular passes. Taboose Pass and Sawmill Pass are two exit/entry options north of Baxter, both very much in the mold of Baxter, perhaps even more physically demanding. They are not recommended.

Beyond Rae Lakes, to the north, the country drops down below 9,000 feet (2,750 m) and changes from the rugged, classic High Sierra. Now you're in the Woods Creek drainage, where the campsites have bear boxes. After crossing a big suspension bridge the JMT heads down a canyon to intersect with the Paradise Valley Trail. The JMT turns northeast up toward Pinchot Pass, scenic and high at 12,100 feet (3,689 m). Lake Marjorie is on the other side. So after a brief foray down low you're right back in the high country. The Taboose Pass Trail intersection is 4 miles (6 km) from Pinchot Pass, from there drop down to cross the South Fork of the Kings River. Here you enter the lower end of the Upper Basin, portal to the Palisades, the second big group of impressive peaks after Whitney. Split Mountain is the first 14,000-foot (4,300 m) peak since Williamson. There are good campsites after you cross the South Fork.

The Upper Basin leads up to 12,080-foot (3,683 m) Mather Pass, the official entry into the Palisades and Evolution Basin, two of the great highlights of the JMT, 5 miles (8 km) from the Taboose Pass

RIGHT: *Backpackers' camp at Palisade Lakes on the John Muir Trail, looking south toward the peaks at Mather Pass.* PHOTO BY PETER POTTERFIELD.

Six days in and heading north, the author catches up on notes.
PHOTO BY JAMES MARTIN.

Trail. Once over Mather Pass, there's good camping at Palisade Lakes, just 4 miles (6 km) north. From Palisade Lakes, the JMT follows the Palisades Creek drainage down to the Middle Fork of the Kings River at the southern end of Le Conte Canyon, down near 9,000 feet (2,750 m).

Le Conte Canyon is a deep valley, quite rugged, with the river dancing down in one waterfall after another. Ten miles (16 km) from Palisade Lakes you come to the Bishop Pass Trail intersection in Le Conte Canyon (ranger station). This trail leads to a pretty good entry/exit point via Dusy Basin and Bishop Pass to the South Lake trailhead. Some say Dusy Basin is worth the side trip. From Le Conte Canyon you find yourself heading back into high country as you go through Big Pete Meadow and approach Muir Pass. As you climb up to the pass at 11,955 feet (3,645 m), 7 miles (11 km) from Bishop Pass Trail, there are big lakes and big basins everywhere.

Once over Muir Pass, the country is even more impressive as you drop down into Evolution Basin, one of the outstanding places in the Sierra, and the third great cluster of peaks encountered on the JMT. All around you are big mountains, very close: Darwin, Mendel, The Hermit, and Spencer. There's a peninsula that goes in to Wanda Lake, an actual dome that is an unreal place to hang out and take in this remarkable basin. Evolution Lake itself, 5 miles (8 km) below, just before you get into forest, is especially nice because it's not as rocky, and yet still outrageously beautiful. Once in Evolution Valley, you drop down out of the high country and into the forest. Here are some exceptionally pretty meadows, McClure (ranger station) and Evolution, 10 and 12 miles (16 and 19 km) from Muir Pass, where you can enjoy an open expanse while looking back at the high peaks.

As you leave Evolution Valley, the JMT veers far to the west of the crest, never really to return until near its terminus at Yosemite. This is the point where the JMT sees a major change in character: The trail not only veers away from the crest, but the crest isn't what it has been, either. Everything tones down at this point. It's pretty, but nothing like you've just been through.

You go off the major maps here as well, in between the Sequoia/Kings Canyon and Yosemite. Beyond are the John Muir and Ansel Adams Wildernesses and the Minarets. Between the Piute Pass Trail, 5 miles (8 km) from Evolution Valley, and Sally Keyes Lakes, there's no water and no camping, but there is an important resupply point just off the trail: 2 miles (3 km) from the Piute Pass Trail, the Florence Lake Trail takes you to the Muir Trail Ranch. Sally Keyes Lakes, 5 miles (8 km) beyond the intersection, has good camping. From there the JMT goes over 10,900-foot (3,323 m) Selden Pass and good camping in 3 miles (5 km) above the expanse of Rosemarie Meadow. From there, it's 6 miles (10 km) up to Bear Ridge, at 9,950 feet (3,034 m), and 4 miles (6 km) farther down to Mono Creek. Just beyond the bridge over Mono Creek is another resupply opportunity: the Lake Edison Trail that leads to the Vermillion Valley Resort in 5 miles (8 km).

The Silver Pass Creek ford, 5 miles (8 km) from Mono Creek, can be dangerous, so take care. The trail winds up and over Silver Divide and down past campsites at Cascade Valley and at Tully Hole, and then descends to popular Purple Lake 10 miles (16 km) from the Divide. Crater Meadow, an important local landmark, is 10 miles (16 km) farther, with trail junctions to Mammoth Pass both before and after the meadows. Reds Meadow is less than 3 miles (5 km) from Crater Meadow, and is a resupply opportunity: This is one of only two places where the JMT crosses a road (the other is at Tuolumne Meadows). Just ¼ mile (½ km) off the trail is Reds Meadow Resort, which offers showers and package pickup. The Devils Postpile, a neat geologic formation, is right here as well; a short shuttle-bus ride can take you to Mammoth Mountain Ski Area and its hordes of summertime mountain bikers.

From the junction with the Devils Postpile Trail, the JMT leaves the San Joaquin as it climbs Volcanic Ridge and down past a number of lakes. Gladys Lake, at 9,580 feet (2,921 m), 7 miles (11 km) from the Postpile Trail, has good camping, with views of 13,157-foot (4,011 m) Ritter and 12,945-foot (3,947 m) Banner, the first big mountains we've seen in a while. (Ritter and the Minarets are metamorphic, much older than the classic Sierra granite, which won't show up again until Rush Creek.) From there it's only 1 mile (1½ km) down to lovely Shadow Lake, no camping allowed. From the lake you go over a series of little passes from one lake to another before reaching Garnett, in 5 miles (8 km), and Thousand Island Lake, 1½ miles (3 km) farther, a highlight of this section of the JMT. From here, views of the Minarets, Ritter, and Banner remind you that you're still in the Sierra, in fact, in the Ansel Adams Wilderness. This is nice country.

From Thousand Island Lake, you cross in 2 miles (3 km) over Island Pass and its outstanding views, and then down into the Rush Creek basin, a landscape more characteristic of the east side: dry and rocky, with east-side flora. From Rush Creek basin you immediately work back up high in just 2 miles (3 km) to 11,050-foot (3,367 m) Donohue Pass. At the top of the pass you enter Yosemite National Park and reenter the classic Sierra country not seen since Evolution Basin. There are great views of Lyell, the highest peak in Yosemite at 13,144 feet (4,007 m), and McLure, and the whole of the Tuolumne high country. This is the home stretch, and it's glorious. You descend via a series of alpine benches into Lyell Canyon, with a look into the largest glacier seen from the JMT, the Lyell.

From Lyell Canyon you could exit to the road (California 120) through Tuolumne Meadows (ranger station) in 12 miles (19 km), or loop south and continue to the conclusion of the JMT two days away in Yosemite Valley. From the road, it's 7 miles (11 km) to Cathedral Pass, the only real elevation gain remaining. From there it's mostly downhill as you pass Echo Peaks, Tressider Peak, and hike into Long Meadow and its legal camping, through sugar pine forest and onto the southern shoulder of Cloud's Rest. From there the trail drops into the Merced River Canyon, right past Nevada Falls, and you're in the valley an hour and half later. So you enter the valley at one of the great waterfalls in America, 620-foot (189 m) Nevada Falls. The last big waterfall you pass is Vernal at a little over 300 feet (90 m). From the classic waterfall view from the bridge across the Merced, it's one mile on asphalt to Happy Isles, where the John Muir Trail officially ends.

Information

YOSEMITE NATIONAL PARK
P.O. Box 577
Yosemite National Park, CA 95389 USA
(209) 372-0200
www.nps.gov/yose

WILDERNESS MANAGEMENT OFFICE
Sequoia-Kings Canyon National Park
Three Rivers, CA 93271 USA
(209) 565-3341
www.nps.gov/seki

Permits

At the Yosemite end, contact the Yosemite Association
Wilderness Management Office
P.O. Box 577
Yosemite National Park, CA 95389 USA
(209) 372-0285
www.yosemite.org

At the Whitney end, contact the private contractor wilderness reservations

P.O. Box 430
Big Pine, CA 93513 USA
(888) 374-3773
www.sierrawilderness.com

Resupply points

VERMILLION VALLEY RESORT, EDISON LAKE
P.O. Box 258
Lakeshore, CA 93634 USA
(559) 259-4000
www.vermillionvalley.com

MUIR TRAIL RANCH
P.O. Box 700
Ahwahnee, CA 93601 USA
(209) 966-3195
Fax: (209) 966-7895
www.muirtrailranch.com

Shuttle services

For shuttles in the Whitney region,
Contact Inyo National Forest
873 Main Street
Bishop, CA 93514 USA
(760) 873-2400
www.fs.fed.us/rs/inyo

For solitude, just climb above the trail. This camp is above Cathedral Pass at Echo Peaks, with the snow-capped Merced Range to the south. PHOTO BY PETER POTTERFIELD.

GRAND CANYON
Rim to Rim to Rim

*Northern Arizona,
United States*

DISTANCE: 44 miles (71 km) round-trip; 21 miles (34 km)
 one-way with shuttle service
TIME: 5–7 days
PHYSICAL CHALLENGE: 1 2 3 4 5
PSYCHOLOGICAL CHALLENGE: 1 2 3 4 5
STAGING: Grand Canyon Village, South Rim, Arizona

The Grand Canyon is the one by which all other canyons are measured, a natural feature big enough to be seen from space but one much better enjoyed at closer quarters. From within, the canyon's staggering architecture and sheer scale can be uplifting, exhilarating, and humbling. Formed at the one place on earth where it could happen, where desert and river—a big one—intersect on a high plateau, the result is the greatest geologic showcase on earth. The rocks at the bottom are 2 billion years old, at the top 5 million, creating a slice through geologic time that defies belief. To walk down through this epic historical record, strata by strata—from Kaibab limestone to Coconino sandstone to Bright Angel shale, right down to the Vishnu complex at the Colorado River—is to take a foot journey unlike any other.

The canyon is, in a word, rugged, so much so it defeated even the hardened Spanish explorers who were the first Europeans to see it, and the first to try to get down into it, in 1550. Since then, the Grand Canyon has attracted people in ever-growing numbers. When Theodore Roosevelt saw it in 1903, he was so moved by this scenic wonder he proclaimed it a game reserve, the best he could do at the time, to protect it temporarily. Eventually, the canyon became a national monument, and in 1919, a national park.

PRECEDING PAGES: **LEFT**: *A hiker on Cedar Ridge, still high on the South Kaibab Trail, O'Neill Butte below.* PHOTO BY PETER POTTERFIELD. **RIGHT**: *The view from the North Rim of the Grand Canyon.* PHOTO BY JAMES MARTIN.

OPPOSITE: *The canyon surprises with creeks and springs, such as this waterfall and pool along the Bright Angel Trail below Indian Garden.* PHOTO BY PETER POTTERFIELD.

ABOVE: *Above the Tipoff, a mule train slowly ascends the South Kaibab Trail on the return from Phantom Ranch.* PHOTO BY PETER POTTERFIELD.

In the century since it was first protected, the Grand Canyon has become one of the greatest tourist attractions of all time. Five million people a year come to take a look.

Fortunately, the innate natural majesty of the canyon overcomes the busy tourist activity along its rim, no matter how many people go there—700,000 per month in July and August alone. The Grand Canyon can withstand insult, as everything else seems insignificant beside it. Reports of hordes on the South Rim are misleading, as fewer than one percent dare to venture a significant distance below the rim, and that's where the magic is. Only 40,000 people hiked down to camp in the backcountry in 2000.

The best way to avoid the crowds in this sprawling, 1.2-million-acre (480,000 ha) park is to hit the trail. While truly wild country elsewhere in the canyon can test the mettle of even the most experienced desert hiker or canyoneer, the main, so-called corridor trails—South Kaibab, North Kaibab, and Bright Angel—afford an opportunity to experience this geologic wonder in an intimate way, but with a degree of safety—with reliable water, known conditions, and good trails.

Any walk in the Grand Canyon is going to rate pretty high on the Richter scale of hikes if only because of the scenery, but to properly absorb the scale and complexity of this incredible landscape invest a little time. To appreciate the canyon, and the forces that created it, you've got to see the river that carved it, the opposing rims, and feel firsthand the dramatic climate shifts between the two. The minimum experience to be considered is to walk it rim to rim, something that can be done comfortably in just three reasonable 7- or 8-mile (11–13 km) days. Better, and much more revealing of the canyon's character, is the trip recommended here: a rim to rim to rim round-trip. This strategy allows for a few extra days to experience the spiritual embrace of the canyon walls—the ambience here deserves some savoring—and to explore new ground as one takes an entirely different route back to the South Rim.

The walk from one rim to the other brings to life the short but colorful human history of the canyon following John Wesley Powell's famous first run through it on the Colorado River in 1869. The Santa Fe Railroad ushered in the modern tourist era in 1901, when it completed a rail spur to the South Rim. Tourists were taken down into the canyon on mules via the Bright Angel Trail, created in 1902 by Ralph Cameron and his brother, who improved an ancient Havasupai route. Cameron charged a $1 toll for its use. The park service finally gained control of the Bright Angel Trail in 1920, after it assumed management of the park, and quickly added a second trail down to the river from the South Rim, the South Kaibab Trail, and the North Kaibab Trail from the Colorado River up to the North Rim via Bright Angel Canyon. The Black Bridge was built in 1928 (using Havasupai laborers), and for the first time the South Rim and North Rim were connected by trail. It remains one of the premier backcountry routes in North America.

LOGISTICS & STRATEGY

The nearest city to the park, Flagstaff, is not convenient for direct-air connections. Most people who come to the park to hike will fly into Las Vegas, probably the easiest city to reach by air, or Phoenix. Both are about a five-hour drive from Grand Canyon National Park and its visitors headquarters, the South Rim's Grand Canyon Village. A predictable, sprawling mini city and motel-hotel strip south of the park boundary on US Highway 180 offers groceries, supplies, and lodging. Arguably a better experience is to choose accommodations within the park itself, in Grand Canyon Village. Expect to pay a little more when staying in one of the concessionaire's hotels or motels, but the advantage of being right on the rim outweighs the expense. Being able to walk to the shuttle bus for trips along the rim, to the backcountry ranger station, or even to many South Rim trailheads keeps you out of the car. Some accommodations in the village, such as the El Tovar Hotel, are quite expensive, but others, such as the Maswik Lodge, feature motel-style parking, reasonable rates, and a cafeteria.

The 44-mile (71 km) route recommended here addresses travel realities in Northern Arizona and takes advantage of the convenient infrastructure on the South Rim. Starting from the South Rim, the hike follows the South Kaibab Trail (the best, shortest, and most direct route from rim to river) 7 miles (11 km) down into the canyon to the Colorado River and crosses via the Black Bridge to Bright Angel Camp. From there, the North Kaibab Trail rises 7 miles (11 km) to Cottonwood Camp, and the following day ascends steeply 7 more miles (11 km) to the North Rim. From the North Rim, the route retraces itself down to Bright Angel Camp and then crosses the Colorado on the Silver Bridge (downstream of the Black Bridge). From the river it ascends to the South Rim via the 9-mile (15 km) Bright Angel Trail, a better, less rigorous route than the South Kaibab for climbing out. This walk takes the hiker down through time and into the unique Colorado River environment of the canyon bottom—twice—on the storied, historic corridor trails, and explores the wilder, higher, and more remote North Rim. A shuttle service makes it possible to halve the suggested itinerary by leaving the trail at the North Rim and traveling back to Grand Canyon Village by van.

Permits are required to hike into the inner canyon, and since permits are in high demand, advance planning is definitely required. The park service issues permits as far as four months in advance. For the best chance to get a permit for the days you want, log on to the Backcountry Information Center's Web site on the first of the month four months prior to your proposed start day, download the permit request form, and submit the request via fax. Three to six weeks after the application, the permit or a denial arrives in the mail. If you are denied an advance permit, you can re-apply for different dates, or take your chances on a limited number of last minute, walk-in permits available at the Backcountry Information Center.

For this hike, you'll need a permit for at least five nights of backcountry camping. From the rim, you'll hike to Bright Angel Camp, an amazingly pleasant place for the amount of traffic it gets. The campground stretches for more than a mile along the west side of Bright Angel Creek under a grove of cottonwood trees. The second night will be spent at higher Cottonwood Camp, 7 miles (11 km) from the North Rim, near Manzanita Canyon and Ribbon Falls. The third night will be spent on the North Rim, in the campground, a backcountry camp, or a park lodging. On the return leg, the first night will be spent back at Cottonwood Camp, the next at Bright Angel Camp. You can adjust this schedule to accommodate layover days, or day trips off the corridor. Water is a huge concern, the overreaching one, when hiking the canyon, and one of the important features of this route is the certainty of potable water at all overnight locations (May to October). In the off-season, the water system is turned off to avoid freezing up.

On the days you'll be at Bright Angel Camp, near the Colorado, you have the option of staying in relative luxury at Phantom Ranch, about a half-hour stroll from the camp. This Mary Jane Colter–designed village, the only commercial lodging in the inner gorge, offers real beds and restaurant meals. But even if you're in a tent at Bright Angel Camp, you can always walk over for a cold beer or a snack at the cantina.

Expect the temperature to change radically in the course of this round-trip adventure. In November, when I last hiked the route, the South Rim (about 7,000 feet, 2,100 m) was near freezing in early morning, but the canyon floor was a balmy 80°F (27°C). During the summer months, temperatures on the South Rim are relatively pleasant, between 50° and 80°F (10–27°C), but the inner canyon temperatures can be extreme, often exceeding 100°F (37°C) at the river. On the North Rim, at about 8,000 feet (2,400 m), temperatures can be 10°F (6°C) colder than on the South Rim.

The corridor trails offer little in the way of significant route variations, which is part of their relative safety and predictability. But you can schedule additional nights on your permit to explore the canyon from any or all of your camps. On the return hike to the South Rim, you can break up the long day on the Bright Angle Trail by scheduling an overnight stop at Indian Gardens Camp, about halfway between the river and the rim.

OPPOSITE: *The "Black Bridge" over the Colorado River, built in 1928, was the first to connect the canyon rims by trail.*
PHOTO BY PETER POTTERFIELD.

HAZARDS

More than 250 Grand Canyon hikers are rescued each year, most succumbing to heat-related problems, poor fitness, or dehydration. Temperatures in the inner canyon can take hikers by surprise because rim temperatures can be 20 or 30°F (11–16°C) cooler. Each uphill day for this hike will cover almost 5,000 vertical feet (1,500 m) and 7 to 9 miles (11–13 km), long days with an equivalent elevation gain to summit day on Mount Rainier. Hiking in the canyon, therefore, requires a good level of fitness as well as basic backcountry judgment. Avoid hiking from rim to river during the hottest summer months, and don't even consider trying a rim to river round-trip in a single day. Plan your hike for spring or fall to avoid hiking out in extreme heat. With proper nutrition, hydration, and fitness, you can make the hike an exhilarating adventure, not a grim ordeal. Be aware that you're going to need a lot more calories—up to 6,000 per day—on your canyon hike than you would at home, and make sure to eat sufficient salty foods to avoid hyponatremia (water intoxication caused by failure to replace salt lost in sweating). Drinking enough water means drinking a quart for every two hours on the trail. In my experience, the best strategy in the Grand Canyon is to use a hydration system, start early in the day, and travel as light as you dare.

Other potential problems facing hikers include lightning strikes (mainly on the rim) and falls. Black widows, tarantulas, scorpions, and rattlesnakes can cause problems, but rarely do.

SEASON

It never ceases to amaze me how many hikers choose the wrong time of year for the best walks on earth, and the Grand Canyon is no exception. By far, a majority of hikers choose to come here in the summer, when conditions are at their most dangerous and crowds at their worst. But off they go, down into the furnacelike canyon, ensuring that the walk back up will be a struggle. Spring and fall are better times to do any Grand Canyon hike, so try to come March through May, or from September through November. Even if you don't have perfect sunshine, you almost certainly will have a more enjoyable hike. Beware that snowfall can close the North Rim road in late spring or early fall, another reason to hike rim to rim to rim: There's no inconvenience if the shuttle services are stopped by snow. Winter can be appealing for hikers who aren't freaked out by cold, short days and long nights, but icy trail conditions up near the rims can make a winter trip unpractical, even dangerous.

A view of the canyon architecture below the South Rim from Indian Garden. PHOTO BY JIM NELSON.

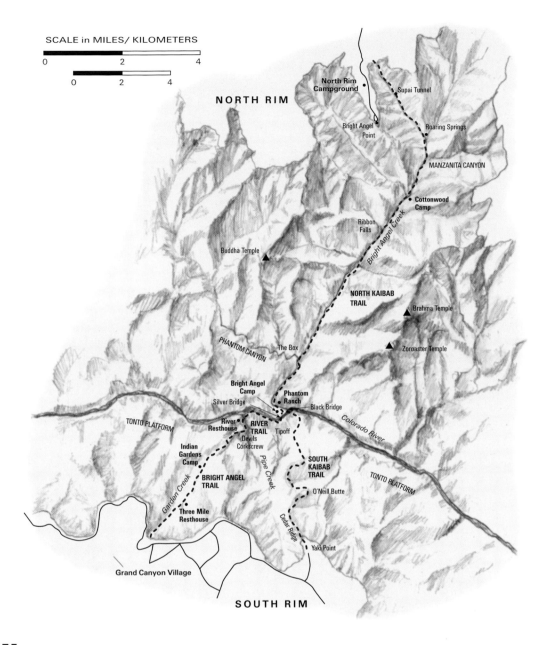

SCALE in MILES/ KILOMETERS

NORTH RIM

North Rim
Campground
Supai Tunnel

Bright Angel
Point
Roaring Springs

MANZANITA CANYON

Cottonwood
Camp

Ribbon
Falls

Buddha Temple

NORTH KAIBAB
TRAIL

Brahma Temple

Zoroaster Temple

PHANTOM CANYON
The Box

Bright Angel
Camp
Silver Bridge
Phantom
Ranch
Black Bridge

Colorado River

TONTO PLATFORM
River
Resthouse
RIVER
TRAIL
Tipoff
Devils
Corkscrew

Indian
Gardens
Camp

SOUTH
KAIBAB
TRAIL

TONTO PLATFORM

BRIGHT ANGEL
TRAIL
O'Neill Butte

Garden Creek
Pipe Creek

Three Mile
Resthouse
Cedar Ridge

Yaki Point

Grand Canyon Village

SOUTH RIM

ROUTE

The park service has closed portions of the South Rim to private
traffic, including Yaki Point, where the South Kaibab trailhead is
located. To get there, you'll need to catch the free shuttle bus from
the Backcountry Information Center to the trailhead, a distance of
about 2 miles (3 km). I suggest taking the first bus of the morning,
which for me meant a dawn start and a beautiful descent over the
South Rim just as the sun blasted over the eastern horizon.

The route passes the mule corrals on the 7,200-foot (2,200 m)
rim and descends the excellent track of the South Kaibab Trail
down through the Toroweap formation on wide switchbacks to
Cedar Ridge, a popular day-hike destination. Below Cedar Ridge,
you climb down through Coconino sandstone, then continue down
on switchbacks to the landmark O'Neill Butte, with its distinctive
cap of Esplanade sandstone. You'll likely be passed by several mule
trains headed for Phantom Ranch on this stretch; if so, just step off

the trail on the uphill side and let the animals pass with their loads
of food, beer, and tourists weaving and swaying atop their mounts.

The steep trail relents as it heads toward the top of the Redwall
Cliff and a set of steep switchbacks working 500 feet (150 m) down
to the Tonto Platform at 4 miles (6 km) and about 4,000 feet (1,200 m).
Soon, you pass the intersection with the Tonto East Trail and reach
the Tipoff, the rim of the inner gorge, where the trail drops 1,600 feet
(490 m) in less than 2 miles (3 km) to the Colorado River, one of the
route's most intriguing sections. The South Kaibab reaches its
junction with the River Trail at 2,700 feet (820 m), where you get your
first view of the Black Bridge. A dark, 200-foot-long (60 m) tunnel
leads to the start of the 440-foot-long (135 m) bridge, swaying 75
feet (23 m) above the river, its support cables anchored in pink
Zoroaster granite. Once across the bridge, follow the trail past the
mouth of Bright Angel Creek about ½ mile (¾ km) north to the small

OPPOSITE: *Deep within its Inner Gorge, the Colorado River is hidden from view for most of the hike down.* PHOTO BY JIM NELSON.

bridge that crosses the creek and leads at 7 miles (11 km) to the campground proper, busy but peaceful, the old cottonwoods swaying in the breeze above spacious and surprisingly private campsites. There is much to explore here in the heart of the inner gorge, including the Colorado River, various side trails, and Phantom Ranch.

From Bright Angel Camp, cross the bridge and turn left onto the North Kaibab Trail to head up Bright Angel Canyon. Less than ¼ mile (½ km) through the cottonwoods brings you to the low, stone and wood buildings at Phantom Ranch, including dormitories, the cantina, and a ranger station. One mile (2 km) beyond Phantom Ranch, above the Clear Creek Trail intersection, the walls of Bass limestone begin to close in as you enter the 4-mile (6 km) section of narrows known as The Box. A wet tread and multiple crossings of Bright Angel Creek mark this section of trail up to the intersection with the trail to 100-foot (30 m) Ribbon Falls, a popular ½-mile (¾ km) side trip. Another 1½ miles (2½ km) takes you to Cottonwood Camp, 7 miles (11 km) and 2,000 feet (610 m) above Bright Angel Camp. Although not as lush, Cottonwood has its own appeal, surrounded by cliffs of Tapeats sandstone and with views up a canyon called The Transept, and higher, toward the trees of the North Rim itself.

From Cottonwood Camp, the trail steepens as it climbs more than 4,000 feet (1,200 m) in just 7 miles (11 km) to the North Rim. The trail crosses a bridge over Bright Angel Creek near Manzanita Canyon 1½ miles (2½ km) from Cottonwood and then gradually leaves the creek as it switchbacks up Roaring Springs Canyon past the spring itself, pouring from Mauv limestone. As you look ahead, the route seems blocked by the sheer rock faces of the daunting and complex North Rim architecture, but the upper North Kaibab trail cleverly penetrates these defenses. The route passes through the Redwall limestone on a cliff carved into the rock, then switchbacks up through the Supai Tunnel (at 5 miles, 8 km) and the Esplanade sandstone into the first conifers of the North Rim. The final section ascends the Coconino sandstone and Kaibab limestone up to the rim itself and the 8,000-foot (2,400 m) Kaibab Plateau.

Here at the North Rim you are 12 miles (19 km) as the crow flies from the South Rim, about 21 miles (34 km) by trail, 215 miles (346 km) by road. The North Rim, at the end of a long, dead-end road, receives only a fraction of the visitors the South Rim does, but the reduced activity is concentrated in a smaller area, so it can still seem busy. You can camp in the North Rim Campground or at large in the backcountry between the North Kaibab trailhead and the park's northern boundary. A permit is required for either option. You can also grab a beer, buy dinner, or even a comfortable room, if you are so inclined, or arrange for a ride back to the South Rim by vehicle.

For a return hike to the South Rim, retrace your steps to Cottonwood Camp and Bright Angel Camp at the Colorado River, the last stop before climbing to the South Rim via the Bright Angel Trail, a longer (by 2 miles, 3 km) but less rigorous route than the South Kaibab. From the campground, head south toward the river, cross Bright Angel Creek on the steel bridge, and hike west ½ mile (¾ km) to the Silver Bridge across the Colorado. The river is visible through

the open grate of the walkway, which is why the mules don't cross on this bridge. Travel west 1 mile (2 km) on the River Trail to its junction with Bright Angel Trail at the River Resthouse (no water). Travel south on Bright Angel Trail up through the canyon of Pipe Creek, crossing the creek several times as you ascend beyond the mouth of Garden Creek and up toward the Devils Corkscrew, a section of switchbacks. The trail above follows Garden Creek for 2 more miles (3 km) up through the Tapeats sandstone cliffs and onto the Tonto Platform, where the big cottonwoods of Indian Gardens come into view. A spring at Indian Gardens was used for irrigation by the Havasupai Indians for hundreds of years, but the cottonwoods were planted by Ralph Cameron, the man who built Bright Angel Trail. The big trees offer welcome shade at this point in the climb, with nearly 5 miles (8 km) remaining to the South Rim. The trail works up a set of switchbacks called Jacob's Ladder, through the Redwall and up to Three Mile Resthouse, where the first day-hikers appear. The trail gets progressively busier with day-hikers as it makes the final, laborious ascent up through the Coconino sandstone and Toroweap formation and, eventually, up the Bright Angel fault into the Kaibab limestone and a final tunnel before reaching the South Rim.

Information

GRAND CANYON NATIONAL PARK
P.O. Box 129
Grand Canyon, AZ 86023-0129 USA
(928) 638-7888
www.nps.gov/grca/index.htm

Permits

Backcountry Information Center
(East of the Maswik Lodge near the railroad tracks)
Grand Canyon National Park
P.O. Box 129
Grand Canyon, AZ 86023-0129 USA
(928) 638-7875 (1–5 PM)
(928) 638-2125 (fax)
Note: This is a busy office, and you may have to try repeatedly to get through by telephone. If possible, use the Web and fax to communicate.
www.nps.gov/grca/backcountry/permit_procedures.htm#p4
www.nps.gov/grca/backcountry/permit_app.htm (permit request page)

FEES: In 2005, cost for permits includes a nonrefundable fee of $10 per permit plus $5 per person per night camped below the rim and $5 per group per night camped above the rim. Permit cancellations incur a $10 cancellation fee. All fees paid to the Backcountry Office continue to be nonrefundable. Frequent users may wish to purchase a one-year Frequent Hiker membership for $25 that waives the initial $10 fee for each permit obtained by the trip leader for 12 months from the date of purchase.

In-park Lodging

For South Rim, North Rim, and Phantom Ranch accommodations, contact Xanterra Parks and Resorts, (303) 297-2757 or 1-888-297-2757, www.grandcanyonlodges.com/dynamic/frameset.htm?page=1.htm.

Shuttle Services

Trans Canyon Shuttle, 928-638-2820

Guide Services

For an up-to-date list of guide services allowed to operate in the park, check www.nps.gov/grca/backcountry/index.htm.

Bright Angel Camp is one of the busiest in the park system, but is still shady, pleasant, and surprisingly private. PHOTO BY PETER POTTERFIELD.

OPPOSITE: *The North Kaibab Trail through Bright Angel Canyon is lush with cottonwoods near the Colorado River.* PHOTO BY PETER POTTERFIELD.

CHESLER PARK
Canyonlands, Needles District
Southern Utah, United States

DISTANCE: 15 miles (24 km) round-trip
TIME: 3–5 days
PHYSICAL CHALLENGE: 1 2 **3** 4 5
PSYCHOLOGICAL CHALLENGE: 1 2 **3** 4 5
STAGING: Moab, Utah

he Colorado River reaches its confluence with the Green River in one of the last relatively undisturbed areas of the vast Colorado Plateau. These rivers and their tributaries meet at a place marked by fantastic natural sculpture—needlelike spires and natural bridges, canyons and mesas and deep river gorges—all carved from the layers of sedimentary rocks that dominate the region. Here is Canyonlands, and Arches, and Natural Bridges—two national parks and a monument that in many ways symbolize the wild beauty of the American Southwest.

Any hike through this surreal red-rock landscape is going to be fascinating, but none more so than the magical journey into Chesler Park. This thousand-acre (400 ha) expanse of open meadow, tucked away among the canyons and slick-rock plateaus and completely encircled by the some of the highest rock spires in the region, is so unlikely that it defies belief. The cowboys who first stumbled into Chesler Park must have been amazed to find a grazing land hidden in the middle of the red-rock desert. Hikers today experience that same sense of discovery when they trudge for miles across the slickrock only to climb through that narrow cleft in the high ramparts and drop into the confounding beauty of this hidden greensward.

Here, just below the point where the Colorado joins the Green, is the heart of Canyonlands National Park, the largest in Utah. Crazy, twisted canyons of the aptly named Maze District lie on the west side of the Colorado River in a place so hard to get to that even today it is virtually unvisited. On the east side of the Colorado stand the Needles, a

Early season in the desert can mean fewer hikers but icy trails, such as this one, half a mile (.80 km) from Chesler Park. PHOTO BY PETER POTTERFIELD.

Chesler Park's distinctive banded pinnacles of Cedar Mesa sandstone characterize the Needles of Canyonlands. PHOTO BY PETER POTTERFIELD.

FOLLOWING SPREAD: *The intriguing landscape of slickrock and eroded sandstone makes hiking to Chesler Park unlike any other adventure.*
PHOTO BY PETER POTTERFIELD.

landscape marked by the distinctive rock pinnacles of Cedar Mesa sandstone, banded in red and white, a landscape deeply cut by labyrinthine canyons. The unlikely expanse of Chesler Park lies among the highest of all the Needles, at nearly 6,000 feet (1,800 m).

The best of the backcountry in the Needles District of Canyonlands National Park is rightfully reserved as a reward to backpackers willing to brave the terrain, the heat, and the lack of water to get into such a place. The hike from Squaw Flat across the slickrock plateaus and down across rugged canyons to Chesler Park traverses some of the most spectacular terrain in Utah. And if the effort seems more taxing than one would expect from a 6- or 7-mile (9–11 km) hike, the payoffs are bigger as well. This sublime rock wilderness rewards with places like Druid Arch, a rare double arch perched at the head of remote Elephant Canyon.

Humans have visited this place for more than ten thou-

sand years, and the ruins of those lost civilizations remain intact. Different groups have moved in and out of this desert, including the Ancestral Puebloan Indians, the same people who populated Mesa Verde and Chaco Canyon. Traces of their lives can be found in the form of dwellings and pictographs, a fact that adds a mysterious appeal to the already wild country. The ruins of one ancient dwelling are tucked away just outside the rocky wall guarding Chesler Park as one travels toward Druid Arch.

In more recent centuries, cowboys roamed this country, eking a living out of the barren but beautiful land, one that is heartbreakingly dry. That ranchers grazed cattle here is evidenced by the old cowboy camp, still visible today, built up against the prominent rock island at the very center of Chesler Park. By World War II, the ranchers were followed by uranium miners. Now a new kind of pilgrim wanders over the slickrock in search of a different treasure: recreation.

No longer a backwater, the wilds of southern Utah have become famous in recent years as their irresistible landscape draws people from all over the world. Tiny Moab, the only real city in the region, is wonderfully set in its valley between red-rock cliffs, the snow-capped LaSalle Mountains rising above in the east. One of the most culturally diverse towns in all of Utah, Moab and its mix of residents and trendy visitors makes a comfortable base for seeing this country.

But the Canyonlands backcountry is a place that demands reasonable judgment and at least some basic expertise to enter safely. A lack of water puts an aura of seriousness on any deep venture into the Needles. A true "high desert," with elevations ranging from 3,700 to 7,200 feet (1,100–2,200 m) above sea level, Canyonlands experiences very hot summers and cold winters. Temperatures may fluctuate as much as 50 degrees F (28 degrees C) in a single day. Less than 10 inches (25 cm) of rain falls each year.

Still, there is life here. Snakes and lizards and squirrels are common sights in the canyons, but if you're lucky you might catch a glimpse of bighorn sheep or a Peregrine Falcon. Take care where you step, as even the soil is alive. Much of the area is covered with a biological soil crust called cryptobiotic soil, a living groundcover that forms the foundation of high-desert plant life in and around Canyonlands. The surprises seem never to end in this red-rock wonderland, a sprawling region of elemental earthworks as fragile as they are breathtaking, natural grand gestures that deserve our best efforts to protect.

LOGISTICS & STRATEGY

Scenic Moab, Utah, is the logical staging area for any hike in Canyonlands National Park. Having come a long way from its days as a remote ranching community and an outpost in the uranium mining industry, this pleasant town on the Colorado River now boasts all the casual creature comforts one could ask for, and more. Some would say it's a little too busy. Moab hums with tourist activity spring through fall as visitors congregate and resupply in town in between visits to nearby Canyonlands and Arches National Parks and the unparalleled hiking, climbing, and mountain biking on other public lands nearby. Astonishingly, even in the deadly heat of southern Utah high-desert summer, people still come to take in the bizarre and beautiful natural features surrounding Moab.

This small town of 6,000 permanent residents is a long way from anywhere. Most visitors arrive via Salt Lake City or Las Vegas, both about six hours away by car. Some come through Grand Junction, Colorado, only half that distance, but a much less convenient airport for most. This remoteness is part of the appeal of southeastern Utah, and one that makes a compelling argument for spending at least a couple of weeks here to see what there is to see, acclimate to the town's laid-back hospitality, and sample the distinctive entertainments—mountain biking, four-wheeling, river rafting, and more. Otherwise you'll find yourself in the uptight position I always seem to end up in: racing from the Salt Lake City airport to get to the Needles District in time to pick up the hiking permit before the ranger station closes in mid-afternoon.

Obtaining a permit for a Canyonlands hike can prove difficult if you don't know the system. These routes have a strong appeal among the cognoscenti, so the permits go quickly, and quirks in the system add a layer of difficulty. All hiking permits are issued at district visitors centers, and all can be reserved in advance. Any permit not reserved in advance is available to walk-ins on a first-come, first-served basis. Walk-in permits are available only the day before or the day of a trip, and in my experience the most appealing

Chelser Park is a thousand-acre expanse of desert meadow encircled by rock spires. PHOTO BY PETER POTTERFIELD.

OPPOSITE: *The desert sun sets on the snow-capped La Sal Mountains, east of Canyonlands.* PHOTO BY PETER POTTERFIELD.

hikes seldom have unused permits in-season. You have to pick up your permit in person, in the district where you're going hiking. If you don't arrive at the district visitors center before it closes on the day of your hike, you risk losing your permit, or at least one night of it.

Reserve your permit early, and try to avoid the busiest times of year, which are spring and fall. You must reserve any permit at least two weeks in advance, and, practically, you need to do it well before that. Permit applications for the following year open on the second Monday of July—so if you want to hike to Chesler Park in March 2006, you can reserve as early as July 11, 2005. The first part of the process is simple: Go to the Canyonlands Web site, download the application form, and fax it in. You can call the rangers to inquire about availability before making your request. The upside of the rigorous permitting process is that you'll never run into crowds in the Canyonlands' backcountry because the rangers precisely control the number of overnight backpackers using the handful of designated camps.

With your reservation in hand, all you have to do is show up at the Needles District visitors center on time to claim the actual permit. Arches National Park and the Canyonlands National Park's Island in the Sky District, where the Colorado meets the Green River, are just outside

Moab. But the Needles District is a significant distance away, some 40 miles (64 km) south on a paved two-lane highway, then another 40 miles on a rougher road to the visitors center, and a few miles yet to the trailhead. So even from Moab you're still two or three hours from the start of the Chesler Park Trail. The best strategy, then, is to arrive in Moab at least a day before your hike, leaving ample time for a relaxed drive down to the Needles. The road to the trailhead is fine for rental cars. From the trailhead six or seven hours on the trail brings you to Chesler Park. If you reserve in advance, you can camp overnight at Squaw Flat Campground, right at the start of the Chesler Park Trail. Although only about 6 miles (9½ km) from the trailhead to backcountry campsite, the route is a convoluted one that for most of the time crosses a surreal slickrock landscape marked by cairns but frequently descends into canyons and shallow drainages along the way. Expect to expend more effort than usual for the miles traveled.

Water is the major consideration when visiting the Needles. Potable water is available at the visitors center, but in this part of Utah everyone should keep a few gallons in the car for unexpected problems. On the trail itself, reliable water can usually be found at Big Springs, 1½ miles (2½ km) from the trailhead, and in Elephant Canyon, one of the drainages crossed en route to Chesler Park and the primary source for drinking water once you've arrived. Sometimes, however, you may have to go a long way up Elephant Canyon to find pools big enough to fill your bottles, so begin the hike into Chesler with all the water you will need the first day and enough to get you out in an emergency. Before you leave the visitors center, inquire at the ranger desk about the availability of water for the duration of your hike. Remember: When hiking in Canyonlands, water rules. On my first hike here my partner and I spent one entire day making the long walk from Chesler Park almost all the way to Druid Arch just to fill our containers. Four gallons (15 l) made for a heavy load on the hike back, but the payoff was two more days in the unparalleled rocky wilderness of the Needles backcountry. Every hiker who spends more than one night in the park can expect to make a similar 4- or 5-mile (6–8 km) water run, so bring containers up to the task.

One or two nights at Chesler Park is the bare minimum time required to experience the unique beauty of the area, but most people spend three or four. A couple of days exploring with day packs reveal stunning formations, such as the Joint Trail, a narrow defile that runs for almost ½ mile (¾ km) between towering sandstone walls mere inches apart. Side canyons and cross-country routes up to the top of the slickrock can keep you busy for a day around the Joint Trail. The standard water run into Elephant Canyon should be combined with the day hike to Druid Arch, an extraordinarily beautiful double arch tucked away at the head of the rugged canyon so far even from Chesler it sees little traffic.

The ultimate day trip out of Chesler is the quest to see the elusive, almost mythical Virginia Park. This pristine but secret meadow is much like Chesler, but smaller and more effectively protected by its higher encircling wall of red-rock towers. Livestock never found a way into Virginia Park, so its native grasses and cryptobiotic soil are treasures the park service protects with vigor. You'll find it marked on no map or mentioned in any park literature, but skilled navigators and careful map readers just might be able to climb in for a look, as it's only a few miles from the camp at Chesler Park.

HAZARDS

The Canyonlands' Needles District is a high sandstone desert cut through with serpentine drainage canyons. In this environment the chief hazards include scarce water, rough terrain, and disorientation. Hikers here must always think about water: Have more than you need and always carry at least enough to get back to the car unless you know for certain the location of a reliable source. Flash floods can be lethal, so stay out of the canyon bottoms if it starts to rain. Canyonlands experiences very hot summers, cold winters, and the temperature may fluctuate as much as 50°F (28°C) in a single day.

SEASON

April and May, and September and October are the busy months in the Needles. Temperatures are mostly moderate, with highs from 80 to 90°F (26–32°C), lows from 40 to 50°F (4–10°C). Some hikers come as late as June, even into July, but heat and lack of water in summer make for a diminished experience. I prefer colder conditions to blazing heat, so my recommendation is to push the limits of the traditional season. Come in March or even earlier, or November or even later, and experience the place with a degree of solitude. Be aware that temperatures can vary wildly in the off- and shoulder seasons, which is why most hikers avoid them. In February, I've seen temperatures as hot as 80°F (26°C) and as cold as 8°F (−7°C), so you have to watch the forecast if you're inclined to come then. Wilderness lovers are often aghast at the southern Utah penchant for vehicles in the backcountry, and that's another reason to come in off-season: The four-wheel aficionados go elsewhere, so you won't hear them grinding away in the distance.

ROUTE

From Moab, drive south on US Highway 191 toward Monticello, Utah. Proceed beyond the turnoff for the well-signed Needles Overlook; at 40 miles (64 km) from Moab turn right, west, onto Utah 211, following signs for the Needles District visitors center. From

TOP: *Morning coffee is on at Big Spring Camp.*

BOTTOM: *Backpackers' camp, nestled among the spires of Chesler Park.* PHOTOS BY PETER POTTERFIELD.

US Highway 191 it's approximately 37 miles (60 km) on the narrow, winding state route to the visitors center. The drive into the Needles passes Newspaper Rock, one of the most important collections of pictographs in this part of the state and one that's worth taking some time to explore. After picking up your permit and ascertaining the status of water availability at the visitors center, follow signs to Squaw Flat Campground, about 4 miles (6 km) away.

From the parking area at the end of the campground road, find the trailhead for the Chesler Park Trail. It can be a little confusing; if in doubt bear right, and don't take the Squaw Canyon Trail by mistake. Look for signs directing you toward Chesler Park or Big Spring.

The route leads southwest from the campground, starting out as a trail across sagebrush flats but soon climbing onto the distinctive sedimentary rock, the famous slickrock of the Canyonlands area. The predominantly slickrock trail is marked by cairns, small stacks of flat rocks. At approximately 1½ miles (2½ km), you reach the intersection with the Big Spring Canyon Trail. When I was last here in March 2003, a good pool of water lay in the canyon near this intersection. From the intersection, cross Big Spring Canyon and continue southwest across the ever-changing slickrock environment, through narrow defiles and over rocky ridges, features that makes hiking in Canyonlands unlike hiking anyplace else.

Approximately 4 miles (6 km) from Squaw Flat Campground you reach an intersection with, confusingly, another trail called the Chesler Park Trail; this one comes in from the north, off the Elephant Hill four-wheel-drive road. Less than 1 mile (2 km) farther, you reach another intersection, this time with the Elephant Canyon Trail. If you were to turn south here down Elephant Canyon (the trail name changes from Elephant Canyon Trail to Druid Arch Trail as you hike south), you'd reach Druid Arch in about 4 rugged miles (6 km). Instead, cross the canyon and continue southwest for 1 mile (2 km), where you begin the climb up into Chesler Park itself. In less than 6 miles (9½ km) you climb up and through a narrow cleft in the wall of needles surrounding Chesler Park at its northern end, an appropriate portal into this hidden place. Within the protective ring of towering needles, the gentle expanse of rolling grasslands and dry sagebrush comes as an unexpected contrast to the rugged landscape you've just walked through. But even after you've entered this high-desert sanctuary, you've still got some distance to go, as Chesler Park is a big place, and the loop trail inside it is almost 4 miles (6 km) long.

Once you enter Chesler Park at its northeast corner, turn left and proceed southwest on the loop trail until you reach your designated campsite in 1 or 2 miles (2–3 km), depending on which one you've been assigned. Some are clustered on the southeast corner of the park; others are placed on the western side of the island of needles that extends into the center of the park. This island or ridge, by the way, makes a great vantage point from which to view the entire park.

From the campsites, the views extend out the open northwest flank of Chesler Park all the way across the Colorado River to the tangle of canyons known as the Maze, reachable only by roads so difficult that few hikers ever go there. Chesler Park itself has a protected and intimate feel, ringed by its imposing wall of Cedar Mesa sandstone. Within Chesler Park itself take care to stay on marked trails so as not to disturb the cryptobiotic soils.

The Joint Trail is easily found in the park's southwest corner, clearly marked by the steps carved into the sandstone that lead down into the narrow slot, a remarkable side trip.

From the cluster of campsites, a well-marked trail leads out of Chesler Park due east for about 1 mile (2 km) to intersect with Elephant Canyon at a point approximately 2 miles (3 km) south of where you crossed it on the way in. Reliable water generally can be found in Elephant Canyon, and Druid Arch lies at the head of the canyon, a two-hour hike from Chesler Park.

Most hikers return to Squaw Flat Campground by simply retracing their steps. A loop trip is possible, however, by returning to Squaw Flat via the Elephant Canyon and Big Spring Canyon Trails.

Information

CANYONLANDS NATIONAL PARK
2282 SW Resource Blvd
Moab, UT 84532 USA
www.nps.gov/cany

Visitor information: (435) 719-2313 (8 AM–12 PM)
Backcountry reservations and permit information: (435) 259-4351 (8 AM–12 PM). Fax permit requests to (435) 259-4285.

Needles District visitors center is open 8 AM–4:30 PM daily.

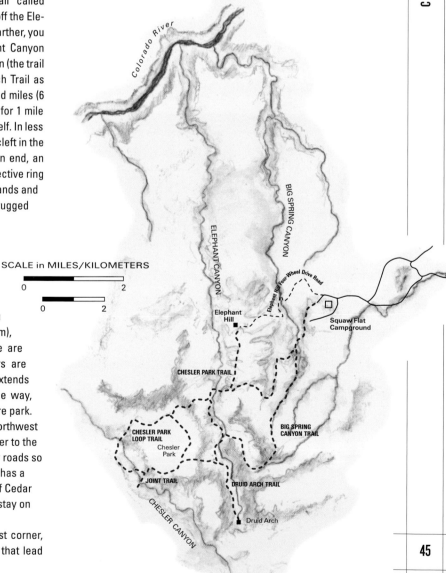

MAROON BELLS CIRCUIT
Maroon Bells Wilderness

*South-central Colorado,
United States*

DISTANCE: 27-mile (43 km) loop
TIME: 4–5 days
PHYSICAL CHALLENGE: 1 2 3 **4** 5
PSYCHOLOGICAL CHALLENGE: 1 **2** 3 4 5
STAGING: Aspen or Glenwood Springs, Colorado

Probably the *ne plus ultra* of Rocky Mountain hiking, the Maroon Bells Circuit is from start to finish a deep immersion in classic Colorado high country. This extraordinarily high route crosses four passes above 12,000 feet (3,650 m) and drops below 10,000 feet (3,050 m) only at the trailhead. The excursion makes a complete circuit around postcard icons, the Maroon Bells, as it winds through high basins, forests of spruce and aspen, and world-class flower gardens. The Bells themselves, side-by-side Fourteeners, are a big part of the draw. Textbook

uplifts, what geologists call faulted anticline mountains, they stand there shoulder to shoulder, like brothers. The peaks are best photographed from Maroon Lake or Crater Lake, both located within the Maroon Bells Wilderness, an expanse of more than 181,000 acres (72,400 ha) in the Gunnison and White River National Forests.

Years ago, I first traveled to the Elk Range in September, for a view of the Bells above forests of golden, whispering aspens, a fact that later elicited actual *sympathy* from a Colorado friend. Flowers are the reason to go there, he told me, and you missed them! Clearly, a return trip was called for. Fields of larkspur, Indian paintbrushes of all colors, alpine sunflowers, fireweed, and columbine in the meadows along the route produce a jaw-dropping display. Your timing has to be right on, however, and even a week can matter. The peak wildflower bloom depends on the previous year's snowfall. In the past decade mid-July has produced the best display. Even through the drought years of the new millennium the flower gardens of the Maroon Bells Wilderness did not disappoint, they just peaked earlier.

This alpine excursion rambles around above tree line for so long that wildflower connoisseurs might never find a better 27 miles (43 km) in the Rockies. But there's more to this route than the flowers. This four-pass loop is concentrated stuff, a fairly short hike that manages to pack a high-octane wallop, from high passes and killer views to open meadows and rolling high country, big lakes, small lakes, jagged peaks,

and high, rounded mountains with abundant wildlife. Pikas and marmots are found throughout the high meadows, but you're also likely to see black bear, deer, and elk. Mountain lions have been seen, but rarely.

It's easy to forget about the altitude until you arrive here from sea level and wonder why you're huffing and puffing. The fact that most of this route is above 10,500 feet (3,200 m) accounts for the high physical challenge rating, but in addition to the altitude it's *work* getting over the passes. On the second day the route crosses two passes over 12,500 feet (3,800 m) within a few hours—not your average backcountry stage.

Because the route is one of the great hikes in a state full of good ones, you can't count on solitude. Still, you may be surprised by the lack of *Homo sapiens* on the back side of the Maroon Bells, which isn't on the way to anywhere and so is visited only by those doing this loop. Gentrification and population growth are issues throughout Colorado, especially here, smack between upscale Aspen and Snowmass Village. If you go on a busy weekend in high summer, expect some company. But a midweek trip at the height of wildflower bloom will have you headed home searching for words to describe what you've seen.

Looking into the Elk Range's Maroon Bells. PHOTO BY BLAINE HARRINGTON.

LOGISTICS & STRATEGY

Flights are available into Aspen, but it's a scary landing and one highly dependent on weather. A more common alternative is to fly into Grand Junction, about two hours away, or even Denver, five hours away, because connections are so much better and flights less expensive. Flights to Grand Junction put you much closer to the action, and the airport is cavernous and easy, the result of oil-shale optimism in the late '70s that didn't pan out with the predicted population explosion.

No matter how you get there, you'll be on the West Slope, very different, the locals are quick to point out, than Denver and its Front Range. This was for decades mining and ranching country, and there's still a lot of that, with values that reflect a working way of life. But the mountains of southern and central Colorado, from the San Juans to the Elk Range and even to the Sangre de Cristos, have also long been a magnet for climbers and hikers and anglers and skiers. This is a place that caters to recreation, a fact that puts a different spin on the social fabric. Aspen has been since the 1950s the archetype of the Rocky Mountain resort town, and gentrification here has reached a fully evolved state that is equaled nowhere else.

Arriving in Aspen can be something of a culture shock. One is hard-pressed to find a more tony town in the American West. It is so full of movie stars and rock stars and celebrity CEOs that it's tough to get reasonable accommodations, a casual meal, or even a parking place. This phenomenon is part of the culture by now, one that is being played out in other mountain towns, from Telluride to Crested Butte to Santa Fe. The glamour can be a lot of fun

A highlight of the Elk Range is its wildflower displays.

for some but off-putting to others. So if upscale isn't your style, Glenwood Springs, while rapidly gentrifying, is a good bet for a base of operations for the Maroon Bells Circuit. A much larger city, Glenwood puts on no airs, is right on the I-70, and remains within an easy drive of the trailhead. Accommodations and restaurants are comfortable and reasonable—for now.

From Glenwood Springs, drive Colorado 82 past spectacular views of Mount Sopris, through the town of Basalt to Aspen (be careful, the winding two-lane road is nicknamed Killer 82 for a reason). Find Maroon Lake Road. It's only a 15-minute drive down the road to the lake, but beware that this, one of the most scenic areas in the Rockies, is a busy place. From Memorial Day to Labor Day, only shuttle buses are allowed on the road from Aspen to the lake during the day, an effort to reduce traffic. The first bus leaves the Aspen Highland Ski Area at 8:30, the last one leaves Maroon Lake at 5 P.M. Three campgrounds are located on the road to the lake; if you want to camp in one of these, tell the person at the gate. From Labor Day to the end of October, there's no restriction on private cars on Maroon Lake Road, an argument for doing the hike off-season.

The usual strategy for the hike is to arrive at Maroon Lake trailhead by midday and plan on camping 1 mile (2 km) or less beyond Crater Lake, or about 4 miles (6 km) from the trailhead. The easy first day sets you up for a tough second day, which crosses West Maroon Pass and Frigid Air Pass, with a camp that night in Fravert Basin. The third day crosses Trail Rider Pass and descends to a camp at Snowmass Lake, where some people take a day to climb Snowmass peak, at 14,092 feet (4,296 m). The final day requires hiking over Buckskin Pass, down through Minehaha Gulch, and back out to Maroon Lake.

On the Maroon Snowmass Trail, en route to Buckskin Pass.

The classic view of the Bells from Maroon Lake. PHOTO BY BLAINE HARRINGTON.

At present, no permit is required for the Maroon Bells Circuit. Any party venturing into the Maroon Bells Wilderness is required to self-register, which is how the rangers get the word out about rules and regulations. At Maroon Lake, find the self-registration kiosk at the overnight parking lot. The route is described clockwise from Maroon Lake, but it obviously can be traveled in either direction.

Maroon Lake is the logical starting point for this hike, but if you prefer to avoid the busy scene in Aspen, you can also enter this loop hike from the Maroon Snowmass trailhead out of Snowmass Village. From there, a 9-mile (14½ km) hike takes you to Snowmass Lake, where you can join the circuit around the Bells. There's another trailhead, the East Fork of West Maroon, off the Schofield Pass jeep road, but that road is rough enough to require a beefy vehicle and, if you go up to Schofield Pass for a look, significant four-wheel-driving skill.

This route has other variations as well. A left turn south of Trail Rider Pass will take you to Geneva Lake, a two-day extension to the hike described here; a turn north at Buckskin Pass takes you to Willow Lake, a side trip that also adds two days.

HAZARDS

In early season, the Maroon Bells Circuit comes with predictably increased dangers related to the previous winter's snowfall: steep hard snow in (and below) the passes, and high-water stream crossings. Avoid these hazards by doing the hike in mid- or late season.

At present, bear-resistant food containers are not required, but they are a good idea, as black bears are frequently seen on the route, particularly in Fravert Basin.

SEASON

Because this route is so high, its opening is dependent on the previous winter's snowfall, or the hiker's ability to travel on snow-covered trails. The Maroon Bells Wilderness high country traditionally opens to hikers in early July, when only the passes still retain snow. Recent low-snow years have advanced the season by at week or two. Significant snowfall occurs by mid-October, so late September is the season's traditional end. Wildflower blooms follow the snowmelt in the high meadows, usually in mid-July. Aspen groves usually reach peak autumn color in late September.

ROUTE

From Aspen drive, or take the shuttle bus from Aspen Highland Ski Area, up to Maroon Lake via Maroon Lake Road. At the Maroon Lake trailhead, take time to enjoy the view of the Bells over the lake. Find the Maroon Snowmass Trail 1975 at the northwest end of the lake and set out.

At 1¾ miles (2¾ km) you reach a trail junction. Turn left onto West Maroon Creek Trail 1970. Go 2 miles (3 km), and 1½ hours from Maroon Lake you reach Crater Lake (10,076 feet, 3,072 m). Camping is not permitted right at the lake itself, so continue on West Maroon Creek Trail 1970. Cross West Maroon Creek just over 1 mile (2 km) from Crater Lake; the creek here is a braided, shallow channel. There are campsites in the trees just beyond, at about 10,500 feet (3,200 m).

Since this is the first day, and you're likely to have started late in the day, making your camp here just beyond Crater Lake is a good idea. The following day is the most strenuous of the entire circuit, taking you up and over West Maroon Pass (12,500 feet, 3,811 m) and Frigid Air Pass (12,380 feet, 3,774 m). Having an easy first day makes even more sense if you're coming from low altitude, as the thin air above 10,000 feet (3,050 m) will take some getting used to. This is a pretty part of the Rockies; there's no need to hurry.

The next day leave the campsites in the trees at 10,500 feet and cross West Maroon Creek a second time. This crossing is more difficult than the first, because the channel is deeper and the water faster. Continue the ascent on big switchbacks. The trail eventually gets quite steep near the top, West Maroon Pass (about 4 miles,

6 km, from and 2,000 feet, 610 m, above Crater Lake). The pass is only a few hundred feet lower than the surrounding peaks, so the views are stunning. The basin on the other side is Schofield, a good one for flowers if your timing is right. From here, the mountain town of Crested Butte is only a day hike away.

Descend the other side, enjoying the staggering color gardens of wildflowers as you hike. After approximately 1 mile (2 km) and 800 vertical feet (240 m), an unsigned (but cairned) trail junction is reached. The trail to the left leads to the East Fork of the West Maroon Creek trailhead. Stay to the right, heading toward Frigid Air Pass on Fravert Basin Trail 1974. More flowers of many varieties light the way as you ascend toward the second pass of the day about 2 miles (3 km) from West Maroon Pass. As you climb, a number of ridges or false passes might be confusing; just stay on the trail and continue up. Just below the pass you'll reach another junction, near a small pond, marked by a cairn; this is a side trail into Hasley Basin. Continue up, bearing right on Trail 1974, toward Frigid Air Pass, which though lower is even steeper for a few hundred feet at the top than West Maroon, but not as sustained. This may be the most interesting of the four passes, rocky and rugged and wild. Once on top, the views into Fravert Basin and into the back side, not the familiar side, of the Maroon Bells are outrageous, well worth all the effort and 4,000-foot (1,200 m) elevation gain.

Descend from the pass via steep switchbacks into Fravert Basin, passing in early season waterfalls big and small on the way down. Descend about 1,600 feet (488 m) to a flat area near 10,800 feet (3,290 m). There's plenty of good camping here, and farther down, before and after the trail crosses the North Fork of the Crystal. This section of the route is probably the most lightly traveled of the

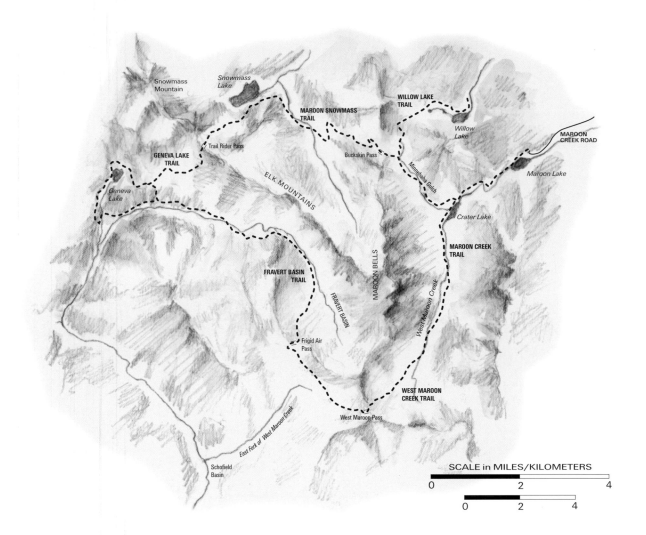

SCALE in MILES/KILOMETERS

entire circuit; it's not on the way to anywhere and so only those doing the circuit pass this way. Fravert Basin makes a scenic camp.

On the third day, leave your basin camp and descend slightly to about 10,400 feet (3,170 m) before starting up again on the long climb to Trail Rider Pass. This is another opportunity for wildflower viewing. In 2 to 3 miles (3–5 km), depending on where you camped, you'll reach an intersection. The left turn goes to a loop around Geneva Lake or out to the Schofield Pass jeep road. Take the right fork, which ascends the steep North Fork Cutoff Trail 1976 from Fravert Basin to the pass. This short section joins the main trail, Geneva Lake Trail 1973, in less than 2 miles (3 km), where the ascent relents at a little plateau with a couple of small lakes. The final climb up to Trail Rider Pass, at 12,400 feet (3,780 m), is not as strenuous as West Maroon Pass. At the top there are wonderful views of Snowmass Lake far below, and of Snowmass Mountain, and back into Fravert Basin. Trail Rider is approximately 7 miles (11 km) from Frigid Air Pass.

From the pass, descend to reach Snowmass Lake in 2 miles (3 km), about 7 miles (11 km) from Fravert Basin. Snowmass Lake is a popular weekend backpacking destination, so try to time your trip so you're camping here midweek. Views of Snowmass Mountain are outstanding, and in fact Snowmass Lake makes a good choice for a layover day, as that allows for an ascent of Snowmass Mountain should conditions and skill level permit. The hike to the top of this Fourteener (14,092 feet, 4,296 m) gains 3,000 feet (910 m) above the lake in a 6-mile (8 km) round-trip. There's a trail most of the way, but steep snow may stop you near the top of the basin. Follow the flower-bordered trail around the left side of the lake. Cairns lead the way through the short sections of talus. A steep section up to the entrance of the bowl may require an ice ax, depending on snow depth, or a prudent retreat. Expect this round-trip hike to take six or seven hours.

On the fourth trail day, leave your camp at Snowmass Lake and find the intersection with Trail 1975; bear right onto Trail 1973 and hike for ½ mile (¾ km). At the second intersection, bear right again onto Maroon Snowmass Trail 1975 and head toward Buckskin Pass, the least strenuous of the four passes on the circuit, approximately 4 miles (6 km) from the lake. The trail ascends gentle,

OPPOSITE: *Ridge camp in the Maroon Bells Wilderness.* PHOTO BY GREGG ADAMS PHOTOGRAPHY.

grassy slopes of the high meadows (with yet more flowers), and then some final switchbacks up to the pass. At the top of 12,462-foot (3,799 m) Buckskin Pass turn to take a final look at Snowmass Mountain, Capitol Peak, and Pyramid Peak. These are some of the best views on the entire hike.

From the pass, descend into the basin, which soon narrows into Minnehaha Gulch. The trail leads down to the intersection near Crater Lake and out to Maroon Lake 4 miles (6 km) from the pass.

Information

ASPEN RANGER STATION
White River National Forest
8006 West Hallam St.
Aspen, CO 81611 USA
(970) 925-3445
www.fs.fed/r2/whiteriver

LEFT: *Hiking the circuit in September means fall color, but no wildflowers.* PHOTO BY GALEN ROWELL/MOUNTAIN LIGHT.

BELOW: *High and wild: the Maroon Bells Circuit dips below 10,000 feet (3,048 m) only at the trailhead, and traverses four passes over 12,000 feet (3,658 m) high.* PHOTO BY TONY DEMIN/NETWORK ASPEN.

BUCKSKIN GULCH
Paria River Wilderness

*Southern Utah,
United States*

DISTANCE: 24 miles (38½ km) one-way
TIME: 3-4 days
PHYSICAL CHALLENGE: 1 2 **3** 4 5
PSYCHOLOGICAL CHALLENGE: 1 2 **3** 4 5
STAGING: Kanab, Utah, or Page, Arizona

Imagine a corridor of stone so long it snakes through the red rock of southern Utah for more than 15 miles (24 km), so deep you cannot see the sky, and so narrow you have to remove your pack in places to get through. This could only be Buckskin Gulch, the most impressive slot canyon in North America, perhaps anywhere. Hiking the length of this sinuous defile is a backcountry experience that will amaze you, and challenge you in unexpected ways.

Centrally located in a fertile area for desert hiking, this surreal set of narrows lies north of the Grand Canyon, east of Zion National Park, and west of Lake Powell. From start to finish Buckskin Gulch takes you on a subterranean tour of the layer cake of the Colorado Plateau, starting in the Chinle and Moenave formations and proceeding upstrata as it travels downhill, so it finishes in the dramatic red rock of

Navajo sandstone. The beauty here is varied, both magnificent and subtle, but always changing. Sections of rock walls are sculpted and fluted, reflecting the bright, indirect southern Utah sunshine in a warm red hue, while in other places the canyon walls are dark and high, even intimidating. But found along its great length are a few delicious surprises. You can suddenly come around a corner to find a fairy tale grotto, a short section aligned just right to make the walls

OPPOSITE: *With more than 18 miles (29 km) of narrows, Buckskin Gulch takes the hiker into an unforgettable corridor of red rock.*
PHOTO BY PETER POTTERFIELD.

Stopping for lunch where the canyon briefly opens up, half a day down the gulch from the Middle Route. PHOTO BY PETER POTTERFIELD.

glow with sunlight, and where a spring gives life to the brilliant green of an old cottonwood tree.

Buckskin Gulch leads eventually to its confluence with Paria Canyon, a bizarre subterranean intersection, a hidden meeting place of two drainages that is as spooky as it is abrupt. The narrows of the Paria extend for another five miles, and when combined with the unrelenting narrows of Buckskin and the unlikely start of this hike through the tight confines of Wire Pass, make a canyon journey of sustained power and impact. On exiting, Paria Canyon at last relents, opening as it becomes shallower, returning the hiker to the world of blue sky, sunshine, and red rock with the feeling of having been through something extraordinary.

Intriguing petroglyphs and rock art seen along the way by observant hikers prove that this canyon has seen visitors for thousands of years. No habitations or other dwellings have been found, but the ancient art carved into the walls reinforces the idea that these canyons were an important travel route between what is now southern Utah and northern Arizona. For a thousand years after the birth of Christ, the Anasazi occupied the region. Much later came the Paiutes, who named the Paria for its salty taste.

A cathedral-like ambience within the deep and quiet canyon enhances the spiritual quality of the hike, but this journey is not without hazards. The dry, sandy floor that snakes along mile after mile makes for easy traveling, but it can be deceptive. Those piles of logs jammed between the canyon walls high overhead show just how high the water in the canyon can get as it roars down in a flood from higher elevations. Buckskin Gulch is not a place to be when it rains, so confirm a dry forecast before hiking. The gulch drains a wide landscape, including areas from Bryce Canyon to Zion. When this slot flashes, the fury of dirty water can change the very features of the canyon.

In fact, a notable landmark, first described by the pioneering canyon explorer Mike Kelsey, was the infamous "cesspool," a chest-deep pool of stagnant water one had to wade as if in an audition for an Indiana Jones movie. But the last time through I was pleased to find the cesspool was gone without a trace, having been scoured out by a recent flash flood. The principle obstacle had become something entirely new—the by-now famous "boulder jam," a blocking puzzle far down canyon that called for patience and powers of observation, not muscle or rope, to surmount.

Expect the unexpected in Buckskin Gulch. Your journey will be unique, which is part of the magic of Buckskin Gulch: It's a different hike every time you do it.

LOGISTICS & STRATEGY

Buckskin Gulch, part of the Paria River Wilderness, cuts through the Colorado Plateau of southern Utah within the boundaries of the newly created Escalante Staircase National Monument. Trailhead access is off US Highway 89, midway between Page, Arizona, and Kanab, Utah. Either town makes a good staging area for this hike, as both have ample accommodations, restaurants, and services. But both are a long way from major airports. The preferred option is to fly into Las Vegas, which is about four hours'

ABOVE: *The Paria River is the only reliable water source on the route.*

OPPOSITE: *Expect an ankle-deep wade from the confluence to the exit at Whitehouse trailhead.* PHOTOS BY PETER POTTERFIELD.

drive from Kanab, considerably better than the six hours or more it takes to drive from Salt Lake City.

The BLM office in Kanab is a good source of information about local conditions in the gulch, and every hiker contemplating this route should call or stop in for an update before venturing into the canyon. The Paria Ranger Station (sometimes called an "information station"), located near the spot where US Highway 89 crosses the Paria River, can also provide information, but the outpost is open only seasonally, doesn't have a telephone, and will definitely be closed when you arrive for a pre-dawn start. The recommended route for Buckskin Gulch ends near this ranger station, but the starting point for the hike, Wire Pass, is located off a good dirt road (fine for rental cars) some 5 miles (8 km) west of the ranger station.

Up-to-date information on Buckskin is essential because the canyon can change dramatically. Obstacles come and go, created and removed by flash floods that can alter the nature of the route literally overnight. Backpackers in Buckskin should expect typical elements of any canyon hike: some wading in muddy water, some log jams, and perhaps a "pour-off" or "dry fall" that requires a shoulder stand or even a short length of rope to surmount. On my last trip, flash floods had hosed the canyon clean, leaving no major pools or obstacles of any sort until a few miles from the end of the canyon. There, a serious log-and-boulder jam required extensive investigation before my partner and I found the keyhole through which we could climb down and through in minutes, lowering our packs on a length of rope.

Further strategizing for a hike through Buckskin Gulch revolves around the fact there is only one exit between either

end. You definitely do not want to be in this historically narrow slot canyon when it rains. Even if the forecast is dry, don't camp on the canyon floor. Instead, spend the first night above the only midpoint exit, known as the Middle Route or at the high-and-dry campsites near the end of the gulch.

The so-called Middle Route is a problematic exit up the north wall of Buckskin Gulch approximately 8 miles (13 km) from the start. This escape chute is difficult to find from the canyon floor and involves some scrambling to ascend. Described as dangerous and hazardous so often, its proper name now seems to be "The Hazardous Middle Route." Nevertheless, the strategy is an appealing one: From the car, proceed 2 miles (3 km) through Wire Pass, hike 6 miles (9½ km) in the gulch itself to the Middle Route exit, climb out of the canyon (carrying sufficient water), and camp safely on the sunny red-rock bench above. The next day, if you're convinced the weather is safe for canyon hiking, descend back into Buckskin Gulch to finish the hike to the Paria.

That plan works only if you manage to find the Middle Route and successfully climb out. Once found, the Middle Route presents difficulties both climbing out and climbing back in (packs must be lowered back down on a rope). The smart call here is to be prepared to hike as far as the campsites near the confluence of Buckskin Gulch and the Paria Canyon, 14½ miles (24 km) from the start, in the event the Middle Route eludes you.

This strategy is quite workable and fun: Sleep at the trailhead the night before (or plan on a pre-dawn arrival) and get a dawn start. Most of the going is on a sandy canyon floor, so barring serious obstacles, the distance to the confluence camps makes a reasonable day, seven to nine hours. You can always keep the Middle Route option open, should you find the way, and find that you can safely climb up it. Whatever you do, don't spend the night on the canyon floor.

Once past the magical, even spooky confluence of Buckskin Gulch with the Paria, any sense of seriousness relents. The Paria narrows are only about 5 miles (8 km) long, and beyond those, Paria Canyon becomes broad and shallow. Good camping can be found in both directions from the confluence, but the closest sites to Buckskin are downstream. That gives you a chance to explore part of Paria Canyon before heading back north to the exit trailhead. The Paria usually has water in it, which makes the final 8 miles (13 km) from the gulch back to White House trailhead an ankle-deep wade. Bring sandals or wading shoes to save your boots.

There is no reliable fresh water in Buckskin Gulch. A seasonal creek near the confluence may or may not flow, so one must start the hike with a two-day supply. Ample water usually can be found in the Paria, a fact that can be confirmed before setting out. Check the Paria where it flows under US 89. If there's water there, there will be water downstream. But because upstream uses may include agriculture, take precautions. I drank a lot of Paria River water, but only after it was both filtered and chemically treated.

HAZARDS

Flash floods are the primary concern in Buckskin Gulch, but to the other, predictable hazards of desert hiking you can add some unusual ones, such as quicksand. There is no confirmed report of a hiker disappearing slowly into the ooze, but partially dried pools can hide mud thick enough to snare and trip up a hiker with a pack. Black widows, scorpions, and rattlesnakes headline the dangerous denizens—along with tarantulas. I've watched them actually swim the river, seeking me out. A tent with mesh renders these dangers mostly moot.

SEASON

Late spring, April through June, is the popular season for hiking Buckskin, but be creative. The hike in fact can be done anytime the trailhead road is open and rainstorms, thunderstorms, or snow don't threaten. Short winter days can really increase the psych-out factor, and high summer is generally too hot, which is why most people hike the gulch in spring or in September and October. I went to Buckskin once in early March and again in late November, and enjoyed stable weather and more solitude as a result.

TOP: *Descending back down the Middle Route after a night camped up on the Dive.* PHOTO BY PETER POTTERFIELD.

ABOVE: *The entrance to Buckskin Gulch through the tight narrows of Wire Pass foreshadows what is to come.* PHOTO BY PETER POTTERFIELD.

RIGHT: *You know you've found the elusive Middle Route when you encounter the unmistakable rock art.* PHOTO BY PETER POTTERFIELD.

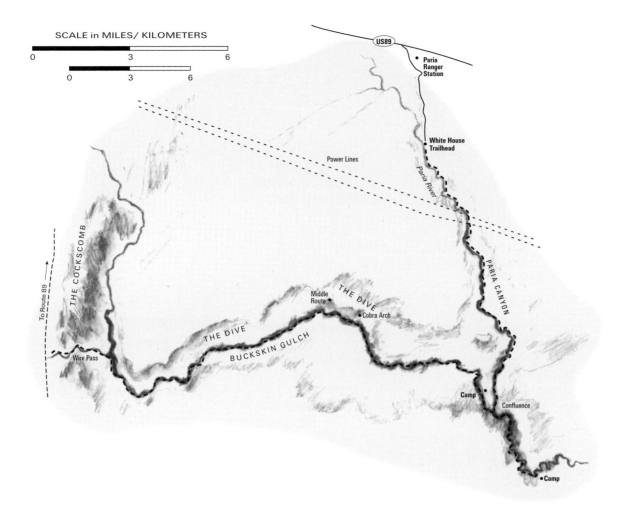

SCALE in MILES/ KILOMETERS

ROUTE

From Kanab, Utah, head east on US 89 to the Paria Ranger Station (44 miles, 71 km); from Page, Arizona, head west (30 miles, 48 km). Leave a second vehicle or a mountain bike at the campground at the White House trailhead, 2 miles (3 km) south of the ranger station, or arrange for a ride with a shuttle provider. The hike will end at this trailhead. Retrace your route onto US 89 east toward Kanab and drive approximately 5 miles (8 km) before turning off to the south on a dirt road between mileposts 25 and 26. About 4 miles (6 km) south of the highway the dirt road actually crosses the upper end of Buckskin Gulch, at this point a broad, sandy wash. You could start hiking here, but few people do as the narrows don't begin for miles. Instead, continue driving south on the dirt road to the signed Wire Pass trailhead and parking lot, almost 10 miles (16 km) from US 89. Sign in at the trailhead register and self-service pay station.

At first light, start hiking through Wire Pass, a short slot so narrow that in places progress is accomplished only by turning sideways. This prelude leads to Buckskin Gulch in less than 2 miles (3 km). Turn right (east) in Buckskin Gulch (look for petroglyphs as you enter) and proceed toward the Paria River, about 12 miles (19 km) distant. There is almost no way to get off route as the sandy canyon floor leads eastward between the walls of this dramatic set of narrows that averages between 10 and 12 feet (3–3½ m) wide for its entire length. Deep, muddy pools may require wading in the first half of the canyon.

Between 6 and 7 miles (9½–11 km) from Wire Pass, the canyon seems to shallow and widen very slightly as it makes a gentle turn to the right below a sharply overhanging wall on the left. This is the point at which the Middle Route descends into the gulch down the north (left-hand) wall. GPS equipment will not work in the gulch, and no distinctive landmark points the way, although there is a beautiful petroglyph about 12 feet (3½ m) off the canyon floor once you find the Middle Route and start up. If your plan is to climb out via the Middle Route to camp on the benches above, watch carefully and move slowly in this section of the gulch. The route is not obvious in any way. If you locate the exit, ascend by climbing a steep cleft that offers some purchase for your boots for about 15 feet (4½ m) to the first sandy ledge, followed by another longer but easier scramble up a rock step. Above the second bench the way opens up and the going is easy. Good campsites can be found on nearby benches and on the north rim (known here as the Dive). To re-enter the gulch the following day, descend the steep sections, lower packs into the canyon on a 40-foot (12 m) length of rope, and continue hiking toward the Paria.

If the way up the Middle Route eludes you, or if you did not intend to leave the canyon at the Middle Route anyway, continue hiking toward the Paria. The canyon walls rise again to several hundred feet as the sandy bottom affords relatively easy travel. You should be prepared for wading the occasional pool, although when I was there in late November 2001 there was no water in the gulch at all east of the Middle Route. About 10 miles (16 km) from Wire Pass, a large log-and-boulder jam blocks the way. The next mile or two (2–3 km) to the confluence with the Paria River are the most stunning of the entire route. In this incredible stretch, the canyon walls soar to their maximum height of almost 500 feet (150 m). Soon, the gulch floor becomes wet and the canyon opens onto a large, sandy hill with cottonwood trees on the left side, harboring several good camp spots well above the canyon floor.

Another few hundred yards leads to the confluence with the Paria. This is a unique place that will take you by surprise: an intersection of two deep, narrow canyons submerged in the Navajo sandstone of the Colorado Plateau. Head upstream (north) toward the exit trailhead, or downstream (south) to take at look at Paria Canyon. Good camping can be found by hiking south; a prominent sand hill on the right bank is reached in less than 1 mile (2 km); approximately 1 mile farther is another outstanding camp with a large cottonwood tree.

The exit to White House trailhead is reached by turning left (north) at the confluence of Buckskin Gulch and the Paria River. Paria Canyon begins to gradually open up in the ensuing 2 or 3 miles (3–5 km), becoming broader and more shallow, and letting in some welcome sunshine. Safe camping options are found along the right (east) bank. Watch for the occasional petroglyph in the high, red rock walls of the canyon on the west side. About 5 miles (8 km) from the confluence, power lines cross overhead; the trailhead is reached approximately 3 miles (5 km) beyond. Watch for a sign on the right-hand bank that points the way out of the riverbed to the White House trailhead and parking lot.

Information

For information, permits, shuttle providers, and current conditions:
KANAB BLM FIELD OFFICE
318 North First East
Kanab, UT 84741 USA
(435) 644-2672
www.ut.blm.gov/kanab/index.html

BLM PARIA INFORMATION STATION
US Highway 89
No telephone
www.az.blm.gov/paria

ST. GEORGE BLM FIELD OFFICE
345 East Riverside Drive
St. George, UT 84790 USA
(435) 688-3246

OPPOSITE: *One of the safe camps in Paria Canyon, south of the confluence with Buckskin Gulch.* PHOTO BY PETER POTTERFIELD.

BELOW: *Though barren, sinewy, and narrow for much of its length, Buckskin Gulch opens up in a few stretches of idyllic grottos.* PHOTO BY ROBERT FARRINGTON.

THE WONDERLAND TRAIL
Mount Rainier

Washington, United States

DISTANCE: 93-mile (150 km) loop
TIME: 12–14 days
PHYSICAL CHALLENGE: 1 2 3 **4** 5
PSYCHOLOGICAL CHALLENGE: 1 2 **3** 4 5
STAGING: Seattle, Washington

More than anything but rain, Mount Rainier symbolizes the Cascade Mountains and the Pacific Northwest. Rising from its lowland valleys like a vision, looking in fact like a papier-mâché stage prop, Rainier shows more local relief than Everest. Even from Seattle, 50 miles (80 km) away, the mountain moves people. The simple desire to climb Rainier was the very thing that put me on an airplane and brought me from New Mexico to the Northwest many years ago. In the beginning, there was only the desire to reach the top of that incredible peak draped in its mantle of glaciers. There I was, puking on the 14,410-foot (4,393 m) summit with the other pilgrims who had climbed too high, too fast. Only later did I get on more intimate—and more rewarding—terms with the mountain, and the wilderness at its feet.

In those intervening decades I've learned to enjoy the backcountry around Rainier as much as its higher slopes. Again and again I'm drawn back to hike through the forests and meadows and gorges and ridges that ring the mountain, to absorb the unique ambience of this wild place, enhanced by the looming presence of Rainier. Scientists say that big mountains actually exert local forces that can be measured on gravity meters, a fact that comes as no surprise to me after hiking on the Wonderland Trail.

To hike all 93 miles (150 km) of the Wonderland is to take the Grand Tour of Mount Rainier's domain. The 360-degree view of the mountain, under varied moods and changing light, is reason enough to come for a look. The cathedral-like ancient forests of Douglas fir and western hemlock, the expanses of lovely alpine meadows (locally called "parks"), the roaring, glacier-fed rivers, and the 35 cubic miles (146 cubic km) of ice draping the rocky flanks of the mountain combine for a landscape of irresistible appeal.

If you spend a half day hiking up through forests of old growth trees so tall they merge in a canopy 150 feet (45 m) above, the moody gloom of the deep woods will suddenly give way to the brilliant sunlight at Indian Henry's Hunting Ground or Klapatche Park. These surprise clearings of open meadow reveal in summer a carpet of mountain lupine, or avalanche lilies, or Indian paintbrush swaying in the breeze. Cross Panhandle Gap and you'll be digging for your Gore-Tex, stopping to watch, mesmerized, as ragged streamers of clouds blow across the glaciers of Rainier's summit dome, seemingly very near to this high, alpine vantage point. Mystic Tarn at dusk will reflect the golden visage of the north side of the mountain, the awesome Willis Wall, as it glows with sunset. The variety of terrain traversed in just a couple of weeks on the circuit around the mountain seems almost unbelievable, even for 370 square miles (960 square km) of mountain splendor.

Just be prepared to do a little work. Distinctive radial ridges called "cleavers" emanate down from high on Rainier right into the backcountry surrounding the mountain. These ridges create serious topography, a successive series of obstructions rising above valleys deeply dug out by raging glacial torrents. These defining features require multiple climbs above 7,000 feet (2,100 m) to surmount, taking the hiker into a high, austere alpine wilderness of ice and rock where summer is an infrequent visitor. The necessity of going up and over these serial ridgelines means that the backcountry traveler who makes a complete circuit of the Wonderland Trail will gain more that 20,000 feet (6,100 m) of elevation in just 90 miles (145 km).

OPPOSITE: *Mount Rainier is surrounded by majestic old-growth forests of Douglas fir, cedar, and hemlock.* PHOTO BY JIM NELSON.

The Ohanapecosh River drains its namesake glacier on the southeast flank of Mount Rainier. PHOTO BY PETER POTTERFIELD.

LOGISTICS & STRATEGY

Completely encircling Mount Rainier, the Wonderland Trail offers unparalleled flexibility. You can do it all at once in a single push, do it in sections over several seasons, or do it over a decade in two- or three-day increments and see the mountain in different conditions and seasons. If you are fit, committed, and willing to walk in all weathers, the Wonderland can be done in as little as eight days. A more reasonable time frame is 12 to 14 days, a period that allows for a more relaxed pace, some time to appreciate the scenery, and a rain day or two. Take even more time if you want to linger near the high-elevation meadows, or make tangential explorations. The Wonderland is an aptly named hiking circuit that accommodates a variety of approaches.

No matter how you choose to do the Wonderland Trail, the gateway to Rainier is through Seattle. The airport is just an hour and a half from Mount Rainier National Park. Many hikers rent a car for the journey to Rainier, the better to explore its environs. Bus service is available, however, from both Seattle and Tacoma to the funky village of Longmire, which lies within the park boundary. This small town, with a grocery and a hotel, is the principle stop for public transportation to Rainier. It also serves as park headquar-

ters. The bus makes sense if you don't want to leave your rental car sitting in a parking lot for two weeks while you're hiking around the mountain.

For those ready to commit a couple of weeks to hike the entire circuit in a single push, one of the challenges is to determine the best strategy. Carrying food for 12 days or more around Mount Rainier is going to make for a heavy pack, a slow pace, and quite likely a diminished experience. Better to stash food beforehand at one or two of the six points where the trail intersects a road, or have friends rendezvous with you at those places with fresh provisions. There is no opportunity along the route to buy food or supplies, other than in Longmire, where selection is limited.

Obtaining the necessary permits is a different sort of challenge. Sixty percent of all wilderness campsites along the Wonderland Trail can be reserved in advance; the remaining 40 percent are issued on a first-come, first-served basis the day of departure. The availability of these on-the-spot permits cannot be counted on when you want to start your trip; they work better for those who are hiking only a section of the Wonderland at a time, and can be more flexible about where they go. Reservations are strongly recommended for hikers who want to travel around Rainier in a single push. Demand is highest in July and August. Off-season hikers will have an easier time getting permits for the dozen or so camps required to complete the circuit.

What permits do you ask for? Hikers on the Wonderland Trail are restricted to camping in designated sites. There are 22 campsites along the route, a situation that spreads out the impact so that every through-hiker is not vying for the same campground every night. The designated camps are not evenly spaced, which means you'll walk right by one as you head to the next, depending on your desired destination and your starting point. Campsites are separated not just by miles but also by substantial elevation gain, which complicates planning. A 3,000-foot (910 m) climb in a single day is not unusual, so be sure to pay attention to elevation between the camps as well as mileage when planning your hike. The route description below can help determine which camps work best.

Each year, backcountry reservations are accepted on April 1 for the entire season through September. The best strategy for obtaining the permits you want is this: Go to the Mount Rainier National Park Web site, download and complete the reservation form, and fax it to the Wilderness Information Center on April 1.

Experienced backcountry enthusiasts who don't mind going a few miles off the trail, or climbing a few thousand feet higher, or camping away from water sources, have another option. A limited number of "cross-country zones" around the mountain can add flexibility, and a degree of solitude, to camping on the Wonderland Trail. Regulations are strict for these zones, group size is limited to five people, and the terrain is often difficult to negotiate. Rangers emphasize that cross-country camping is suitable *only* for those adept with map and compass, and in excellent physical condition for enduring the additional challenge. Contact the Wilderness Information Center to inquire about the availability of cross-country zones.

With your permit in hand, you're ready for the Wonderland Trail itself. My suggestion for a complete circuit is to start in Longmire and do the trail clockwise. The rhythm of the hiking works well that way, starting on the busy south side of the mountain, where most visitors arrive, before moving up around the scenic west side to Mowich Lake, a good resupply point. From there, the route travels on to the wild, remote north side of the mountain to White River, another good resupply point. The route then runs down the east side, where some of the route's most scenic hiking is to be found, to Box Canyon. From there, the route parallels the Stevens Canyon Highway back to Longmire.

In truth, it matters not where you start or which direction you hike, or whether you do it all at once or in a dozen two- or three-night trips. This walk in the shadow of Mount Rainier will pay off no matter how you go. If you have less than a week to spend at Rainier, I suggest sampling the Wonderland Trail by one of three options: hiking from Ipsut Creek to Mystic Lake, a two- or three-day round-trip; from Longmire to St. Andrews Park, a four- or five-day round-trip; or from the White River Campground Road to Summerland and Panhandle Gap, a two- or three-day round-trip. With a second car, the last trip can be extended to Indian Bar and Cowlitz Divide, with an exit at Box Canyon.

A hiker crosses the Wonderland Trail suspension bridge over Tahoma Creek. PHOTO BY PETER POTTERFIELD.

The backcountry at the foot of Mount Rainier's steep north face is among the wildest in the park. PHOTO BY PETER POTTERFIELD.

A hiker works up through Moraine Park on the Wonderland Trail, bound for Mystic Lake. PHOTO BY PETER POTTERFIELD.

HAZARDS

The eruption of Mount St. Helens in 1980 proved without a doubt that the Cascade volcanoes remain active. For that reason, the Wonderland Trail comes with a set of hazards unique to hiking in North America: mud flows, glacier outburst floods, lahars, pyroclastic flows, and other events relating to Rainier's volcanic origins. While it is unlikely an eruption will happen without warning, mud flows and other glacier-generated floods can and do happen suddenly, so every hiker must come to grips with this weird reality. If you do go, rangers recommend that should you hear rumbling or see rivers rise rapidly, do *not* run downstream, but move to higher ground as fast as possible.

Winter lasts nine months a year on Rainier, and summer only a few weeks, so climate can be hazardous any time of year. Catching all the wind and rain that rolls in from the Pacific, Mount Rainier generates its own weather, much of it bad. Newcomers are aghast at how quickly a hot, sunny day can turn into a cold whiteout, particularly at higher elevations such as Panhandle Gap. Snow can fall in such places any time of year, clouds can hide landmarks, and chilly, damp weather can cause hypothermia in the unprepared.

Proper clothing and good equipment can protect you from the elements, and a map and compass, or GPS receiver—as well as the experience to use them—can help you find the way in a cloud.

Glacier-fed rivers pouring off the mountain can take out bridges or trails on the route. Most of the bigger rivers on the Wonderland have by now been crossed by substantial suspension bridges that have made round-the-mountain progress more predictable than ever before. Check with park rangers when you arrive to ascertain that the Wonderland Trail crossings are "in."

While black bear live in the park they seldom cause problems; still, be sure you take the precaution of hanging your food bags out of reach when in camp. Cougars are regularly but infrequently seen.

SEASON

The best weather in the Pacific Northwest almost always comes in July and August, so that would seem the time to do the route. But those months are also the busiest by far. If you want to hike the Wonderland in the prime of the summer, you'll need to get an early start on your hiking permit, and be prepared to have company along the trail. An alternative plan might be to go early in the season, if you've got the

Glacial meltwater flows over Wauhaukaupauken Falls at Indian Bar. PHOTO BY PETER POTTERFIELD.

A hiker takes a breather at St. Andrews Lake on Rainier's west side. PHOTO BY PETER POTTERFIELD.

backcountry skills, including proficiency on snow-covered trails and route finding. Another option is to go later in the season, when fall color, cool temperatures, and stable weather patterns can make for ideal hiking conditions and snow-free travel. In general, the Wonderland Trail is in hiking condition most years from late June to October, but beware that heavy snow years can delay its opening, and early snow can close it prematurely.

BELOW LEFT: *When the snow melts, Mount Rainier's meadows for a few weeks each year become spectacular flower gardens.* PHOTO BY PETER POTTERFIELD.

BELOW RIGHT: *A backcountry camp near Panhandle Gap, the highest section of the Wonderland Trail.* PHOTO BY PETER POTTERFIELD.

FOLLOWING SPREAD: *Liberty Ridge and the Willis Wall are reflected in Mystic Tarn.* PHOTO BY JAMES MARTIN.

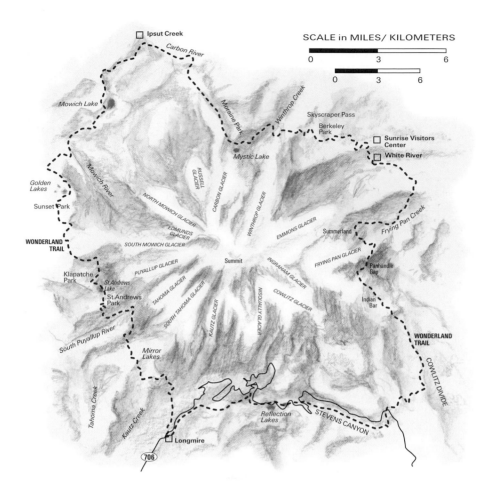

ROUTE

In terms of attractive features on the flanks of Mount Rainier, the 93-mile-long (150 km) Wonderland Trail can be broken down into the ten useful sections listed below. Allowing for both trail mileage and elevation gain, the following route description can be used for trip planning: Determine the features near which you wish to camp, how many overnight stays you're contemplating, and then decide which camps best serve your purposes. With that information, you can apply for your permit.

Given the unusual amount of elevation gain and loss on the Wonderland Trail, most hikers find 9 to 12 miles (14½–19 km) per day a reasonable distance, although fit backcountry travelers certainly can do more. The Wonderland is a route that calls for some free time, however. Build in time at the end of the day to take in the scenery and to think about what you've seen, and schedule a layover day or two to allow for some rest and contemplation, not to mention tent-bound storm days.

Longmire (road access) to Indian Henry's Hunting Ground, 6½ miles (10½ km) The in-park town of Longmire features a hotel, museum, ranger station, and the Wilderness Information Center. If you haven't received your permit in the mail, you'll need to pick it up here before finding the trailhead at the northeast end of town. The route starts in deep forest and climbs up and over Rampart Ridge and down to Pyramid Creek Camp (3 miles, 5 km), near Kautz Creek. From the camp, the route ascends 1,200 feet (360 m) to Devils Dream Camp (5 miles, 8 km), and higher still to the meandering meadows (with outrageous flower gardens in season) at Indian Henry's Hunting Ground (6½ miles, 10½ km) and nearby Mirror Lakes, both with unobstructed views into the southwest flank of the mountain.

Indian Henry's to Klapatche Park, 10½ miles (17 km) From the open high country near Indian Henry's the trail descends sharply 1,700 feet (518 m) in 1½ miles (2½ km) to the swaying suspension bridge at Tahoma Creek. From this memorable bridge the route climbs out of the river drainage for 1,400 feet (420 m) and 2 miles (3 km) to Emerald Ridge, and then down once again 1,000 feet (300 m) to the South Puyallup River and the South Puyallup Camp, 6½ miles (10½ km) from Indian Henry's, and the first backcountry camp since Devils Dream. From the South Puyallup, the Wonderland Trail gains 2,000 feet (610 m) to the high country at St. Andrews Lake and St. Andrews Park, with awesome views of the mountain, before descending slightly to Aurora Lake at Klapatche Park and the nearby Klapatche Park Camp, one of the most scenic camps on the entire route, 10½ miles (17 km) from Indian Henry's.

Klapatche Park to Golden Lakes, 7½ miles (12 km) The Wonderland Trail drops 1,900 feet (580 m) from Klapatche Park, working back into the ancient forest, reaching the North Puyallup Camp in 3 miles (5 km) before regaining 1,200 feet (365 m) as it climbs into Sunset Park and Golden Lakes Camp, 7½ miles (12 km) from Klapatche Park. Be sure to hang your food and take other bear precautions, as in my experience there is as much bear activity here at Golden Lakes as anywhere in the park.

OPPOSITE: *A hiker climbs out of the forest above Mowich Lake.* PHOTO BY JAMES MARTIN.

Golden Lakes to Mowich Lake (road access), 10½ miles (17 km) From Golden Lakes, the route drops quickly out of the high meadows 2,400 feet (730 m) into the forest and on to Mowich River Camp at 7 miles (11 km) before climbing steeply once again, recovering 2,300 feet (700 m), to Mowich Lake Campground. There is an unpaved road all the way from WA 165 to Mowich Lake, which makes this stop a potential resupply point—the first since Longmire. The road also means cars, people, and noise, a slightly shocking reality check after a wild and scenic 35 miles (56 km) afoot.

Mowich Lake to Ipsut Creek Campground (road access), 5½ miles (9 km) From Mowich Lake, the route rises slightly to Ipsut Pass before dropping 2,500 feet (760 m) to Ipsut Creek Camp at 5½ miles (9 km), a relatively easy day. Ipsut Creek Campground is accessible to automobiles via the Carbon River entrance to the park, and so is a resupply alternative to Mowich Lake.

Ipsut Creek to Mystic Lake, 7½ miles (12 km) The next two sections are among the most remote and appealing on the Wonderland Trail. From Ipsut Creek, the Wonderland Trail ascends the Carbon River Valley for just under 3 miles (5 km) to the Carbon River Camp under the Echo Cliffs. Above the camp, the route crosses the Carbon River via a suspension ridge, then rises alongside the snout of the Carbon Glacier for a steep 1½ miles (2½ km) (hot and dry in summer), ascending 1,800 feet (550 m) to Dick Creek Camp. From Dick Creek, the route ascends 3½ miles (5½ km) into gentler terrain, through meadows and into Moraine Park, before cresting a ridge and dropping down to Mystic Lake, with its sublime views of the Willis Wall, and Mystic Camp, 7½ miles (12 km) from Ipsut Creek.

Mystic Lake to Sunrise (road access), 9 miles (15 km) From Mystic Camp, the route descends to cross Winthrop Creek (check that the creek has not washed out the crossing) before rising 1,000 feet (300 m) to Granite Creek Camp at 4½ miles (7 km). The Wonderland climbs out of Granite Creek and up 500 feet (150 m) to Skyscraper Pass, one of the highest points on the route at 6,740 feet (2,055 m). The trail then passes through the meadows of Berkeley Park to Frozen Lake, and on to Sunrise Camp at Shadow Lake, 8½ miles (13¾ km) from Mystic Camp. If you're going to resupply at the Sunrise Visitors Center, or just want to take a look, it's ½ mile (1 km) off the Wonderland Trail. Take the ½-mile (1 km) spur trail signed SUNRISE found 1 mile (2 km) beyond Shadow Lake.

Sunrise to White River Campground (road access) and Summerland, 10½ miles (17 km) From Sunrise, hike 3½ miles (5½ km) and 2,000 feet (610 m) down to White River Campground, a major staging point for climbing Rainier via the Emmons Glacier route, and a busy campground and access point. Some hikers choose to start the Wonderland Trail here. From the campground, find the Wonderland Trail from the campground loop, and follow it as it parallels the road for 1½ miles (2½ km); it's an additional 5 miles (8 km) contouring around Goat Island Mountain and hiking up Frying Pan Creek to reach the meadows at Summerland, more than 2,000 feet (610 m) above White River, 10½ miles (17 km) from Sunrise.

Summerland to Box Canyon (road access), 12 miles (19 km) From Summerland, the Wonderland Trail rises to its highest point, Panhandle Gap, at 6,750 feet (2,058 m). Look for mountain goats here. From the gap, the route traverses boulder fields, possible

snow slopes, and terraced bowls as it descends to Indian Bar, a small, picturesque meadow bisected by the gravel-strewn Ohanepecosh River bar, tucked deep in a canyon more than 1,500 feet (450 m) and 4 miles (6 km) below. The camp here is one of my favorites. From Indian Bar, the route climbs 500 feet (150 m) up to the crest of the spectacular Cowlitz Divide and the beginning of a superb ridge walk offering nonstop views of Rainier, and the Tatoosh Range to the south, as the trail descends along the Divide more than 2,500 feet (760 m) to Nickel Creek Camp, 11 miles (18 km) from Summerland, or down a final mile (2 km) to Box Canyon and road access.

Box Canyon to Longmire (road access), 13½ miles (21½ km) From Box Canyon, the Wonderland Trail crosses the Stevens Canyon Highway and proceeds west toward Longmire on the south side. It's heresy to say so, but in many ways, this section of the route is the least interesting part of the Wonderland, paralleling a busy highway full of noisy recreational vehicles and other park traffic, and crossing it several times. If you're going to skip a section, skip this one. The route reaches Maple Creek Camp in 2½ miles (4 km) of easy hiking. The next 8 miles (13 km) can be hot, dry, and strenuous as the Wonderland climbs 2,200 feet (670 m) to Reflection Lakes (crossing the highway again) and on to Paradise Creek Camp. The final 3 miles (5 km) is a downhill run back to Longmire.

Information

MOUNT RAINIER NATIONAL PARK
Tahoma Woods, Star Route
Ashford, WA 98304-9751 USA
Headquarters:
(360) 569-2211, (360) 569-2177 (TDD); visitor information,
(360) 569-2211, ext. 3314
www.nps.gov/mora

Permits can be obtained from the park's Longmire Wilderness Information Center, (360) 569-4453, (360) 569-3131 (fax);
www.nps.gov/mora/recreation/wic.htm

Grand Park is a worthwhile two-day detour off the Wonderland Trail, but camping on any meadow is no longer permitted by the park.
PHOTO BY JAMES MARTIN.

OPPOSITE, TOP: *The forests of the Carbon River drainage, on the mountain's wet north slope, are among the most verdant in the park.* PHOTO BY JAMES MARTIN.

OPPOSITE, BOTTOM: *Rangers post current hiking information at the twenty-two designated camps along the Wonderland Trail.* PHOTO BY PETER POTTERFIELD.

DIABLO LAKE TO LAKE CHELAN
North Cascades

Washington, United States

DISTANCE: 28 miles (45 km) one-way
TIME: 3–4 days
PHYSICAL CHALLENGE: 1 2 3 4 5
PSYCHOLOGICAL CHALLENGE: 1 2 3 4 5
STAGING: Seattle, Washington, or Vancouver, British Columbia

When you travel from north to south along the Cascades of the Pacific Northwest, the nature of the range undergoes an elemental change. Big volcanoes such as Hood, Adams, Rainier, and Glacier Peak gradually give way to the rugged, dramatic climax of the North Cascades. This cluster of wild mountains and their companion glaciers, hard against the Canadian border, has been called the Switzerland of America. A hundred miles of sharp, jagged, ice-draped rock spires with names like Forbidden, Eldorado, Fury, and Terror are hidden here, in secret, behind an impenetrable moat of dense forest. These are among the biggest nonvolcanic peaks in the range; some are so remote they cannot be seen from any road.

Separating these awesome ridges of alpine peaks are deep, low-altitude river valleys of old-growth forests. Many of these valleys are so choked with slide alder and devils club a mile (2 km) a day is good time for anyone game enough to take them on. The going here can be so difficult that one almost mythic group of craggy summits less than 10 miles (16 km) from the North Cascades Highway—the storied Picket Range—remained virtually unvisited until the 1960s. Well protected by these long, difficult approaches, the North Cascades remain, arguably, the most pristine mountain wilderness in the lower 48 states.

Thanks to the grit of 19th-century miners, however, a way into this sanctuary exists. By following Thunder Creek drainage up toward its sources among the peaks and glaciers, you can not only penetrate miles into these magnificent ancient forests, but keep going, farther and higher, to greater rewards. Working up the mountain slopes at the head of Thunder Creek, this route rises with the terrain to traverse alpine basins and climb into the spectacular high country of the North Cascades—and from there down the

other side into a completely different eco-zone. The result is a rare crossing of the Cascades, from the "wet side," where the water flows west to Puget Sound, to the "dry side," where the waters flow east to fjordlike Lake Chelan. Together, the Thunder Creek and Park Creek Pass Trails create a 28-mile (45 km) journey through the heart of this remote range.

Looking into the chasm of Thunder Basin, with Forbidden Peak on the ridge to the left, the spires of Klawatti Glacier above the hiker.
PHOTO BY PETER POTTERFIELD.

OPPOSITE: *A hiker reaches the crest of Park Creek Pass.*
PHOTO BY PETER POTTERFIELD.

For more than 18 miles (29 km) from Diablo Lake, the well-built Thunder Creek Trail follows a mostly moderate grade through some of the biggest and oldest trees in the Pacific Northwest. From the valley floor this classic route finally works out of the misty forests into the bright sunlight of the alpine zone. Once above the trees, an entirely new reality, a landscape of fearsome spires, is revealed—Forbidden, Boston, Buckner, Logan, and Goode—classic North Cascades "nine-thousanders" all, thrusting skyward from a sprawling foundation of hard blue glacial ice. The trail finally climbs steeply to arrive at Park Creek Pass, a narrow, 6,000-foot (1,830 m) col between Buckner and Logan, one of the most dramatic vantage points in the Cascades. From this visual climax, the route plunges back down the other side of the mountains into a forest of pine, not Douglas fir and hemlock, and eventually to the tiny settlement of Stehekin, which seems a remnant from another century.

Prospectors and trappers opened Thunder Creek. In fact, just beyond Skagit Queen Camp, 13 miles (21 km) up the valley, relics from turn-of-the-century mining development can still be seen. The water-powered generator ran a compressor, which supplied piped compressed air to drill rigs up Skagit Queen Creek. More signs of mining activity can be found farther along the trail. Much effort and money were expended

The ramparts of Mount Buckner, from a camp high above Park Creek. PHOTO BY PETER POTTERFIELD.

before developers left this remote and rugged land. Thunder Creek Trail is the unlikely legacy of these mining days.

This hike from the turquoise waters of glacier-fed Diablo Lake, milky with "rock flour," to the funky mountain village of Stehekin covers the gamut of Cascade Range wonders in just a few days. The finish comes with an unexpected flourish. The descent from Park Creek Pass eventually spills out into the Stehekin River valley, where an unlikely and frequently washed-out road leads 19 rough miles (30 km) to Stehekin. The village itself is not accessible by any road, so the only way out to town is on a North Cascades National Park shuttle bus that was barged up for this purpose. Stehekin itself, with just a ranger station and some accommodations, is not the end of the line, but the beginning of the next leg of the journey. The only way out is via a boat ride (or perhaps float plane flight) down the 50-mile (80 km) length of Lake Chelan, a stunning body of water that fills a mountain gorge deeper even than the Grand Canyon.

There is no better way than hiking this route to see the hidden magnificence of remote and seldom-visited North Cascades National Park. Created in 1969 with an emphasis on wilderness preservation, the mere existence of the park

may be one of the most significant conservation achievements of the modern environmental movement. Snatched from the jaws of development and timber interest, the 700,000-acre (280,000 ha) park is the brightest jewel in a region of great parks. From the old growth forests of Thunder Creek to the high hidden peaks of Park Creek Pass and the spectacle of Lake Chelan, this hike shows why.

LOGISTICS & STRATEGY

North Cascades National Park is three hours from Seattle by car, and about the same from Vancouver, British Columbia. One of the reasons this area remains unspoiled is simply this: The place is remote. Virtually no place in the park is accessible via public transportation. You really need a car to see the park and get to the trailhead. For the route described here, the most convenient strategy is to have two cars in your party, but it can be done with one.

This spectacular North Cascades excursion starts from Washington 20, known locally as the North Cascades Highway. It ends 47 miles (76 km) away in the village of Stehekin, at the head of Lake Chelan. The final 19 miles (30 km) is covered via park service shuttle. Stehekin itself is not accessible by road, so from there you've either got to walk, ride a horse, take a float plane or—and this is what just about everyone does—take one of the regularly scheduled passenger ferries down to the city of Chelan, Washington. At the opposite end of the 50-mile-long (80 km) lake, Chelan is 150 miles (241 km) from Seattle, via US Highway 97, US Highway 2, and I-5.

The route can be hiked in either direction, but it works better starting at Lake Diablo and finishing in Stehekin. The tranquil miles through this remnant of ancient forest are the perfect setup for the rugged mountains of Park Creek Pass. The hiking ends where the Park Creek Trail intersects the Stehekin River Road. Note that "road" is something of a misnomer; this 19-mile (30 km) section of unpaved road is completely cut off from any other road or highway. The only vehicles on it are owned by the park service or by the few dozen full-time residents of remote Stehekin. The short Stehekin River Road is, however, a crucial element that makes remote sections of North Cascades National Park accessible. The park service shuttles that deliver hikers and climbers to a half dozen trailheads open up hundreds of square miles of otherwise inaccessible wilderness.

To take advantage of this amenity you'll need to reserve seats on the shuttle in advance. The village became an in-holding settlement when North Cascades National Park was created in 1966, and there's little here save for the park service ranger station, a few accommodations for visitors, and, in season, a restaurant and bakery. In high summer, the scene here is festive and casual. The village becomes the jumping-off place for true wilderness adven-

tures, or a destination for day hiking, mountain biking, and kayaking. Reserving overnight accommodations in Stehekin for the day of your arrival allows for a comfortable conclusion to the hike, with the final boat ride down to Chelan reserved for the following day. There are three options for the voyage (reservations recommended for all): the venerable *Lady of the Lake*, which makes a slow, four-hour trip; a faster ferry that completes the route in only two and a half hours; and a high-speed catamaran, which makes the 50-mile (80 km) run in just an hour. Another option is to book a flight on one of the Chelan Airways De Haviland Beavers.

The most straightforward approach is this: Leave Seattle with two cars and make the three-hour drive in caravan over Stevens Pass to Chelan, Washington. Leave one car in this small city in the heart of Washington State apple country, and continue north on US Highway 97 to Pateros, Washington, at the confluence of the Columbia and Methow Rivers. Turn northwest here on Washington 153 and follow it to Twisp, Washington, and the intersection with the North Cascades Highway (Washington 20). Follow the North Cascades Highway westbound over Washington Pass to milepost 131. Just beyond the milepost, turn south into Colonial Creek Campground and the trailhead for Thunder Creek Trail, about two-hour's driving time from Chelan. When you return to Chelan by boat at the

A backpackers' camp in upper Park Creek, with Mount Buckner behind. PHOTO BY PETER POTTERFIELD.

conclusion of the hike, retrieve the other vehicle and retrace the driving route to pick up the second car.

North Cascades National Park requires that you get a backcountry camping permit for any overnight backcountry hike, and you have to do that in person. Backcountry permits may be obtained up to one day in advance at the Wilderness Information Center in Marblemount, Washington, at milepost 106 on the North Cascades Highway; at the North Cascades National Park Visitors Center in Winthrop, at milepost 120 on the North Cascades Highway; or at the Stehekin Ranger Station in Stehekin, if you're starting from there. If you've dropped a car at Chelan, you can pick up a permit in Winthrop and reserve a seat on the shuttle.

If you have only one car in your party, consider this option: On arrival at the Stehekin River Road take the shuttle to the village of Stehekin for a look at this unique "bush" settlement. After a few hours rest and a meal, or an overnight, take the shuttle back out on the river road, but not to Park Creek. Instead, get off one stop before at Bridge Creek, where the Pacific Crest Trail intersects the road. Take one or two days to hike the Pacific Crest Trail for 13 miles (21 km) (Six Mile and South Fork Camps are both good overnight locations) out to Washington 20, about 2 miles (3 km) east of Rainy Pass, and approximately 30 miles (48 km) east of your car at Colonial Creek. Try to catch a ride with other backpackers from the Rainy Pass parking lot back to your car, or if that fails, hitchhike back to the trailhead.

HAZARDS

The chief hazard facing hikers on this route is going up and over a snow-covered Park Creek Pass. In season, a trekking pole and moderate caution are usually all that are required, and by the end of the season, the pass may be entirely free of snow. Hikers who wish to do the route earlier than July should know how to use an ice ax.

In this wild part of the Cascades encounters with black bear, deer, and other wildlife can be expected, but seldom present any danger. Persistent rumors of grizzly bear sightings in this area lead some biologists to think a remnant population, or visitors from Canada, may pass through the area.

SEASON

The critical factor that determines when this route opens is the amount of snow at Park Creek Pass. This rare crossing point in the Cascades typically has snow in it until August, but most seasons is hikable by early July. If you want to carry an ice ax (and know how to use it), the pass can be crossed in late June. July to September is the traditional season for this route, but, weather permitting, it can be done as late as mid-October.

Monkey flower (top) and penstemon (bottom) thrive in the lush valleys of the North Cascades, a world-class habitat for many varieties of alpine wildflowers. PHOTOS BY JAMES MARTIN (top) AND DAVE SCHIEFELBEIN (bottom).

OPPOSITE: *Iconic Thunder Creek flows through the primeval forests of the North Cascades.* PHOTO BY JIM NELSON.

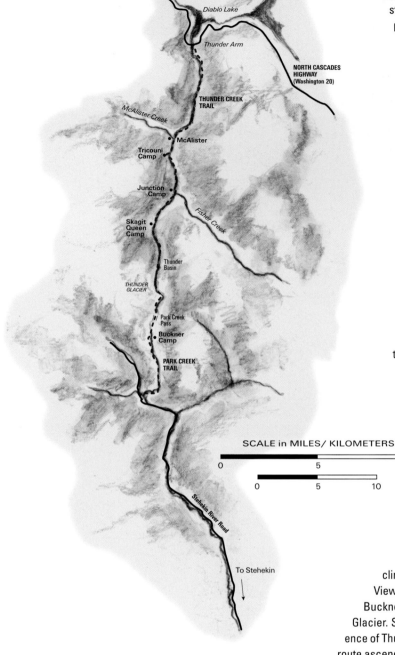

Diablo Lake

Thunder Arm

NORTH CASCADES
HIGHWAY
(Washington 20)

THUNDER CREEK
TRAIL

McAlister Creek

McAlister

Tricouni
Camp

Junction
Camp

Fisher Creek

Skagit
Queen
Camp

Thunder
Basin

THUNDER
GLACIER

Park Creek
Pass

Buckner
Camp

PARK CREEK
TRAIL

Stehekin River Road

To Stehekin

SCALE in MILES/ KILOMETERS

0　　　　　5　　　　　10

0　　　　　5　　　　　10

ROUTE

From Seattle, follow I-5 north to near Burlington, Washington. Take the Cook Road exit, number 232, and proceed east to Washington 20, the North Cascades Highway. Follow the highway for 70 miles (113 km) to Colonial Creek Campground on Diablo Lake, just beyond milepost 130, and find the Thunder Creek trailhead at the east end of the campground, at 1,200 feet (360 m).

The trail begins in the Colonial Creek Campground and travels along the western shore of Thunder Arm before crossing Thunder Creek to head south along the east side of the creek. The startling turquoise color of Thunder Creek comes from its heavy load of rock flour, ground by the many glaciers of the creek's headwaters. Before starting this hike, gaze upward to some of the sources: the glaciers on looming Colonial and Pyramid Peaks.

Meandering through a cathedral of old-growth forest, the trail passes burned-over groves where old-growth survivors tower over younger trees. If you get a late start, two good forest camps offer good stopping points early on. Thunder Camp is just 2 miles (3 km) from the trailhead, Neve Camp just 1 mile (2 km) farther. These areas offer glimpses into the Cascade giants of Snowfield and Colonial Peaks. Follow the easy trail through the forest as it ascends imperceptibly, reaching McAlister Creek in 6½ miles (10 km). A bridge crosses Thunder Creek here, leading to another forest camp at McAlister Creek in ½ mile (¾ km).

One mile (2 km) beyond McAlister Creek, Thunder Creek Trail reaches the traditional first night's stopping point, Tricouni Camp, among the great deep-forest camps in the American West. At the confluence of two fast wilderness rivers, Thunder Creek and Fisher Creek, it is nestled among the old tress below Tricouni Peak, Primus Peak, and the Austera Towers to the south, and Red Mountain to the north. Above this camp, the route ascends 1,000 feet (300 m) in 2 miles (3 km) to follow Fisher Creek, and thus avoid a large swampy area in the valley bottom, before leveling off again at Junction Camp, at 3,000 feet (910 m), 9 miles (15 km) from the trailhead. From this ridge, views open up to Boston Glacier and Tricouni Peak. The Fisher Creek Trail heads east to Easy Pass and back to Washington 20, while the Thunder Creek Trail continues toward the head of the valley and the wild peaks above. A side trail leads to some old cabins down in the swampy area, which is itself a thing of wild, creepy beauty, the largest marsh in the North Cascades.

From Junction Camp, the trail dips slightly before climbing steadily once again toward Thunder Basin. Views begin to open up toward Boston Peak and Mount Buckner, and, finally, the great expanse of ice that is Boston Glacier. Skagit Queen Camp is 4 miles (6 km) from the confluence of Thunder and Fisher Creeks, still at 3,000 feet (910 m). The route ascends more steeply for the next 2 miles (3 km) to Thunder Basin at 4,300 feet (1,310 m), 15 miles (24 km) from the trailhead. The basin makes a good camp for savoring the views above before working up and over Park Creek Pass the next day.

Thunder Creek Trail concludes by climbing steeply more than 3 miles (5 km) up across the broad shoulders of Mount Logan and a final, even steeper section up to Park Creek Pass at 6,040 feet (1,841 m). The pass itself is a narrow defile that typically is filled with hard snow even in August; in early season, the amount of snow may require the use of a ski pole or ice ax. From the pass, descend into high open meadows and rolling, grassy slopes, with views of 9,000-foot (2,750 m) peaks all around: Storm King, Booker, Goode, and Buckner.

Follow meadows, heather slopes, and wildflowers in-season down through the rolling high country. Camping isn't permitted on the fragile alpine meadows, but if you're an experienced off-trail hiker, cross-country camps can be found ½ mile (¾ km) off the trail southwest and northeast of the pass (permits required). The closest established camps to the pass within the trail corridor are Thunder Basin, 2 miles (3 km) back at Thunder Creek, and Buckner Camp, 3 miles (5 km) down the Park Creek side. Five Mile Camp is just below Buckner Camp.

Below the 6,040-foot (1,841 m) pass the trail meanders down through the high, open parklands for 1 mile (2 km). Here, at about 5,700 feet (1,740 m), the trail descends more steeply, eventually leaving the high, hanging valley of the pass, and descends steeply via switchbacks down to Park Creek itself, about 3 miles (5 km) from the pass, crossing avalanche tracks on the way. Once at the creek, you quickly reach Buckner Camp, the highest legal camp on the Park Creek Trail, and just below that, Five Mile Camp; farther down is the unmistakable horse camp. From Five Mile Camp, the trail descends gradually beside Park Creek for another 2 miles (3 km). Five miles (8 km) from the pass, a hard-to-find climbers' track leads east and up to the shoulder of Mount Goode and some scenic campsites. This steep, strenuous 3-mile (5 km) route is for experienced hikers seeking high-country views and a genuine wilderness experience before leaving the Cascades.

Below the Goode climbers' track, pass the final established camp on the Park Creek Trail, 6 miles (9½ km) from the pass, and descend via a steep, switchbacked trail down to Park Creek Campground near the Stehekin River Road, at 2,300 feet (700 m). This is where you'll catch the park service shuttle to Stehekin, about an hour's drive on the rough road. With an early start, you can camp as high as Five Mile Camp on your last night in Park Creek and still make it down to the road in time to catch the first shuttle to town.

Information

NORTH CASCADES NATIONAL PARK
810 State Route 20
Sedro-Woolley, WA 98284-1239 USA
Headquarters, (360) 856-5700; visitor information, (360) 856-5700;
www.nps.gov/noca

MARBLEMOUNT RANGER STATION
7280 Ranger Station Road
Marblemount, WA 98267 USA
(360) 873-4500 ext. 39

STEHEKIN RANGER STATION
(360) 856-5700 ext. 340

CHELAN RANGER STATION
(509) 682-2549

For park service shuttle bus schedule and reservations to and from Stehekin, call (206) 470-4060.

LAKE CHELAN PASSENGER FERRIES
(509) 682-4584
www.ladyofthelake.com

FLOATPLANE SERVICE BETWEEN STEHEKIN AND CHELAN
Chelan Airways: (509) 682-5555

Scenic Fisher Creek, a tributary to Thunder Creek, offers a route variation to the North Cascades Highway. PHOTO BY DAVID SCHIEFELBEIN.

WHITE MOUNTAIN TRAVERSE
White Mountains

New Hampshire, United States

DISTANCE: **53 miles (85 km) one-way**
TIME: **6–8 days**
PHYSICAL CHALLENGE: **123**4**5**
PSYCHOLOGICAL CHALLENGE: **12**3**45**
STAGING:**Manchester, New Hampshire; Portland, Maine;**
or Boston, Massachusetts

This long traverse through New Hampshire's White Mountains has been the comeuppance of many an arrogant hiker from outside New England. Deep, in-cut valleys combine with the highest peaks in the East to make for daunting elevation gains and heartbreaking losses, even for those who honed their hiking abilities in the Sierra or the Cascades. Add to that the potential for some of the worst weather on the continent and you've got a wilderness outing of both serious challenge and epic appeal. With high ridge walks, rocky summits, expansive views,

and a chance to sample one of the most spectacular sections of the legendary Appalachian Trail, who can resist?

The real highlight of this 53-mile (85 km) route is the vaunted Presidential Range Traverse, perhaps the most difficult and dangerous section of the 2,000-mile (3,220 km) Appalachian Trail. The route climbs over a succession of peaks more than 5,000 feet (1,500 m) high, and one over 6,000 feet (1,830 m). Mount Washington, at 6,288 feet (1,917 m) the undisputed monarch of the Presidentials, has been branded the stormiest place in the world, a reference to its record for the highest wind speed ever recorded, 231 miles per hour. Conditions are seldom that bad, but the potential for sudden, severe weather means this hike calls for prudence over valor. The Presidentials can be wet and windy and cold, even in summer. These treacherous conditions frequently result in injuries to hikers, even deaths.

It would be a mistake to view this stunning route as some sort of grim ordeal. Summers can be mild, and while you have to be wary of potential storms, this long wilderness walk—much of it above tree line—can be a glorious if strenuous jaunt. Adding to the allure is the fact that the Appalachian Mountain Club (AMC) has developed along this route a system of refuges that is unusual in the American backcountry. Six European-style huts, offering meals, bunks, and provisions, are spaced roughly a day's hike from each other. Lodging can be reserved in advance, meaning you can do this physically demanding hike in relative comfort, and with a lighter pack. But this is an area just as well suited to camping. Using your tent and stove, where permitted, is a good way to experience the terrain in a style in keeping with its wilderness heritage.

For all but the final few miles, the route follows the Appalachian Trail. This oldest and best-known of America's

ABOVE: *Mount Washington at sunrise.* PHOTO BY RICHARD J. BAILEY.

OPPOSITE: *The famous "Worst Weather" sign on the Edmands Path, which connects to the Appalachian Trail just above Mount Eisenhower.* PHOTO BY RICHARD J. BAILEY.

long-distance continental routes runs for 2,167 miles (3,488 km) along the ridge crests and across the major valleys of the Appalachian Mountains from Mount Katahdin, in Maine, to Springer Mountain, in northern Georgia. The AT, as the route is universally known, began as a vision of forester Benton MacKaye. It was opened as a continuous trail in 1937 and designated as the first National Scenic Trail by the National Trails System Act of 1968. There's more history here: Part of the White Mountains route, from Crawford Notch to Mount Washington, follows the Crawford Path, the oldest continuously maintained foot trail in America, dating from 1819. In fact, the extensive trail system in the White Mountains predates the AT by a century, and most of the trail signs here carry both the local trail name as well as the AT symbol.

LOGISTICS & STRATEGY

The route recommended here covers 27 miles (43 km) from Franconia Notch to Crawford Notch, and another 26 miles

(42 km) from Crawford Notch to the Appalachia trailhead on US Highway 2. While the hike can be done in either direction, it is described from south to north, as that is the better strategy. Going that way gives the hiker a few days to warm up on the slightly less strenuous southern section before tackling Mount Washington and the rest of the Presidential Traverse proper.

This is New England, where nothing is too far from anywhere else, and so Bostonians and New Yorkers will drive to the trailheads. For those coming from farther afield, Boston is a good choice of airports; from there it's a three-hour straight shot up I-93. Airports at Manchester, New Hampshire, and Portland, Maine, also are within a three-hour drive. The route begins off the Franconia Parkway, at the Flume trailhead parking area in Franconia Notch Park, and ends at the Appalachia trailhead, on US Highway 2, about 5 miles (8 km) west of Gorham. The AMC also operates a shuttle service between popular trailheads in the White Mountains, making it easy to get back to your car—or get to the trailhead from which you want to start. Shuttle rides can be reserved in advance.

At present, no permit is required to hike the route from Franconia Notch to Appalachia, but you will need to follow the rules on backcountry fires and camps. These regulations, which change yearly, are posted on the White River National Forest Web site under "Rules for Campers." Keep in mind that much of the Presidential Range is designated either as wilderness or other restricted-use status, where camping is controlled or prohibited. The route also passes through three state parks, which have different regulations. You will need to buy a Forest Pass, a parking permit that can be purchased on an annual or weekly basis, if you intend to park at Franconia or Appalachia.

Six of the eight huts operated by the AMC—Greenleaf, Galehead, Zealand Falls, Mizpah Spring, Lakes of the Clouds, and Madison Spring—are spaced along this route. The huts offer bunkroom accommodations, running water, basic provisions, and breakfasts and dinners prepared by the hut crew. From Franconia Notch to Appalachia, the huts make it unnecessary to bring a tent or brave nighttime temperatures, a fact that opens up the possibility of doing this route a bit earlier or later in the season. You'll need to know that you have a bunk, so if you intend to stay at the huts be sure to reserve in advance through the club's telephone reservation system. It is possible to purchase space on arrival, but that depends on vacancies, a rare thing at the popular huts during summer. At about $70 per night, the huts may seem expensive, but you get a lot in return, including a kitchen staff; meals are included in the cost of accommodation.

Be aware that this is a rugged route despite the proximity of huts and other surprising amenities, such as the cafeteria near the summit of Mount Washington. The section from Franconia Notch to Crawford Notch traverses 27 miles (43 km) of hardwood and coniferous forests and crosses high summits, including Mount Lincoln (5,089 feet, 1,552 m) Mount Lafayette (5,249 feet, 1,600 m) South Twin (4,902 feet, 1,495 m), and Mount Guyot (4,560 feet, 1,390 m). Conditions here, though not as bad as in the Presidentials, can be dangerous on the exposed portions. Significant elevation gain results from the steep ascents and descents over summits along the way. From Crawford Notch to Appalachia, you're on the Presidential Traverse proper, one of the most difficult sections of the AT. Much of the 26 miles (42 km) is above tree line, where camping is strictly prohibited. The weather can be horrible, even dangerous. Elevation gain and loss on this section are extreme, so allow a few days to traverse this route over peaks such as Mount Eisenhower (4,780 feet, 1,452 m), Mount Franklin (5,004 feet, 1,526 m), Mount Washington (6,288 feet, 1,917 m), and Mount Madison (5,363 feet, 1,635 m).

The start of the hike is in Franconia Notch State Park, second only to the Mount Washington area as the most popular hiking destination in the White Mountains. The most famous feature here, the Old Man of the Mountain, sadly came to a bad end in the spring of 2003, when its craggy features collapsed.

HAZARDS

Weather in the Presidentials can be deadly, and for that reason this hike isn't recommended for novices. Mount

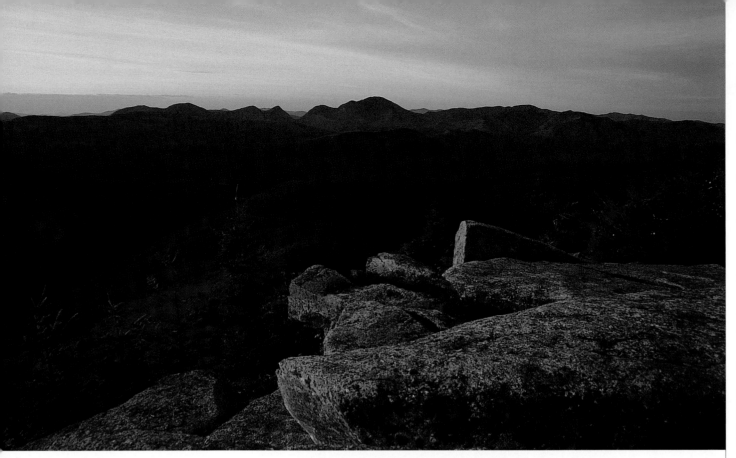

An early morning view from the top of Zeacliff into the Pemigewasset "Wilderness." PHOTO BY RICHARD J. BAILEY.

Washington weather is indicative of what you'll face in the Presidentials. The summit lies in the path of historic storm tracks, and because of its elevation, the peak is biologically and ecologically similar to the subarctic zone. Washington has received measurable snowfall during every month of the year, and average annual snowfall is more than 250 inches (6.35 m). As of 2003, the highest temperature ever recorded on the summit was 72°F (22°C), but the annual average temperature on the mountain is only 27°F. The summit is in cloud 70 percent of the time, and hurricane-force winds—75 miles per hour (120 kph) or higher—occur on average an unbelievable 104 days per year. Hikers contemplating this route must come prepared to deal with extreme conditions. In the 150 years that records have been kept, more than 100 hikers have perished from falls, weather, exposure, and other factors.

One often overlooked hazard is the nuisance of mosquitoes and blackflies. These insects can be unbearable without appropriate measures, such as effective repellent and head nets.

SEASON

The hiking season in the White Mountains is June through September, with July usually seeing the warmest temperatures.

September, and even October, can have some of the best hiking conditions, with stable weather patterns, clear skies, and fall color. April and May often produce difficult conditions, with deep, wet snow. Winter months are surprisingly busy in these mountains, as hikers, skiers, and snowshoers with appropriate skills venture in as weather permits. At any time of year, however, severe storms can produce dangerous conditions.

ROUTE

The start to the hike is found within Franconia State Park, on the east side of the Franconia Parkway, at the Flume Trailhead parking area. From the parking lot, take the access trail about ½ mile (1 km) to the Appalachian Trail, here signed the AT/Liberty Spring Trail. Turn right on the trail and ascend toward Franconia Ridge, passing the Liberty Springs campsite and hitting the ridge just north of Mount Liberty, (4,459 feet, 1,359 km), on the southern section of Franconia Ridge, about 3 miles (5 km) from the parking lot. At the junction of the AT/Franconia Ridge Trail, turn left to follow the crest of Franconia Ridge as the AT runs along the narrow ridgetop, finally coming out of the trees at Little Haystack, (4,800 feet, 1,463 km). From here you can see Mount Washington behind the Twins. The route continues up through this scenic section, crossing Mount Lincoln (5,089 feet, 1,551 m), the second tallest peak in New Hampshire outside the Presidentials. From here you get views into the Pemigewasset Wilderness, locally known as the Pemi, and its prominent peaks of Garfield and Owls Head.

From Lincoln, you continue north on the ridge to cross Mount Lafayette, (5,260 feet, 1,604m), about 7 miles (11 km) from the trailhead. Along the ridge leading to Lafayette you can see Greenleaf

OPPOSITE: *Mount Madison and the Madison Springs hut, viewed from the Gulfside Trail.* PHOTO BY RICHARD J. BAILEY.

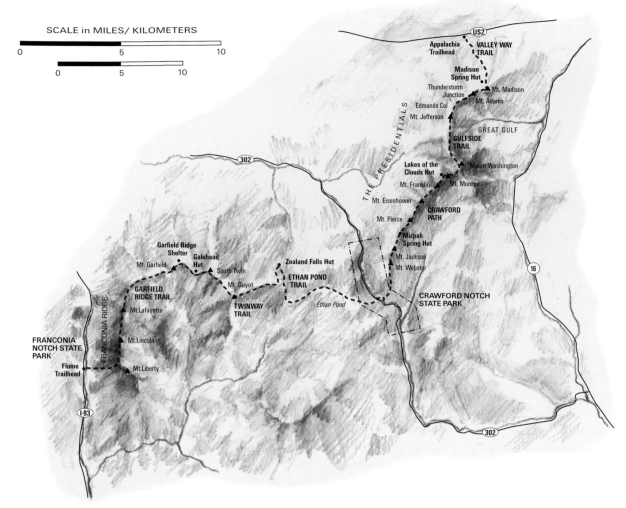

Hut to the west, exposed on a westerly ridge a 1½ miles (2½ km) and 1,000 feet (300 m) below the summit of Lafayette on the Greenleaf Trail, about 8 miles (13 km) from the parking lot. From the summit of Lafayette, the AT descends over large boulders to below tree line on rugged Garfield Ridge. This section, fabled for its exhausting topography, descends almost 2,000 vertical feet (610 m) to the Lafayette-Garfield Col before climbing up to Mount Garfield (4,500 feet, 1,372 m), an open summit between Franconia Ridge and the Twins. Past the summit of Garfield, the Garfield Ridge Shelter is to the north on a small spur trail. The trail descends again to a major col before climbing gradually up to the completely rebuilt Galehead Hut, perched on the ridge at 3,800 feet (1,159 m), with good views into the Pemi. This is one of the most remote huts in the system, almost 15 miles (24 km) from the Franconia Notch trailhead, just over 7½ miles (12 km) from Greenleaf hut.

From the hut, the AT/Twinway trail gains 1,100 feet (370 m) as it ascends sharply to the summit of South Twin, 4,902 feet (1,494 m), in about 1 mile (2 km). The route then winds towards Mt Guyot. At the junction with the Bondcliff Trail, which heads east to Mount Bond, the AT/Twinway turns left and climbs gently to the exposed summit of Guyot and spectacular views. At the summit, the AT drops again before climbing steeply to a high point on the shoulder of Mount Zealand. A small spur trail leads to the true summit at 4,260 feet (1,299 m). The AT continues to Zeacliff, high above Zeacliff Pond. From Zeacliff, take in spectacular views of the Pemi, an impressive chunk of "wilderness" here in long-settled New England. (The Pemi is not true wilderness; it was heavily logged around 1920, and is not a designated federal wilderness area.) After descending for more than 1 mile (2 km), the Twinway crosses Whitewall Brook, here a shallow

stream flowing over rock slabs, and reaches the venerable Zeeland Falls Hut, at 2,780 feet (850 m), 7 miles (11 km) from Galehead Hut.

Beyond the hut, the AT follows the Ethan Pond Trail as it goes through Zeeland Notch and along the grade of an old logging railroad. This wide, easy track is a pleasure as it heads towards Ethan Pond and the Ethan Pond shelter and campsite, about 5 miles (11 km) from Zeeland Falls Hut. From the campsite, it's 3 miles (8 km) and 1,800 feet (550 m) down to Crawford Notch State Park on US Highway Route 302. The Appalachian Trail crosses railroad tracks and enters a parking lot off the highway. On the east side of the highway, the AT/Webster Cliff trail crosses the Saco River and climbs up to fine views of Crawford Notch. Above, the route turns northward and continues climbing over several steep knobs on the way to Mount Webster.

From Crawford Notch a very tough five hours and more than 3,000 feet (910 m) of elevation gain lead up and over a number of false summits to the top of Mount Webster at 3,910 feet (1,192 m). From the top, the trail descends slightly along the ridge only to climb up again toward the summit of Mount Jackson, 1½ miles (2½ km) distant. Jackson is only 200 feet (60 m) higher than Webster, but it's a strenuous climb from the col over boulders to reach the top (4,310 feet, 1,438 m). There are good views of the entire Presidential Range, notably Mount Washington, and even the Mizpah Springs Hut on the side of Mount Pierce. From Jackson's summit, the trail descends slightly to reach the Mizpah Springs Hut, 6½ miles (10½ km) from the parking lot at Crawford Notch State Park, and 10 miles (16 km) from Zeeland Falls Hut. Built in 1965, the Mizpah Springs Hut is one of the most modern on this section of trail. The Nauman campsite is next to the hut.

The 5-mile hike (8 km) from Mizpah Springs Hut to Lakes of the Clouds Hut is a highlight of the Presidential Range Traverse, traveling the entire way above tree line and offering the summits of Mounts Pierce, Eisenhower, Franklin, and Monroe. But beware, this bald ridge can be extremely exposed in bad weather, so be prepared for temperatures on the ridge to be 20 or even 30°F (11–17°C) colder than at the hut. From Mizpah Springs Hut, the AT/Webster Cliff Trail climbs steeply to the bare rock summit of Mount Pierce (4,310 feet, 1,438 m) and good views of Eisenhower, Franklin, and Washington. Just past the summit the trail drops, and at a junction on a shoulder connecting Pierce and Eishenhower the route turns right and becomes the AT/Crawford Path, which leads all the way to Mount Washington.

The AT goes not to the top of Eisenhower, but around the peak, so take the short Mount Eisenhower Loop Trail if you want to go to the 4,780-foot (1,457 m) summit with its great views. The AT/Crawford Path traverses the east flank of Eisenhower and continues over Mount Franklin (5,004 feet, 1,526 m). Beyond, the AT traverses the east flank of Mount Monroe, so take the Mount Monroe Loop Trail if you want to enjoy the view of Mount Washington from the 5,385-foot (1,642 m) summit of Monroe. The AT/Crawford Path reaches the Lakes of the Clouds Hut, on the broad flank of Mount Washington, 5 miles (8 km) from Mizpah Springs Hut.

This hut, so close to Mount Washington's summit, is one of the largest and most popular of all the huts along the trail, hence its nickname, Lakes of the Crowds. Though it has a capacity of almost 100 people, it is frequently full. If you arrive here without reservations, be prepared to be turned away, except in emergencies, when the hut crew may let you pay for a sleeping space on the dining room floor.

From the Lakes of the Clouds Hut the AT/Crawford Path winds between the two Lakes of the Clouds and starts the ascent of Mount Washington's summit cone. The upper part of the mountain is basically a big boulder field up which the trail climbs with only a few switchbacks. The way through the rocks is marked by white-painted blazes that identify the AT route.

Mt. Washington's summit, which is also a New Hampshire state park, is a busy place. There's a road as well as the venerable Cog Railway; the railway, built in the 1860s, is said to have the steepest grade of any railroad in the world—14 percent. There is also a visitors center, cafeteria, a weather observatory and various structures including radio antennas. Wilderness it is not. The summit is visited by up to 250,000 people per year, about a quarter of whom are hikers. Though the area is famous for having the worst weather in the world, Mount Washington's most notorious conditions occur during winter storms, although summer storms can be severe as well. Conditions are legendary for turning very bad very quickly. The entire route from Pierce to Madison is exposed to weather, so be prepared.

From the summit, continue on the AT/Trinity Heights Connector for a few hundred yards to where it ends at the AT/Gulfside trail. Turn right here. The AT will follow the Gulfside for the rest of the Presidential Range traverse to Madison Springs Hut.

The summit of Mount Washington, showing the weather observatory and the Northern Presidentials beyond. PHOTO BY RICHARD J. BAILEY.

FOLLOWING SPREAD: *The well-worn trail along Franconia Ridge, second in popularity only to trails on Mount Washington.*
PHOTO BY RICHARD J. BAILEY.

The rocky trail drops steadily from the summit of Washington, crosses under the cog railroad tracks, and skirts the Great Gulf on the way to Washington-Reagan col. The Great Gulf is the largest ravine in the White Mountains. Washington and the peaks of the northern Presidentials (Jefferson, Adams and Madison) arc around to form its headwall. The AT winds around the west side of the recently renamed Mount Reagan (formerly Clay) and down to Sphinx Col, then along the ridge to the junction with the Mount Jefferson Loop Trail. The loop trail leads over the summit with its great views, while the AT/Gulfside passes to the east of the summit and drops steadily to Edmands Col. Several trails meet at Edmands Col, including the north end of the Mount Jefferson Loop. The AT continues, ascending from the col past Storm Lake (a seasonal pond) and on to a place famous for bad weather, Thunderstorm Junction, a major trail intersection marked by a gigantic cairn.

From here the Lowes Path goes up Mount Adams, to the south. (The Lowes Path and the Air Line Trail can be used as a loop over the summit of Adams for more great views.) The AT/Gulfside descends to Madison Springs Hut in the col between Adams and Madison. The historic hut, built in 1888, was rebuilt in the 1940s after fire destroyed the original.

If you don't want to go to the summit of Madison, take the popular Valley Way Trail 3½ miles (5½ km) from the hut to the parking lot at Appalachia. Take care to stay on the Valley Way as there are many trail junctions on the way down. The summit of Madison, 5,367 feet (1,626 km), is ½ mile (1 km) above the hut via the AT/Osgood trail. If you go to the top, the easiest and most protected—if slightly longer—route down is to take the AT/Osgood trail back to the Madison Hut and pick up the Valley Way Trail for the descent to Appalachia. Appalachia is on the south side of US Highway 2, approximately 5 miles (8 km) west of Gorham and 1 mile (2 km) east of Lowe's Country Store.

Information

WHITE MOUNTAIN NATIONAL FOREST
Federal Building
719 North Main Street
P.O. Box 638
Laconia, NH USA 32460
(603) 528-8721
www.fs.fed.us/r9/white

New Hampshire Division of Parks and Recreation
www.nhstateparks.org/parkspages/parks.html

HUT AND SHUTTLE INFORMATION
AMC hut reservations and trailhead shuttle service 603-466-2727, Monday to Saturday, 9 AM to 5 PM, (603) 466-3871 (fax)
www.outdoors.org/

McGONAGALL PASS
Denali National Park

Alaska, United States

DISTANCE: 38 miles (61 km) round-trip
TIME: 4–5 days
PHYSICAL CHALLENGE: 1 2 3 **4** 5
PSYCHOLOGICAL CHALLENGE: 1 2 3 **4** 5
STAGING: Wonder Lake Campground,
    Denali National Park, Alaska

B ackcountry travel in Alaska can be habit forming. So much of the terrain remains in a pristine state that hiking through it resets your threshold for what constitutes wilderness. No place in the state is more spectacularly beautiful than the Alaska Range, 600 miles (950 km) of glacier-covered mountains, rolling taiga, and expansive tundra stretching from Mentasta, east of Mount Deborah, to the Tordillo Mountains, west of Denali Park. Mount McKinley—the locals prefer its Athabascan moniker, Denali—regally reigns over the entire range. At 20,320 feet (6,100 m), the peak is the highest point in North America, and from Wonder Lake one of the most transforming views on the continent. From the 2,000-foot (600 m) lowlands at the lake—as close as you can get on a road—the mountain shows more than 18,000 feet (540 m) of vertical relief. When the clouds suddenly part to reveal Denali, it is always much higher than you expect, its icy ridges soaring into the heavens so far it defies belief.

But even from Wonder Lake, Mount McKinley is almost 30 miles (48 km) away. The hike to McGonagall Pass covers that final, wild divide, taking you across the tundra wilderness right to the very ice and rock of the mountain. McGonagall Pass is the small notch in a 20-mile (32 km) wall of granite that stretches along the north side of the Muldrow Glacier from Anderson Pass to Gunsight Pass. The Muldrow here flows down off the northern flank of Denali in one of the heaviest ice flows in the Alaska Range, moving down toward Anderson Pass, where the big glacier makes its famous right-angle turn. And even though you're in a national park, with rules and rangers and people, this hike is so out there it challenges the imagination while

Wonder Lake and Mount McKinley, a classic wilderness view in North America and the start of the hike to McGonagall Pass.
PHOTO BY PETER POTTERFIELD.

ABOVE: *The 89-mile (143 km) Denali Park Road, no private vehicles allowed, provides access to Wonder Lake.* PHOTO BY PETER POTTERFIELD.

OPPOSITE TOP: *Clusters of lupine along the McKinley River.*
PHOTO BY PETER POTTERFIELD.

satisfying even a voracious lust for the wild. Big rivers, rolling tundra, and wild animals are just part of the show here, as the immense and inspiring bulk of Denali fills the forward horizon.

In the early days, climbers used this route to reach the mountain and ascend to its summit by following the Muldrow to its high-altitude origins. This is a historic route, the way by which Archdeacon Hudson Stuck came on his first ascent of the peak in 1913. Since then, the Wonder Lake–to–McGonagall Pass route was the mountain's primary access until the Talkeetna bush-plane scene became popular in the 1970s. Climbers still use this route, but rarely, and now only when traversing the peak. It has become instead the ultimate venue for those who seek true wilderness. There is an irony here: In a park famous for being trail-less, this route has a pretty good track from start to finish.

Physically, the hike is not demanding, with less than 20 miles (32 km) of moderate tundra and about 3,800 feet (1,140 m) of elevation gain. But there are two elements that change the nature of this excursion. First, you've got to cross the braided channels of the McKinley River, a potentially dangerous enterprise if you don't have the skill and judg-

ment to do it safely. Second, you've got to come to terms with the fact that you're walking through prime grizzly bear habitat. While there has never been a bear fatality in the park, the mere presence of thousand-pound carnivores torques the feel of the adventure. These sobering realities seem not so unreasonable when put in perspective: Dangerous bears roam in lots of places, including the Rockies and the Sierra. And the fact is, there are no wild places in Alaska without big rivers and big wildlife. This is, after all, one of the last wild places, and that's the reason to come here. If you're going to do an Alaskan hike, you might as well do one with an Alaskan character, and this one fills the bill in spades.

The opportunity to see Denali National Park is also part of the allure. Wonder Lake is near the end of the 89-mile-long (143 km) Denali Park Road, and is in itself an adventure. The ride from the park entrance to the lake is a rare opportunity to see this sprawling habitat, and its denizens living unmolested on their native ground. You'll see taiga, and tundra, and the ecotone in between. There are drunken forests, where trees tilt at crazy angles from melting permafrost, and miniature forests, stunted by the arctic environment. Tundra dominates, however, with its ubiquitous

ABOVE: *Grizzly bears in significant numbers roam the tundra of Denali National Park and change the nature of the hiking here.* PHOTO BY PETER POTTERFIELD.

RIGHT: *The recently improved McKinley Bar Trail now includes sections of boardwalk over boggy areas.* PHOTO BY PETER POTTERFIELD.

a similar distance from the park entrance, so you'll need to allow for travel time when planning the hike.

For most, the journey starts at the airport in Anchorage and the rental car garage. It's possible to make the journey to Denali National Park by train, or by bus, but the backcountry gear you'll need on the hike and the provisions you'll need while camping at Wonder Lake can make for an awkward amount of baggage. Before leaving Anchorage it's a good idea to stop at a major supermarket for provisions, and at one of the outdoor stores, such as REI, for camping gas or any other equipment you couldn't bring on the airplane. Beyond Anchorage, the next opportunity will be in the strip malls around Wasilla, about an hour away, where selection is more limited. At the park itself, the village outside the entrance at present lacks the necessary range of products.

From Anchorage, follow the George Parks Highway (AK 3) north toward Fairbanks 240 miles (385 km) to the town of Denali Park, gateway to Denali National Park. The drive will take longer than you think because there is serious construction along this busiest of Alaskan highways during the short summer months. Plan on five to six hours and count yourself lucky if it goes quicker than that. Denali Park itself is not a thing of beauty, with motels, restaurants, and souvenir shops lining both sides of the highway, even climbing up the hillsides. The place does kind of grow on you, though, for the creature comforts and casual succor it provides with a funky frontier flavor. Since you'll be camping for a week or more, it makes sense to spend this first night in a comfortable lodging and indulge yourself before the long bus ride out to Wonder Lake the following day.

willows, dwarf birch, and ponds full of beaver and muskrat. Birders come here for the eagles and Sandhill Cranes, Long-tailed Jaegers and ptarmigan. But it's the larger wildlife, from grizzly and wolf to moose and caribou—and the almost certainty of a sighting—that makes Denali a great American wilderness.

LOGISTICS & STRATEGY

The hiking route to McGonagall Pass starts at Wonder Lake Campground, near the end of the Denali Park Road, and takes a couple of days each way. Most people will make a midpoint camp somewhere around Clearwater Creek, both coming and going. With the exception of the river crossings, the hiking is not strenuous. McGonagall Pass is so wild and scenic you may wish to spend a full day there, giving you two opportunities to view sunset and sunrise on the mountain at extremely close range. Five days is the usual amount of time allotted for the hike. The park entrance is a half-day drive from Anchorage, however, and Wonder Lake

Crossing the McKinley River and Clearwater Creek can be the most challenging element of the hike to McGonagall Pass. PHOTO BY ERIC SIMONSON.

The route to McGonagall Pass: the brief stretch of forest, the McKinley River bar, the tundra rise of Turtle Hill, and finally the low peaks along the Muldrow Glacier. PHOTO BY PETER POTTERFIELD.

Private cars are not allowed in Denali National Park beyond Savage River, 15 miles (24 km) from the entrance, so to get to Wonder Lake you'll need to do what everybody else does: ride the park's vast fleet of shuttle buses. To do that you'll need an advance reservation. You'll also need an advance reservation for a camping permit. Months before you arrive—in fact as soon as reservations open in December for the following season—call the park or go online to reserve your tickets and campsites. You'll need to reserve a seat on the camper bus to Wonder Lake for the day you wish to go there; the return ride is a more flexible, first-come, first-served, no reservation required or accepted. You also need to reserve a tent site at Wonder Lake Campground. I recommend at least a couple of nights at the campground before departure for McGonagall Pass, as Wonder Lake is a terrific place to hang out, do some day hikes, and get acquainted with the local landscape and the creatures in it. You may also wish to reserve another night or two at Wonder Lake to unwind after the hike, before the bus ride out to the park entrance.

Finally, you need to get a backcountry permit for the hike to McGonagall Pass, but you can't do that until you arrive at the park. Get the permit at the backcountry desk in the main visitors center near the village. The process takes about an hour, during which you watch a video about safe practices in bear country, river crossings, and animal encounters, and receive one or more bear-resistant food containers. It is possible your permit will be issued for a day or two later than you wanted, particularly in high summer. That's okay because you'll have reserved a few days to spend out at Wonder Lake. With your permit and tickets in hand, you're ready to catch the early camper bus the next morning.

RIGHT: *When hiking on the north side of Denali, the mountain exerts a palpable presence.* PHOTO BY JAMES MARTIN.

BELOW: *Camp above Clearwater Creek near the tundra rise known as Turtle Hill.* PHOTO BY BRIAN OKONEK.

Riding the bus in Denali turns out to be a mixed bag of drudgery, high excitement, and interesting human interaction. You'll be on the camper bus, which is a totally different experience to that of the regular buses, and arguably more fun. The last seven or eight rows of seats are removed to accommodate all the backpacks, tripods, and duffle bags, and the passengers are serious outdoors types—climbers, photographers, hikers, biologists, bikers, and the like—of varied age, wit, and nationality. The drivers are genuine Alaskan characters themselves, and many say they prefer the clientele on the camper bus to that of the regular tour buses, full of mere sightseers. These funky vehicles—basically just school buses—grind slowly along the bumpy, winding gravel road, dropping off and picking up hikers along the way, while driver and passengers all carefully watch for wildlife. Any sighting brings an immediate halt. I've seen wolves feeding on a kill, grizzlies, moose, caribou, and sheep from the camper bus, sometimes just a few feet from the window. Since Wonder Lake is near the end of the road, a trip there shows you the whole thing, from Sable Pass to Polychrome Pass, Highway Pass, Stony Dome, and eventually the Eilsen Visitors Center and then Wonder Lake. At almost 90 miles (145 km), this is a long strange ride, a trip that usually takes about six hours.

Camping at Wonder Lake is unique in the world, and more fun than you might think. It's not car camping, but it's not backpacking either, so think of it as "bus camping," which can be pretty comfortable. The veterans are the ones with the rolling duffle bags full of food, fuel, beer, and other essentials. The camper bus drops you off about 100 yards (90 m) from the campground. Once you've claimed your tent site, immediately store *all* your food and toiletries in the big, grizzly-proof walk-in locker between the covered cooking shelters. Part of the reason there has never been a bear fatality in the park is that the rules about food handling are very strict, and hefty fines are levied on those who transgress. The living is easy here, with side trips to Wonder Ridge and Wonder Lake itself, all dominated by the looming presence of Denali. If it rains, and it will, just gather under the cooking shelter with the rest of the pilgrims. People who make it out this far can be an entertaining bunch. On my last trip, in 2002, one meal under the shelter introduced me to a biologist studying Sandhill Cranes, a German wildlife photographer, an American landscape photographer, and a University of Fairbanks professor who had been one of the first women to climb Denali.

The route to McGonagall Pass starts just outside the Wonder Lake Campground at a well-marked trailhead, and there's a pretty good trail through the tundra most of the way. The first section, the 3 miles (5 km) from Wonder Lake to McKinley Bar, has been improved recently, with boardwalks bridging the swampy areas. On the other side of the McKinley Bar a visible track in the tundra (it may be difficult to find at the start) leads to the rocky ravine that works up to McGonagall Pass itself, some 19 miles (31 km) away.

Crossing the McKinley River, and sometimes Clearwater Creek as well, is the crux section of the hike. There are well-tried techniques for crossing wilderness rivers both for solo hikers and for groups—the tripod, the arm link, the stick brace, and more. Learn and practice them on smaller rivers before you go to Denali. As for the bears, while the mere presence of these creatures can be daunting, many people hike every year in the park without serious incident. The critical thing is to know what you're getting into and to make a decision you can live with. Once you're on the trail, it's too late for second thoughts.

HAZARDS

The braided stream of the McKinley River, nearly 1 mile (1½ km) wide, is the greatest hazard on this route. The river flow fluctuates; you could find a cold wade or a dangerous torrent requiring skill and patience. Go early in the day, when flows are usually lowest, wait for the river level to go down after a heavy rain, and take the time to find the safest route across. A long hot spell can cause the river to rise to dangerous levels. In certain situations, the river may not be passable, but that's rare. The backcountry ranger desk at the visitors center can provide current water-volume information—but there's no guarantee that will reflect what you find at the river days later.

Bears and other wildlife are a potential hazard. Park rules mandate you stay at least ¼ mile (½ km) away from bears, but the smart course of action is to aggressively avoid any close encounter with a grizzly. Other animals, such as moose, can be even more dangerous, so keep your distance from all wild animals in the park. The pre-hike video shows rules and proper techniques for dealing with animal encounters. Heed the information.

SEASON

June to late August is high season in the park, and there's only a week or two on either end of that range when a visit is practical. The weather is warmest and the days longest (up to 16 hours) in June and July. But those are also the rainiest months, and the time of year when mosquitoes and flying insects create such a nuisance that head nets, sometimes even full bug suits, are essential. The bugs abate a bit in late August and may be gone by early September, a good time to visit the park despite the fact that significant snow can fall.

ROUTE

From Wonder Lake Campground, hike east down the spur road ½ mile (¾ km) to the well-signed McKinley Bar trailhead. Follow the trail over a couple of low ridges and then through the spruce forest (extensive boardwalks here are helpful in marshy areas) for just under 2½ miles (4 km) to the north bank of the McKinley River. The traditional route is to follow the bank about a ½ mile (¾ km) to the left, or southeast, before starting across. The river is in a braided channel; many strands compose the total flow of the river. Don't be deceived. The first few channels are often smaller ones;

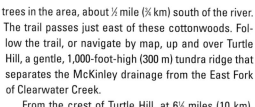

Wonder Lake Campground

MCKINLEY BAR TRAIL

DENALI PARK ROAD

McKinley River

▲ Turtle Hill

Clearwater Creek

Cache Creek

McGonagall Canyon

Oastler Pass

MULDROW GLACIER

McGonagall Pass

TRALEIKA GLACIER

▲ Mount Brooks

Mount Tatum ▲

Mount McKinley ▲

the big one (or big ones) is likely to be near the middle or toward the south shore of the mile-wide McKinley Bar.

Cross the river carefully. Eric Simonson, who has crossed it five times while traversing Denali, said the river has never stopped him. His advice is to take it slow and make a thorough recon before you commit yourself. "The trick is, take time to cross the river, don't just barge across or you'll find yourself up to your crotch and then you've got a real problem. Take time at each channel, take hours, move upstream and downstream, look carefully for the best place to cross."

Long-time McKinley guide and Alaska outdoorsman Brian Okonek says it's a good idea to unbuckle your pack's sternum strap and waist belt when crossing, and to make sure camera straps and other paraphernalia won't impede you from getting your pack off quickly. If you do go down, Okonek's advice is to kick for the shallows on the *inside* of a channel's bends, using your pack for floatation.

Once across the river, look for the crucial, historic landmark: a grove of a half dozen or so cottonwood trees, the only deciduous

trees in the area, about ½ mile (¾ km) south of the river. The trail passes just east of these cottonwoods. Follow the trail, or navigate by map, up and over Turtle Hill, a gentle, 1,000-foot-high (300 m) tundra ridge that separates the McKinley drainage from the East Fork of Clearwater Creek.

From the crest of Turtle Hill, at 6½ miles (10 km), descend via trail or open tundra to Clearwater Creek at 10½ miles (17 km). (Clearwater Creek is the halfway point in the hike, and many parties camp near the crossing.) Cross the Clearwater (make noise and watch for bears in the brushy areas) and traverse toward the right, west, to get around the bluff on the far side of Clearwater Creek before turning left, south, again to start up toward Cache Creek. The area is brushy, so try to stay on the trail as it leads up out of the Clearwater drainage, still east of Cache Creek. Reach Cache Creek about 1 mile (1½ km) from Clearwater, opposite the high bank on your left, which is actually an old moraine. Cross Cache Creek here to its west side.

The route ascends along the west side of Cache Creek, eventually crossing the creek at approximately 13 ½ miles (22 km), about 4 miles (6 km) from the Clearwater. The trail from here begins to climb in earnest up toward the pass as the valley narrows. At 16 miles (26 km), Cache Creek forks. Stay with the trail as it follows the left fork. In another ½ mile (¾ km), just 2 miles (3 km) below the pass, the creek forks again. The left fork leads to Oastler Pass, the right toward McGonagall Pass. There is good camping here, on meadows, with water, but most people prefer the view from higher up.

The trail continues up through rocky McGonagall Canyon and eventually to the pass at 5,730 feet (1,720 m), just above the mighty Muldrow Glacier. Camps at the pass are scenic but may be windy and cold. Water is problematic. Small runnels can be found, but the prudent course might be to carry water from Cache Creek. The glacier is only 200 feet (60 m) below, winding its way down the northern flank of the mountain, but don't venture onto the ice unless you've got the necessary skills.

Retrace your steps for the return trip. Make sure to cross Cache Creek to the correct, west side, at about 5½ miles (9km), before the creek gets to be too big to cross easily.

Information

DENALI NATIONAL PARK
P.O. Box 9
Denali National Park, AK 99755 USA
Visitor information: (907) 683-1266
Park headquarters: (907) 683-2294
www.nps.gov/dena

SHUTTLE AND CAMPGROUND RESERVATIONS
Doyon/ARAMARK Joint Venture
241 West Ship Creek Avenue
Anchorage, AK 99501 USA
(907) 272-7275, 1-800-625-7275, (907) 264-4684 (fax)

OPPOSITE: *McGonagall Canyon, the final steep defile below McGonagall Pass, and upper Cache Creek.* PHOTO BY BRIAN OKONEK.

WEST COAST TRAIL
Pacific Rim National Park

British Columbia, Canada

DISTANCE: 47 miles (76 km) one-way
TIME: 6–8 days
PHYSICAL CHALLENGE: 1 2 3 **4** 5
PSYCHOLOGICAL CHALLENGE: 1 2 3 **4** 5
STAGING: Victoria, British Columbia

A week on the West Coast Trail is unlike any other backcountry journey. This rugged, 50-mile (80 km) route along the wild west coast of Canada's Vancouver Island will show you the famous "shipwreck coast" of the Pacific, a place so stormy and wild that dozens of sailing vessels met a violent end here in the 19th century. Braving this physically demanding route gets you a rare glimpse into a pristine low-elevation old-growth temperate rain forest of spruce, cedar, and hemlock, and a coastal zone complete with sea stacks, sandstone bluffs, sandy beaches, and deep-cut surge channels.

But it is the unusual features of the long hiking route itself that make this journey so interesting. Where else can you pull yourself across coastal coves in rudimentary cable cars; climb high, slippery, dangerous wooden ladders with a heavy pack; ascend slimy boulders as big as trucks on a windswept beach; or risk being caught by high tides between insurmountable headlands? Where else can you see

black bear and gray whales before lunch, then observe starfish and other marine life in a tidal pool while your dinner simmers? Finish it off with sunset over the Pacific, a driftwood fire blazing merrily below the tide line, and you have the makings of a unique backcountry experience.

The West Coast Trail is not for everyone. This strenuous route offers all the variety you could ask for, and maybe more challenge than you want. Sea stacks, dramatic headlands, and long stretches of sandy beach make a nice foil to the magnificent ancient forest at the ocean's edge. For most of the trail's length, you have a choice between walking the rocky coast or the forest trail—depending on tide—a two-for-one sort of deal. But newbies who hear about the ladders and the boardwalks and arrive thinking the trail is a groomed route are in for a rude surprise.

The arduous physical demands of the route are exacerbated by the potential for really nasty weather. Sections of this coast receive more than 100 inches (2½ m) of rain per

OPPOSITE: *The rocky beach at Camper Creek Camp on the West Coast Trail.* PHOTO BY DAVE SCHIEFELBEIN.

BELOW LEFT: *A backpacker on the West Coast Trail passes some of the ubiquitous debris of this infamous "shipwreck coast."* PHOTO BY DAVE SCHIEFELBEIN.

BELOW RIGHT: *A hiker catches up on his notes at a beach camp near Walbran Creek.* PHOTO BY DAVE SCHIEFELBEIN.

ABOVE: *Crossing Cullite Creek in a cable car, one of the West Coast Trail's unique elements.*

BELOW RIGHT: *Negotiating a surge channel near Owen Point.*

OPPOSITE: *Ladders near Cullite Cove, one of the many extensive ladder systems that makes the route passable.*
PHOTOS BY DAVE SCHIEFELBEIN.

year, and even in summer the hike can be wet and exposed for days on end. The weather's violence is proved by the fact the route was built as the Dominion Life Saving Trail. In the early 1900s, the trail was created to connect patrol cabins and lighthouses, offering a route for life-saving crews and shipwrecked sailors to make their way back to civilization. Native people, lighthouse keepers, shipwreck survivors, homesteaders, prospectors, and missionaries traveled this route for a century before it became one of the recreational wonders of Vancouver Island. The West Coast Trail is part of Pacific Rim National Park Reserve, which was established in 1970.

Even today sections of this wild coast remain so remote that you can glimpse something of the Coast Indian way of life that has existed here for centuries. Parks Canada has struck a unique collaboration with First Nation peoples, Native Americans, whose ancestors have lived along this coast for centuries. Members of the Pacheedaht, Dididaht, and Huu-Ay-Aht bands serve as trail guardians and operate services along the trail.

The sense of remoteness extends to the small settlements

at either end of this long route. Port Renfrew and Bamfield, reflecting the timber and fishing heritage of frontier Canada, have little in common with the Anglophile tea and crumpets crowd just a few hours away in Victoria. But part of the appeal of the West Coast Trail is the opportunity to come to Vancouver Island, to sample some of the charms of the provincial capital, and then head out for a backcountry journey unlike any other.

LOGISTICS & STRATEGY

Access to the West Coast Trail is through Victoria, British Columbia. Vancouver Island has pretty good access: car ferries from Vancouver, British Columbia, and Annacortes, Washington; high-speed passenger ferries from Seattle; scheduled flights into Victoria International Airport; and float plane flights from Seattle and Vancouver into Victoria's Inner Harbour.

From Victoria, there are multiple options for getting to the two trailheads—Port Renfrew at the eastern end and Bamfield at the western. Since this is the west coast of Vancouver Island, it would seem that the trail would run north and south, but a look at the map shows that the coast here runs more east and west, starting out alongside the Strait of Juan de Fuca at Port Renfrew, but finally curving around to flank the Pacific Ocean as it rises toward Bamfield.

Whether you start in Bamfield and travel east or start in Port Renfrew and travel west is a matter of personal preference. The hike is described here from east to west, but you can do it either way. The eastern end is definitely more difficult, so your decision comes down to whether you want to get the hardest work over with or save it for last.

Shuttle services operate daily in-season between Victoria and the trailheads. A water taxi operates between Port Renfrew and Bamfield as well. These options create many possibilities for getting to and from the West Coast Trail. If you have a car, you can drive to Port Renfrew, do the hike, and on arrival in Bamfield take the water taxi back to your car. Or you can take the shuttle bus to Port Renfrew, do the hike, and take the shuttle bus from Bamfield back to Victoria.

The season for hiking the West Coast Trail runs from May 1 to September 30, with the peak season being from June 15 to September 15. Wardens (rangers) at Pacific Rim National Park say off-season hiking on the trail is hazardous, due to violent Pacific storms, and is not recommended. All people using the West Coast Trail must obtain a Park Use Permit, even day-hikers. If you're hiking the whole trail, you've also got to get the appropriate Overnight Use Permit. A growing awareness of this trail's powerful allure has made permits more difficult to obtain.

If you want to hike during the period of the best weather, from July 15 to September 15, you'll need to take advantage of Parks Canada's advance reservation system to get the dates you want. Reservations are accepted up to three months in advance. Some spaces in peak season, however, are allocated to standby permits. To get one of those, just show up at the West Coast Trail Information Centre in either Port Renfrew or Bamfield and apply for your permit. You may have to wait a day or two, but you'll probably get one.

Another effective strategy is to try to do the hike in the so-called shoulder seasons, May 1 through June 14 and September 16 through 30. There is still a limit on the number of hikers during these periods, but in most cases there are not enough hikers at these times to surpass the limit. Parks Canada says there is seldom a wait during these off-season periods. So for shoulder season, just show up at one of the West Coast Trail Information Centres to get your permit. Maximum group size at any time is ten people, and fees for a week on the trail as of 2003 were about Can $140, which covers the cost of both ferry crossings required during the hike.

Whether you arrive hoping for a standby permit or reserve one in advance, you won't get your permit until you show up in person at one of the information centers in Bamfield or Port Renfrew and participate in the required orientation session. The session prepares hikers for the arduous journey to come, the unique elements (such as ladders and cable cars), wildlife encounters, the dangers presented by tides, and the potential for severe weather, or just plain cold and wet weather. The session also emphasizes camping techniques to reduce environmental impacts on this fragile ecosystem. The sessions serve to remind hikers about the considerable dangers of the trail. About 1 percent of hikers who attempt it end up being evacuated.

A forest trail runs the entire 47-mile (76 km) length of the route, but in many cases the more scenic coastal or beach route paralleling the trail is feasible. But hiking on the coast (sometimes a rocky shelf, sometimes a sandy beach, sometimes a boulder field) entails a number of hazards: dangerous surge channels, up to 15 feet (4½ m) deep, must be crossed, and tides must be monitored. In fact, coastal hiking on this route is all about tides. You must time the beach sections to coincide with low tide, or risk being caught between insurmountable headlands by a rising tide. If

Spectacular Tsusiat Falls on the West Coast Trail. PHOTO BY DAVE SCHIEFELBEIN.

that happens, you can die. If you decide to take a coastal section but find your way blocked by a surge channel you discover you can't safely cross, your retreat might be blocked by a rising tide, presenting another potentially deadly situation.

Within the park, you can legally camp most anywhere you want. The fact that most people use established camps underscores the fact that they are often in the best places, have bear lockers or bear poles for hanging food, and are conveniently spaced at appropriate distances. But this route definitely harbors opportunities for solitude if you're willing to look for it. Fires are allowed, and ample quantities of driftwood can be found to use as fuel. Build your fire below the high tide line, however, so you don't trash the beach. The route crosses several First Nation reserves, so be respectful in these areas and obey the rules.

There's a character to the West Coast Trail: The eastern, or Port Renfrew, section is the so-called hard end. That's where most of the ladders are; that's where the dangerous surge channels are; that's where the hiking is most difficult. The western, Bamfield, end of the hike presents fewer difficulties. Both of the trailhead towns have North American frontier flavor that can seem exotic to foreign visitors.

Port Renfrew is reminiscent of some places in Alaska, a town at the end of the road that just happens to be at the start of a great hiking route. Bamfield is a pleasant place that takes advantage of the world-class fishing, kayaking, and hiking nearby, and makes a good hub for hanging around before or after the hike. A trailhead information center, open 9 A.M. to 5 P.M., is located in both towns, where you'll apply for, pick up, or drop off your trail permit.

HAZARDS

For a lowland hike, the West Coast Trail is surprisingly difficult and dangerous. Approximately 1 percent of all the hikers who set out on this route require evacuation. Injuries include fractures from falls from the slippery ladders and on the muddy trails and mangled hands from improper manipulation of the cable cars. Hypothermia and other weather-related problems are common. During 2001 and 2002, 180 hikers were evacuated from the trail—mostly from the more difficult eastern section. Know what you're getting into when you embark on this hike, and take care when you're on it.

The park wardens are responsible for assisting injured hikers. If you do get injured, watch for their red or gray Zodiac boats beyond the breakers and wave something bright over your head to signal them to come to shore. You may also be advised or assisted by the Qu'uas Guardians, members of the Pacheedaht, Dididaht, and Huu-Ay-Aht First Nations who work in partnership with park wardens on hiker rescues. Evacuations are more frequent during bad weather. Understand that bad weather can tie up the park wardens and delay assistance. Be prepared to pay for the evacuation's cost if you make the call.

Bears can appear anywhere along the route; protect your food. Most established camps have trees for hanging food bags or bear-proof lockers. You need to boil or treat all your water.

SEASON

The West Coast Trail is open for hiking from May 1 to September 30. Travel during the off-season is hazardous and not recommended. Peak season runs from June 15 to September 15; make advance reservations at this busy time or be prepared to wait a few days for a standby permit.

ROUTE

The first two days of the route are the most demanding, and the first, arguably, has the additional whammy of being the least rewarding.

In Port Renfrew, ask at your lodgings about how best to get to the trailhead, which is actually a boat launch about 4 miles (6 km) from town. You'll cross the Gordon River in a boat or canoe operated by a band of the First Nation people. The cost is included in the fee you paid for the permit. It's important to get an early start, so take care of your permit business the day before.

The trail from the Gordon River to the first camp at Thrasher Cove is a veritable obstacle course through the dense second-growth forest. You'll be walking over (and even under) huge roots, up slippery slopes and muddy switchbacks, crossing creeks by wading or balancing on wet logs. Expect to take most of the day on this 4-mile (6 km) introduction to the West Coast Trail before arriving at Thrasher Cove, at the bottom of a long ladder. The small camp, right on the beach, looks across the bay of Port San Juan toward Port Renfrew. Be sure to camp right up against the driftwood, to be out reach of the high tide.

From Thrasher Cove, it's 5 miles (8 km) to Camper Bay by trail. That's the safer (but not necessarily easier) way to go on this sec-

A typical itinerary would be to arrive at one of these trailhead towns in the afternoon, pick up your permit and attend the briefing, enjoy a relaxed evening and the biggest dinner you can find, then start early in the morning. If you're starting from Port Renfrew, I highly recommend taking the earliest ferry across the Gordon River, because the first day is a bear. From there, most people take about a week, making five or six camps on their way to Bamfield.

You'll need a seam-sealed tent, lots of rain gear, stout gloves for pulling yourself along in the cable cars, and 30 feet (10 m) of climbing rope to get into and out of surge channels if you want to walk the coastal shelf.

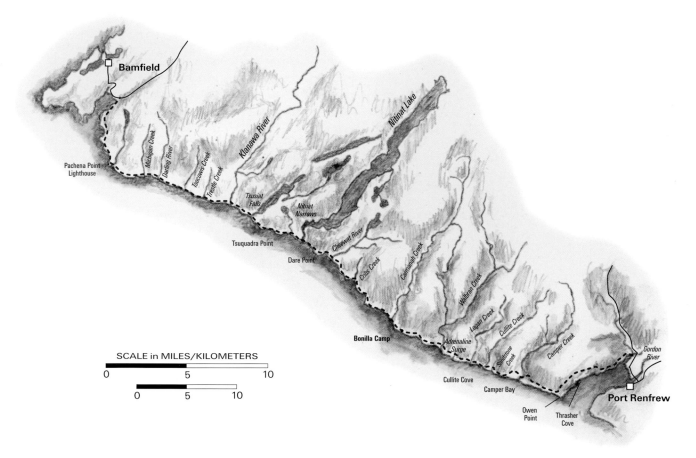

Bamfield

Pachena Point
Lighthouse

Michigan Creek

Darling River

Tsocowis Creek

Trestle Creek

Klanawa River

Tsusiat
Falls

Nitnat
Narrows

Nitnat Lake

Tsuquadra Point

Dare Point

Cheewat River

Cribs Creek

Carmanah Creek

Walbran Creek

Logan Creek

Cullite Creek

Bonilla Camp

Adrenaline
Surge

Sandstone
Creek

Camper Creek

Gordon
River

Cullite Cove

Camper Bay

Port Renfrew

Owen
Point

Thrasher
Cove

SCALE in MILES/KILOMETERS

0   5   10

0   5   10

tion. The trail completely bypasses Owen Point, however, a high-light of this part of the coast. If you can time your arrival at Owen Point, four hours distant, to coincide with low tide, consider the coast route, which follows a boulder-covered beach and coastal shelf littered with driftwood logs, slippery boulders, seaweed, and kelp. Potentially dangerous surge channels cut through the shelf, requiring that you climb into and across them. Despite these obstacles, the beach route is more scenic and open; the forest trail is safer, but just as physical, going up and down ladders (with a heavy pack), and through the mud and roots, much like yesterday's hike, only longer and harder.

Owen Point is a neat place, with enormous sea caves and, fre-quently, sea lions on the beach and whales beyond the breakers. Here you see the magic of the West Coast Trail. Climb about ¹/₂ mile (1 km) beyond the point up to the forest trail at the first marked exit. Back on the forest trail, big ladders and your first cable car (you can also wade here unless the creek is especially high) get you to Camper Bay. Old hands say this is where the torture ends and the fun begins. Camper Bay is open and scenic, with a creek suitable for bathing, a sandstone bluff, and a blowhole shooting up like a geyser. Gray whales are often seen here, where the *John Marshall* went down in 1860.

From Camper Cove, start out on the forest trail; dangerous surge channels and a really tough scramble into Sandstone Creek make the beach route impractical. The trail is strenuous, but once across Sandstone Creek on the bridge it presents few problems to Cullite Cove camp, on the east side of the creek. Beware that the ladders down to Cullite Cove are long. You can pass Cullite Cove camp and continue on to Logan Creek camp, just 1 mile (2 km) far-ther, about 4 miles (6 km) from Camper Bay. From Cullite Cove, cross the creek on the cable car and take the board-walked trail through

the weird stunted forest of a bog. You'll climb a lot of ladders on this section of the route. If you're camping at pleasant Logan Creek camp, don't cross the long suspension bridge, but descend to the camp via the big ladders east of the bridge.

From Logan Creek camp, climb back to the trail, cross the long, swaying bridge, and follow the muddy forest trail to Walbran Creek. Avoid the coastal shelf between Logan and Walbran Creeks; it is crossed by Adrenaline Surge, almost certainly the most dangerous surge channel of the entire route. At Walbran Creek, about 2 miles (3 km) from Logan Creek, the camp is east of the river but close to the beach, so be sure your camp is high enough to stay dry when the tide comes in. If the tide permits, a good day hike from Walbran Creek camp is to walk down the shelf for a look at Adrenaline Surge.

From Walbran Creek camp, go back to the forest trail and cross the creek via the cable car. If the tide is right, you could start out on the coastal shelf, wade the creek, and follow the coastal route to Bonilla. The route here is mostly on a sandy beach, a nice change from the tough going so far. In fact, many people consider Walbran Creek the dividing line between the "hard" and the "easy" ends of the trail. Two shipwrecks happened at Bonilla Point, the *Lizzy Mar-shall* in 1884 and the *Puritan* in 1896.

Bonilla camp and its waterfall are 4½ miles (7 km) from Walbran Creek, but most people just keep chugging up the beach another mile (2 km) to Carmanah Creek, though it can be a tough go in the soft sand. Everybody likes to camp at Carmanah Creek, sometimes for several nights, because of the roomy, lovely setting and proxim-ity to a Chez Monique. A restaurant in the wilderness may seem like heresy, but beer and burgers at Chez Monique is a tradition, and a welcome respite from the hardship so far endured. (The restaurant is near the lighthouse, about 1 mile [2 km] from camp.) Some people spend several nights here, about midway through the trip, to savor the relative comfort.

From Carmanah Creek camp, climb back up to the trail and take the cable car across the creek, past the well-kept lighthouse and grounds near Carmanah Point, which marks an important dividing line. From here to Bamfield you'll be walking beside the Pacific Ocean, not the Strait of Juan de Fuca. Fill up your water bottles at the lighthouse and climb back up to the forest trail for the pleasant hike to Cribs Creek camp (and the natural stone breakwater) 3 miles (5 km) from Carmanah. (Some people prefer the beach route between the lighthouse and Cribs, so check the tide situation.) Cribs is a popular camp with good water. Potable water can be a problem in the section west of here, so some hikers carry water from Cribs Creek to Nitinat Narrows.

From Cribs Creek, the coastal shelf is tempting, but the undulating forest trail is quite scenic and probably the better way to go, because there is a potentially difficult surge channel on the coastal route. Several camps are found near Dare Point, named for the ship that wrecked here in 1890, 2½ miles (4 km) beyond Cribs camp. From Dare Point, continue on the forest trail across the long bridge above the salty Cheewat River, in 2 miles (3 km); from the graceful bridge it's another mile (2 km) (much of it board-walked) to the ferry at Nitinat Narrows. The only way across the swift water here is via the ferry. Operated by a band of First Nation residents, the ferry runs from 9 A.M. to 5 P.M. If it is nowhere in sight when you get there, don't worry, it soon will be.

West of the Narrows is some of the most straightforward hiking of the trip so far—Tsuquadra Point in 2 miles (3 km) and Tsusiat Falls 2½ miles (4 km) beyond. Camping is found on the beach on both sides of the Tsusiat River. These are popular spots because impressive Tsusiat Falls pours right onto the beach, right there. Don't miss the huge cave on the trail between Tsuquadra Point and Tsusiat Point. Spend some time here, and walk out to the beach when you can between the Narrows and Tsusiat Falls. This is a pretty part of the coast.

From the falls, climb the ladder back to the trail and head west. You're on the home stretch now. You'll reach the cable car over the Klanawa River in 1 mile (2 km), and here there's no choice but to use it. The river is too dangerous to wade. Once on the Bamfield side, it's easy to move between the trail and the beach, so hike on the beach when possible and get back on the trail when you need to. Make sure to get down on the beach to see the anchor on the west side of Trestle Creek, 2 miles (3 km) from the Klanawa. Between Trestle Creek and Tsocowis Creek are some outstanding vantage points from the trail. This is a scenic stretch of the coast, and a real cruise compared to the first grueling days.

Tsocowis Creek, 2½ miles (4 km) from Trestle Creek, makes an excellent camp. Cross the bridge to the campground, where bear lockers protect your food. The waterfall is just a stroll upstream. From here, the trail leads in 2 miles (3 km) to Darling River camp, and in a half mile (1 km) to Michigan Creek camps, on both sides of the river. This is one of the best whale-watching spots on the trail, but Michigan Creek is an extremely popular site as it's the first camp from the Bamfield end of the West Coast Trail.

From Michigan Creek it's only 7½ miles (12 km) to the end of the route. An excellent trail (part of it is an old road bed) leads out to Pachena Point Lighthouse, and then the overgrown road leads to the Pachena Bay trailhead, just off the Bamfield road. You're still 3 miles (5 km) from town; locals sometimes wait here to drive weary survivors back to town, for a fee. If no one is available, you have to walk. The trail information center is open from 9 to 5; be sure to drop off your permit.

Information

PACIFIC RIM NATIONAL PARK
Box 280
2185 Ocean Terrace Road
Ucluelet, British Columbia V0R 3A0 Canada
(250) 726-7721
www.pc.gc.ca/pn-np/bc/pacificrim/activ/activ6a_e.asp

BAMFIELD INFORMATION
bamfieldchamber.com//directory.html

PORT RENFREW INFORMATION
www.portrenfrew.com/renfrew.html

Permit information

PARKS CANADA
From Canada and the United States, 1-800-435-5622; from Greater Vancouver, (604) 435-5622; from all other countries, (250) 387-1642.

Ferries and Shuttle

British Columbia Ferries (Vancouver to Victoria car ferry), (250) 386-3431, www.bcferries.bc.ca

Washington State Ferry System (Annacortes to Victoria car ferry), (206) 464-6400, www.wsdot.wa.gov/ferries

"Victoria Clipper" (Seattle to Victoria passenger ferry), (206) 448-5000 in Seattle, (250) 382-8100 in Victoria, www.victoriaclipper.com

West Coast Trail Shuttle Express (Victoria to Port Renfrew and Bamfield), (250) 477-8700

Bamfield–Port Alberni Ferry, www.ladyrosemarine.com

Port Renfrew–Bamfield Water Taxi, www.islandnet.com/~jberry/juanfuca.htm

Fires below the tide line, such as this one near Walbran Creek, are legal on some sections of the trail. PHOTO BY DAVE SCHIEFELBEIN.

THE ROCKWALL TRAIL
Yoho and Kootenay National Parks

Alberta and British Columbia, Canada

DISTANCE: 45 miles (81 km)
TIME: 6–7 days
PHYSICAL CHALLENGE: 1 2 3 4 5
PSYCHOLOGICAL CHALLENGE: 1 2 3 4 5
STAGING: Banff, Alberta

The hike from lovely Floe Lake to the frankly awesome Rockwall of Kootenay National Park and then down into Yoho National Park shows you the flip side of the Lake Louise basin, where the scenery rivals most anything in the Canadian Rockies. In the course of a reasonable, weeklong backpack, this extraordinary excursion samples the best features of this famous mountain park and World Heritage Site. The distinctive thrust-fault peaks of the Continental Divide, the limestone edifice of the Vermilion Range's Rockwall, a brace of spectacular mountain lakes, and a rich roster of wildlife combine here for a major-league wilderness experience.

For most of its length, the route follows the Canadian Great Divide Trail, a network of trails running along the crest of the Continental Divide. Combining the Floe Lake, Rockwall, and Goodsir Pass Trails, the route has several exit options. Before 1997, the most scenic variation picked up the McArthur Valley Trail to Lake O'Hara, but frequent trail closings and lack of maintenance have made that option more difficult. Whichever way you finish it, this route is as remarkable for its diversity as it is for its scenery. Part of that owes to the fact you won't for long maintain a steady elevation on this hike. It climbs and descends with abandon, ranging from just over 4,000 feet (1,219 m) to almost 8,000 feet (2,438 m). The Rockwall Trail ascends to three high passes and dives into three deep drainages as it flanks the Vermilion Range. Expect big elevation gains as you travel from trailhead to ice-bound alpine lakes, across rolling meadows to high passes, and, eventually, down each night to creek-side camps in the forest.

The waterfalls, glaciers, wildflowers, and snowy summits seen on this traverse symbolize the region. For more than a century, the magnificent aspect of the Canadian Rockies has attracted attention from mountain lovers, even from a great distance. European guides came here from the Alps as early as the 1890s. Since then, the Canadian railway hotels at Lake Louise, Banff Springs, and Jasper have strengthened this tradition of mountain recreation on a grand scale. Taken together, the parks embrace a landscape of stunning beauty that is deservedly famous. The ambience is distinctively Canadian, but with a European flavor, resulting in a comfortable and civilized setting adjacent to a challenging wilderness.

I first hiked here in 1975, when Banff was a funkier place and reservations to go hiking were not required. Much has changed, but one thing has remained constant: the presence of grizzly bears in declining but sufficient numbers to not only affect backcountry policy, but to give even experienced hikers pause. These creatures are powerful icons of the North American wilderness, but sharing the backcountry with grizzlies changes the nature of a hike. Every hiker must assess his or her own comfort level before embarking on a weeklong hike in an environment where humans are not at the top of the food chain.

LOGISTICS & STRATEGY

Banff, Kootenay, and Yoho National Parks are best reached from Calgary, Alberta, and its large international airport, only two hours by car from the mountains via the TransCanada Highway. The parks are contiguous, abutting each other and the border between the provinces. Banff and

OPPOSITE: *Lake O'Hara (on the right) and Mary Lake (on the left) as seen from the West Opabin Plateau Trail.* PHOTO BY ROGER HOSTIN.

Kootenay are on the Alberta (east) side of the Continental Divide, Yoho on the British Columbia (west) side. One entrance fee allows you to enter all the parks.

The town of Banff, busy in summer and popular with Japanese and European travelers year-round, is the local center for tourism and the most convenient staging area for the hike. Accommodations and meals can be expensive, some would say unreasonably so, but its proximity to the trailheads, and its many lodgings, cafés, and restaurants, make Banff the logical choice for your base. The smaller town of Field, British Columbia, on the west slope of the Rockies within Yoho National Park, is closer to the finish of the hike, but no closer to the start below Floe Lake. Both

Hikers stop at Goodsir Pass for a view of the Goodsir Peaks.
PHOTO BY HANS FUHRER.

private and national park campgrounds nearby provide alternatives to lodging in town.

The combined allure of the Rockwall Trail and Floe Lake has of late put the permit for the hike in higher demand. The safe strategy is to reserve your permit early: The park's backcountry offices are open June to September, but the Lake Louise Trail Office handles backcountry reservations year-round. Reservations are accepted up to three months in advance. The reservation fee is over and above the daily backcountry fee, but by reserving in advance you can be assured of getting the permit for when you want to go.

The Floe Lake trailhead is 36 miles (57 km) from Banff on Highway 93 in Kootenay National Park. Here, within the park boundaries, the Vermilion River drains the valley between the peaks of the Continental Divide and those of the Vermilion Range. The hike enters this high valley at Floe Lake and follows the eastern escarpment of the massive Rockwall of the Vermilion Range north. Rather than stay high, the trail ascends to three passes and descends into three drainages as it punches north into Yoho National

Park. Named for a Cree word meaning "awe," Yoho is a rugged landscape of glacier-clad peaks, rock walls, waterfalls, and glacial lakes. The hiking route crosses the Continental Divide at Goodsir Pass; from there, the route retreats back to Helmet Creek and out via the Paint Pots trailhead, or down into Yoho and out via the Ottertail River Trail, or, if you are lucky, on to one of the crown jewels of the Canadian parks, Lake O'Hara.

Floe Lake—so named because of the little icebergs floating around in it—lies at timberline, set between the forests, the glacier on its far shore, and the 3,000-foot (900 m) cliffs of the Vermilion Range. Reached by a steep but well-maintained 7-mile (11 km) trail, Floe Lake is the scenic first camp on this traverse. On successive nights, backcountry sites at Numa, Tumbling, and Helmet Creeks offer comfortable wilderness camps. A final night at McArthur Creek is the last stop before a strenuous day out the Ottertail River Trail or up and over McArthur Pass to splendid Lake O'Hara.

In recent years, there's been a new twist to the final day of this hike: During summer, the rangers sometimes close the McArthur Creek Valley to hikers when grizzly bear activity warrants. If your hike conflicts with a trail closing, you'll miss taking a wilderness route to Lake O'Hara, one of the unique aspects of this excursion. Recommended workarounds, however, add no mileage to the route: From McArthur Creek Camp, you can hike out via the Ottertail River Trail to the TransCanada Highway, or, from Goodsir Pass, retreat to Helmet Falls Campground and make your exit from there out to Paint Pots trailhead on Highway 93. Even if trail closings block the final day to Lake O'Hara, you still get a long traverse through one of the most amazing mountain landscapes in North America.

If the route to Lake O'Hara from Goodsir Pass is open when you go, you'll finish this great alpine route with a flourish. Lake O'Hara is nestled high in its classic alpine bowl. Rocky peaks lean in from above, multiple waterfalls—including the magical Seven Veils Falls—pour into it. The sharp spire of Cathedral Mountain, Mount Odaray, dripping with waterfalls, and complex Wiwaxy Peak are just some of the mountains that ring this sparkling gem. Wilderness it is not, however, as a private lodge perches on its shore, serving afternoon tea if you arrive in time to get a table. Shuttle bus service between the lake and the highway, 7 miles (11 km) below, must be reserved in advance, or you can take the Cataract Brook Trail the final 8 miles (13 km) down to a bus depot on the highway.

HAZARDS

Grizzly and black bears are among the abundant wildlife found in the Canadian Rockies. Grizzly bear sightings are uncommon, and attacks on hikers in the Canadian Rocky Mountain parks are rare, but they do happen. Protect yourself by being wary when hiking, avoiding areas of known

Numa Pass above Floe Lake. PHOTO BY HANS FUHRER.

activity, and by keeping food a safe distance from your camp. The backcountry camps on this route are equipped with bear poles with wires and pulleys, which enable you to store your food, toiletries, and garbage out of harm's way. Use them. Talk to rangers about bear safety and bear activity along the route. Other wildlife, including coyotes, wolves, cougars, and elk, can present a danger as well, so keep a respectful distance.

The Canadian Rockies have not escaped the scourge of waterborne giardia, so treat or filter your water. Weather in the mountains can change suddenly, particularly at the high elevations reached on this route, so come prepared for cold and wet weather, even in summer.

SEASON

Mid-July through mid-September is the traditional hiking season in Banff's high country, but the high passes on this route can be snow-covered as late as August. That fact tends to compress most hiking activity into August, when, on average, the Rockies see their best weather of the year. September makes a good time to come, as a hike in late season avoids the busiest weeks. October can be even better, if you

luck out with Indian summer weather, as permits are easier to get and most trail closings are over by then.

ROUTE

The Floe Lake trailhead is in Kootenay National Park, on the west side of Highway 93, 14 miles (22 km) from the Banff-Kootenay park boundary at Vermilion Pass. The well-maintained trail crosses the Vermilion River and follows a gentle grade for the first few miles but then starts steeply uphill. At 5 miles (8 km), the trail ascends more than 2,000 feet (600 m) via a series of switchbacks up the headwall below the lake. When the terrain finally levels out, the trail passes through a high (more than 6,500 feet, 900 m) alpine setting to a broad ridge above Floe Lake to the campground, 7 miles (11 km) from the parking lot. Set at the base of the cliffs of the Vermilion Range, towering more than 3,000 feet (900 m) above, Floe Lake makes a scenic camp, complete with a small glacier and floating icebergs.

From the lake, the Rockwall Trail proper begins, taking you up through thinly forested slopes and alpine meadows to 7,700-foot (2,320 m) Numa Pass, the highest point on the entire Rockwall Trail. Set high among the familiar peaks of the Canadian Rockies, Numa Pass is a stupendous vantage point, so high and open it looks right into the Rockwall itself, Floe Lake, and northward along the crest of the Continental Divide, the mountain-sides draped in ice. From Numa Pass, the trail descends steeply on switchbacks an unreal 5,000 feet (1,500 m) down into Numa Creek and a meadow below a waterfall.

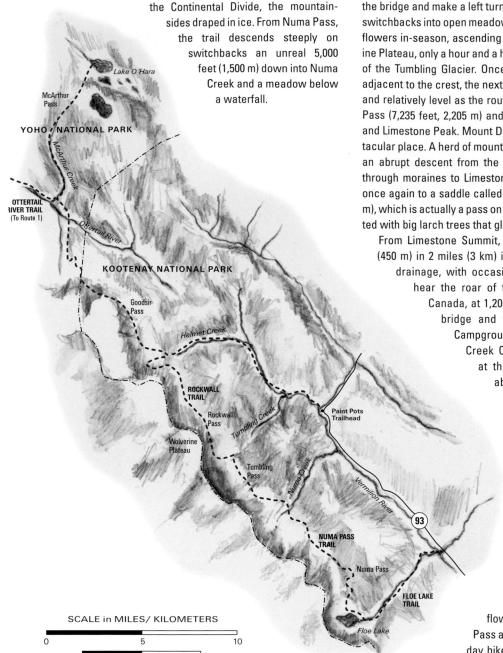

YOHO NATIONAL PARK

McArthur Pass

Lake O'Hara

McArthur Creek

OTTERTAIL RIVER TRAIL (To Route 1)

Ottertail River

KOOTENAY NATIONAL PARK

Goodsir Pass

Helmet Creek

ROCKWALL TRAIL

Rockwall Pass

Tumbling Creek

Paint Pots Trailhead

Wolverine Plateau

Tumbling Pass

Numa Creek

Vermilion River

93

NUMA PASS TRAIL

Numa Pass

FLOE LAKE TRAIL

Floe Lake

SCALE in MILES/ KILOMETERS

0   5   10

0   5   10

the bridge and make a left turn onto the Rockwall Trail, climbing on switchbacks into open meadows full of Indian paintbrush and other flowers in-season, ascending 1,250 feet (375 m) up to the Wolverine Plateau, only a hour and a half from camp, and more good views of the Tumbling Glacier. Once up here on this extended plateau adjacent to the crest, the next 3½ miles (5½ km) remain high, open, and relatively level as the route ascends only slightly to Rockwall Pass (7,235 feet, 2,205 m) and its superb views into the Rockwall and Limestone Peak. Mount Drysdale looms above. This is a spectacular place. A herd of mountain goats is often spotted here. After an abrupt descent from the pass, the trail meanders over and through moraines to Limestone Meadows, then ascends slightly once again to a saddle called Limestone Summit (7,118 feet, 2,170 m), which is actually a pass on the shoulder of Limestone Peak, dotted with big larch trees that glow golden in the fall.

From Limestone Summit, the route drops almost 1,500 feet (450 m) in 2 miles (3 km) into the forest of the Helmet Creek drainage, with occasional views of Helmet Falls (you'll hear the roar of the water), the second-highest in Canada, at 1,200 feet (365 m). The route crosses a bridge and then descends into Helmet Falls Campground, 7½ miles (12 km) from Tumbling Creek Camp. Just before the trail arrives at the campsites, a side trail leads in about 15 minutes to the base of the falls.

Helmet Falls Camp marks the end of the Rockwall Trail proper; from there, the route follows the Goodsir Pass Trail north over Goodsir Pass and into Yoho National Park. From your camp at Helmet Falls, descend to cross the bridge by the patrol cabin and continue down to the intersection with the Goodsir Pass Trail. The trail climbs up for 1,500 feet (450 m) and 2.5 miles (4 km) to the wide, flower-filled alpine meadows of Goodsir Pass at 7,200 feet (2,200 m). The pass, just a day hike from Helmet Falls Camp, offers an outstanding vantage point into the twin towers of Mount Goodsir (11,700 feet, 3,510 m), the highest peak in Yoho National Park, and one of the prettiest in the area. Behind you, the amazing Rockwall's impressive architecture stretches all the way back to Foster Peak.

From Goodsir Pass, the recommended route leads to one more camp at McArthur Creek, where it meets the Ottertail River, then up and over McArthur Pass to the terminus at Lake O'Hara. However, in recent years, park wardens have closed the route up McArthur Creek during summer months in an effort to minimize hiker encounters with grizzly bears, and the park has stopped maintaining the trail. (You'll know whether the route is open to Lake O'Hara when you get your permit.) If travel to McArthur Creek is prohibited, you have two good alternatives. From McArthur Creek Camp, hike the Ottertail River Trail for 9 miles (15 km) out to the trailhead on the TransCanada Highway, 5 miles (8 km) west of Field. Or, from Goodsir Pass, exit via the 9-mile (15 km) route from

Boardwalk trails cross over to Numa Creek Campground, the only camp on the Rockwall Trail low enough for legal fires, 6 miles (9½ km) from Floe Lake.

From the camp, walk beyond the campground and down to the signed intersection, where the Rockwall Trail turns left and begins to climb toward Tumbling Pass. The trail ascends steadily to the north on switchbacks, finally entering a steep section of meadow leading to Tumbling Pass (7,250 feet, 2,200 m), and more views of the looming Rockwall and the Tumbling Glacier, with Foster Peak dominating the view to the south. The trail then descends via moraines and switchbacks, dropping 1,500 feet (450 m) into the forest. Tumbling Creek Camp is reached in 5 miles (8 km).

From Tumbling Creek, the trail climbs up to Rockwall Pass, what many consider the highlight of the traverse. From the camp, cross

Floe Lake and alpine larch trees in autumn livery, as seen from near Numa Pass in the early morning. PHOTO BY ROGER HOSTIN.

Helmet Falls to Paint Pots trailhead parking lot: Descend from Goodsir Pass back to Helmet Falls Camp, hike down through the forest 5 miles (9 km) on the Helmet Creek Trail to Helmet Ochre Camp, and out via the Ochre Creek Trail to the Paint Pots trailhead on Highway 93 in 4 miles (6 km).

If your permit allows you to hike from Goodsir Pass down into Yoho Park and on to Lake O'Hara, follow the Goodsir Pass Trail as it leads north and ascends slightly from the pass before descending down into the forest. The 6-mile (9 km) descent to the Ottertail River is long, strenuous, and without reliable water until you reach the river itself. Near the bottom, hike past the junction for the Ottertail Falls Trail and continue northward to the river; the route crosses the bridge and turns downstream past the McArthur Creek warden cabin to the campground in its dense, lodgepole pine forest. The McArthur Creek Camp is 6½ miles (10 km) from Goodsir Pass.

From the camp on McArthur Creek, only a day's hike and one pass remain before reaching Lake O'Hara. From your camp, make the arduous 7½-mile (12 km) ascent up the McArthur Creek Valley Trail to McArthur Pass. As you ascend the trail along McArthur Creek, gaining more than 2,400 feet (720 m), views of Mount Goodsir make this tough uphill route a little easier to bear. The heavily vegetated avalanche chutes are excellent grizzly bear habitat, so be extra wary as you ascend this valley.

Once you get to McArthur Pass at 7,250 feet (2,228 m), you're only a short walk from Lake O'Hara, 1½ miles (2½ km) away. Descend through forest, passing Schaffer Lake first, then the Elizabeth Parker Hut, before continuing down the trail to the warden cabin at Lake O'Hara situated on one of the prettiest lakes in the Rockies. The campground here is a good place to spend a night or two (with prior reservations) to savor completing this outstanding route.

You still need to reach the highway in the valley below. With reservations, you can ride the bus, but without, the bus ride will be problematic. You could walk the Lake O'Hara access road (7 miles, 11 km), but that would be a let-down from the world-class wilderness route you've just completed. The most appealing route is to descend the trail on the west side of the Cataract Brook Valley.

Cataract Brook is Lake O'Hara's outlet, and this route, mostly in forest, provides good views of the peaks around the lake and above the creek as it descends. It's 8 miles (13 km) to the trailhead at the end of the Great Divide walk, right on the TransCanada Highway, where you can catch a bus to Lake Louise or Banff.

Information

KOOTENAY NATIONAL PARK
Box 220
Radium Hot Springs, British Columbia V0A 1M0 Canada
(250) 347-9615
E-mail: kootenay.reception@pc.gc.ca
Backcountry permit and camping reservations: June to September, (250) 347-9505; September to May, (403) 533-1264

YOHO NATIONAL PARK
Box 99
Field, British Columbia V0A 160 Canada
(250) 343-6783, (250) 343-6012 (fax)
E-mail: yoho.info@pc.gc.ca
Backcountry permit and camping reservations: June to September, (250) 343-6783; September to May, (403) 533-1264

LAKE LOUISE TRAIL OFFICE
(403) 522-1264 (year-round)

Lake O'Hara bus and campground reservation line: (250) 343-6433

LAKE O'HARA LODGE
May through October and February through April, (250) 343-6418; other months, (403) 678-4110

Hikers along Helmet Creek, near the Helmet Falls warden cabin. Helmet Falls is in the distance. PHOTO BY ROGER HOSTIN.

Two

SOUTH AMERICA

FITZ ROY GRAND TOUR
Parque Nacional
Los Glaciares
Argentine Patagonia

DISTANCE: 36-mile (58 km) loop
TIME: 4–7 days
PHYSICAL CHALLENGE: 1 **2** 3 4 5
PSYCHOLOGICAL CHALLENGE: 1 **2** 3 4 5
STAGING: El Chalten, Santa Cruz Province, Argentina

The profile of the Fitz Roy group—a dramatic, ascending ridge formed by the rock spires of Cerro Torre, Poincenot, St. Exupery, and the magnificent arrowhead of Fitz itself—appears out of the plain more abruptly even than that of the Grand Tetons in Wyoming. Towers of pink-tinged gray granite take your breath away, rising in impossibly sheer faces from a surrounding pedestal of ice. The eastward aspect of these storybook mountains opens onto the broad Patagonian plain, exposed to sunrises that paint them brilliant orange to blood red. It is a sublime view, a spectacle, a reason to come.

The peaks lie within the boundaries of Parque Nacional Los Glaciares, one of the biggest national parks on the continent—more than 124 miles (200 km) long with 2,000 square miles (6,000 square km) in area. World Heritage Site status was bestowed here in 1982, and if Fitz Roy is the star of the show, the big glaciers to the south are major players and actually draw more visitors. Both Lago Viedma and Lago Argentino, their waters turned by glacial sediment into a surreal blue, lap up against the ice cap where huge glaciers spill into them. These wild, windswept steppes of Patagonia harbor some of the largest bodies of ice outside the polar regions, and the flowing rivers of ice and soaring rock towers combine for an irresistible backdrop to a hiking adventure.

Explorer Francisco Moreno named Fitz Roy for the captain of Charles Darwin's famous vessel, the *Beagle*, which sailed within sight of the peak in 1834. At 11,073 feet

PRECEDING SPREAD: *The Fitz Roy group.* PHOTO BY PETER POTTERFIELD.

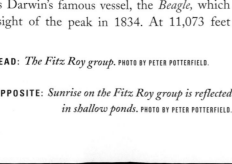

OPPOSITE: *Sunrise on the Fitz Roy group is reflected in shallow ponds.* PHOTO BY PETER POTTERFIELD.

TOP: *Hikers pass Campamento Rio Blanco, the historic "climbers' camp," on the way to Laguna de los Tres.* PHOTO BY PETER POTTERFIELD.

ABOVE: *On the rough trail from Campamento Poincenot to Laguna Sucia.* PHOTO BY PETER POTTERFIELD.

(3,322 m), the mountain the local Indians called Chalten isn't big on the Himalayan scale, but because it rises from a gently rolling plain, it shows more relief than most world-renowned peaks. In the 1950s and '60s, these mythic towers drew climbers from all over the world, including Frenchman Lionel Terray, Italian Walter Bonatti, Argentine José Fonrouge, Scot Dougal Haston, and American Yvone Chouinard.

Those visits explain the plethora of French, British, Argentine, and Californian place-names that dot the map around here. Alpinist still come, and in greater numbers, but the weather is kinder to hikers than to climbers; the hilly, beech-covered plain—*meseta* in Spanish—east of the Fitz Roy massif demands little elevation gain, making for unusually pleasant and consistently interesting backpacking. Backcountry travel here is not physically demanding, and yet comes with a huge payoff in terms of scenery, and, lately, ever-increasing creature comforts.

In fact, traveling to Patagonia is much easier and more fun than it was even five years ago. El Chalten, the tiny village at the base of the Fitz Roy group and the entrance to the national park, has changed dramatically with the opening of a new airport at nearby El Calafate. So many new lodges, restaurants, and other amenities (including bookstores, grocery stores, and a microbrewery) have sprouted in El Chalten that it no longer feels like a remote outpost, but a cosmopolitan mountain village of some civility. Bus transportation between town and the airport is frequent and convenient, and once you get here, the hiking is so close by there's no need for a car.

The major trailheads are within a few blocks of each other. These trails lead through beech forests to some of the most impressive views in the hemisphere. Like much of the history down here, the trails are a recent development. None of them existed when the great mountaineers first ventured to Fitz Roy to make attempts on the peaks. The hiking routes developed more or less organically, connecting what is now El Chalten with the mountains, and with the best viewpoints. This hike—in fact, this place—is all about enjoying the view of Fitz Roy and its scenic neighbors. And even today, surprisingly few people come. You bump into the lucky ones, backpackers from Europe, Australia, America, Japan, and Buenos Aries, who trod the trails in pairs and small groups toward Fitz Roy and Cerro Torre, winding through the gnarly beech trees of the Patagonian forests, the dramatic peaks soaring above them.

LOGISTICS & STRATEGY

As late as 2000, getting to Fitz Roy and Parque Nacional Los Glaciares was an authentic adventure. When I made the journey in 1996 with photographer Art Wolfe, we flew from Buenos Aires to Rio Gallegos, a windswept town on the South Atlantic coast of southern Argentina, and spent the entire next day driving on unpaved roads to El Calafate on Lago Argentino. After a night there, it was another five hours on gravel roads to El Chalten, a town established in 1985 to confirm Argentina's claim on the area over that of Chile.

The journey became easier when the airport at Calafate opened in 2001. Direct flights from Buenos Aires take you to within five hours of the mountains, and El Chalten, which has metamorphosed, chrysalis-like, into a pleasant mountain resort town. The improving infrastructure is a clear testament to the draw of this outrageous landscape, and has made the journey to Patagonia reasonable in terms of effort and expense. Some of the best hiking and climbing on earth are to be found here at Los Glaciares, and without question, more people will come as the word spreads. The recent monetary crisis in Argentina has saddened and angered the Argentines, but the result is that for Europeans

OPPOSITE: *Lunch stop with a view of the Fitz Roy massif.*
PHOTO BY PETER POTTERFIELD.

and North Americans this civilized country is now a better bargain than it's been in a decade.

International flights usually arrive in Buenos Aires mid-morning, but the Calafate flights leave the city early in the day, which means a mandatory overnight stay in BA—lucky you. I've done this a few times and have it wired: Check into a good but reasonable hotel near San Martín Plaza, then walk along Avenue Florida (one of the miles-long pedestrian shopping ways) to a luxurious dinner at one of the good restaurants in the Puerto Madero district, maybe a tango bar after that if you're man or woman enough. Then up for an early cab ride to the airport—not back out to Ezeiza, the international airport, but Aeroparque, the domestic terminal on the banks of the muddy Río de la Plata, with Uruguay just across its wide mouth.

From the sparkling new airport at Calafate, find the bus for El Chalten and sit back for the five-hour ride to the village, which lies just within the boundaries of Parque Nacional Los Glaciares. You could rent a car, although you won't need it once you get to the village, or hire one of the accommodations or guide companies in El Chalten to pick you up at the airport. There's no longer any real reason to go

to Calafate itself, aside from curiosity, for the ever more comfortable El Chalten is your base for everything necessary to hike the trails around Fitz Roy.

New lodges in El Chalten open every year. Check with the El Chalten Web pages to find one that suits your style, or simply pitch your tent in one of two large, free campgrounds in town. On recent visits I've stayed at El Puma, an established, civilized lodge that has private rooms as well as doubles and triples, serves breakfast, has a bar, and is practically next door to most of the new restaurants. El Puma is operated by a venerable El Chalten operation called Fitz Roy Expediciones, which offers climbing and hiking guide services, horse-packing, and can even arrange airport transfers and hotel reservations in Buenos Aires.

Once you've arrived in El Chalten, you're ready to explore the hilly terrain below Fitz Roy and indulge in some glorious backpacking. The whole point of being here is to savor the landscape, one dominated by the granite towers of the Fitz Roy group, but the feature I like best is that you go where you want when you want. You don't need a permit or official sanction of any kind (about the only rule is no fires in the backcountry). Simply tell the people

at your accommodations where you're going and when you'll be back, and off you go. Your only foreseeable problem is the potential for wind and rain.

Weather in any mountainous region can be bad at times, but down here, conditions in the shadow of Fitz Roy can be consistently awful. Frequent storms with interludes of sun in between is the norm. In 1996, I was here for a week in late summer—late February and early March—and never took off my down jacket. The weather was cold, wet, and windy. I managed to hike every day, but each night crawled into a meticulously staked-down tent. On the moraine at Laguna Torre, the wind blew my loaded pack away like it was a candy wrapper. Be prepared—but also be aware there's a gentler side to Fitz Roy. I was hiking out of El Chalten in 2002 during that record-breaking summer, when day after day of 75°F (24°C) temperatures and perfect sunshine had the locals shaking their heads in disbelief. That year, Patagonia in February was like the Sierra or the Dolomites in August.

There is no signature round-the-mountain hike for the Fitz Roy massif. The only way to circumnavigate the mountain is to venture out on the ice cap, where glacier-travel experience is required. The hiking route instead is a physically easy 36-mile (58 km) foot journey through the distinctive beech forests—*las lengas* to the locals—that visits all the major viewpoints of the scenic plain on the east side of the Fitz Roy group.

The hike begins with an easy 7-mile (11 km) day to Cerro Torre, probably the most awesome rock spire in the world, and the glacier-fed lake at its feet. A 3-mile (5 km) side trip from Campamento Jim Bridwell leads to an even better viewpoint near the site of Italian climber Cesare Maestri's old camp. From there, it's another short day, less than 5 miles (8 km) on a good trail, to Campamento Poincenot, where a stay of one or two nights allows for trips to Laguna de los Tres and an up-close view of sunrise on the Fitz Roy massif; a second side trip takes experienced hikers to the wild and seldom-seen shore of Laguna Sucia. From Campamento Poincenot, a 6-mile (9½ km) route follows the western bank of the Río Blanco (past the turnoff for Glaciar Piedras Blancas) to its junction with the Río Eléctrico Trail and a third camp at Piedra del Fraile for another night or two. From there, the hike returns to El Chalten via a final camp at picturesque Laguna Capri, perhaps the prettiest overnight camp of all.

HAZARDS

With no bears, no bugs, and no snakes, there's not much to worry about down here except breaking your ankle or other-

Laguna
Eléctrico

Piedra
del Fraile

Río Eléctrico

23

Río Blanco

GLACIAR
PIEDRAS BLANCAS

Laguna
Piedras Blancas

▲ Fitz Roy

Laguna
de los Tres

Camp
Poincenot

▲ Poincenot

Campamento
Rio Blanco

▲ Rafael

▲ St. Exupery

Laguna Sucia

23

GLACIAR
RIO BLANCO

GLACIAR TORRE

Laguna
Madre

Laguna
Capri

Laguna
Hija

Camp
Laguna Capri

Laguna
Nieta

Río de las Vueltas

Laguna
Torre

Camp
Jim Bridwell

□ El Chalten

Río Fitz Roy

23

SCALE in MILES/ KILOMETERS

0   2   4

0   2   4

wise doing yourself in by injury. To date, giardia have not been reported in the streams around Fitz Roy. The biggest risk factor is without a doubt the fickle Patagonian weather. Hikers must come prepared to deal with windy, cold, and wet conditions.

SEASON

The austral hiking season is October through April, and that's the time to be here; the most reliable sun is generally found December through February, but, ironically, those can be the windiest months. In Patagonia, the weather is notoriously unpredictable; you can luck out with good weather early or late in the season but encounter ferocious winds in high summer. Come prepared. As recently as 2002, crowding was not a problem, even in high season, so weather is the overriding consideration for deciding when to come.

OPPOSITE: *Sunrise on the entire range. From left to right, the high peaks are St. Exupery, Rafael, Poincenot, and Fitz Roy.*
PHOTO BY PETER POTTERFIELD.

ROUTE

The hiking route, which starts and ends in El Chalten, is best experienced as one continuous backpack. But, if weather intervenes, it can be broken up by a return trip to El Chalten from Camp Poincenot.

From El Chalten, find the main trail to Laguna Torre below the northwest end of the village near a white house and a national park sign prohibiting fires. The well-traveled track ascends steeply at first, offering good views overlooking El Chalten and the valley of the Río de las Vueltas. In less than two hours and about 2 miles (3 km) from town, the trail reaches a small rise affording good views of Río Fitz Roy and Cerro Torre itself. The route levels out and continues for 4½ miles (7½ km) to the outlet stream at Laguna Torre and Campamento Jim Bridwell (named for an American climber). Set up your camp here and spend the rest of the day exploring. With day packs, continue up over the moraine and along the north side of Laguna Torre for an incredible view: Cerro Torre and the spires of Egger, Standhardt, and Bifida, and higher up, the glacier to the Adelas Range's Cerro Grande. Vantage points such as this are exactly what bring hikers to Patagonia. This side trip has historical interest, as it leads to the site of Cesare Maestri's camp. The Italian climber's 1950s claim on the first ascent of Cerro Torre was later discredited.

St. Exupery and Poincenot emerge from the mists above Laguna Sucia, one of the most impressive mountain cirques in Patagonia. PHOTO BY PETER POTTERFIELD.

For day two of the hike, depart Campamento Jim Bridwell and retrace your steps from yesterday for approximately 2 miles (3 km) until you reach the intersection with the trail to Campamento Poincenot, which at last visit was well marked. Take the trail leading north by turning left; the way may seem faint at first, but it soon becomes a good track. The trail leaves the valley floor and begins to climb steeply for about 1 mile (1½ km) to a plateau, ascending part of the way through a beech forest. Once on the plateau, the route passes tiny Laguna Nieta on your right and the bigger Laguna Hija on your left, and, finally, the southern tip of Laguna Madre before descending to the intersection with the main trail between El Chalten and Camp Poincenot, at 4 miles (6 km) from Laguna Torre. Turn left at the intersection and continue on the well-traveled trail through low trees, crossing the Río del Salto, and on to Camp Poincenot, 5 miles (8 km) from Campamento Jim Bridwell.

Camp Poincenot, the so-called backpackers' camp, with its view of the tops of Fitz Roy and Poincenot Spire, is bordered by a dense, twisted beech forest, a Harry Potter landscape if there ever was one. One of the busiest camps in the park, Poincenot can serve as home for at least one and perhaps two nights; it serves as the base camp for two of the hike's most scenic legs. The trail up toward Laguna de los Tres can clearly be seen from camp as a steep, 1,300-foot (400 m) climb rising straight up to the lake tucked in at the foot of Fitz Roy. The route follows the well-defined trail from camp, crossing the Río Blanco on a good log bridge, and ascending to Campamento Río Blanco, the so-called climbers' camp, closer to Fitz Roy but without a view, in about ½ mile (¾ km). The obvious trail ascends almost straight up from there, with very few switchbacks, up and over the lip of a moraine and into the small basin that holds Laguna de los Tres, about 2 miles (3 km) from Campamento Poincenot. It's a great hike whenever you do it, but the view from Laguna de los Tres is best appreciated at sunrise. Your options for sunrise are to hike up, traveling light, during late afternoon or early evening and bivy at the lake to wait for dawn. That's what some of my companions did. Or, you can do as I did: Eat and sleep well in your comfortable base camp, rise for an early start to make the two-hour hike by headlamp in time for sunrise on the towers. I've seen a lot of great sunrises in the mountains, but none beat dawn on Fitz Roy from the shores of Laguna de los Tres.

The second hike to consider from Poincenot Camp is the trip to Laguna Sucia, a glacier-fed lake tucked at the bottom of one of the most wild and scenic cirques in Patagonia. The three-hour trip is best suited for those accustomed to off-trail travel, but there is a pretty good track most of the way, with only a few steep sections that present problems. The route is obvious at first: Cross the bridge across the Rio Blanco, turn left on the good trail traveling southwest along the river's north shore, and follow it for 1 mile (1½ km) or so through a particularly beautiful beech forest. Beyond the trees, the route traverses a huge boulder field, the way marked by cairns, before the river narrows into a gorge, requiring some easy but unsavory scrambling on moss-covered rocks. Follow the moraine to the lake's outlet and stupendous views of Poincenot and Glaciar Río Blancas. You're in a wild place here, so turn back if the going becomes uncomfortable. Expect big, down-slope winds in attention-getting gusts, a reminder that you're in Patagonia.

The next stop is Piedra del Fraile on Río Eléctrico, a downhill run. From Campamento Poincenot cross the Río Blanco and travel due north along the good trail on the west side of the river. (There are trails on both sides of the river; make sure you follow the one on the west side.) One mile (1½ km) down the trail you'll see the creek coming from Laguna Piedras Blancas, at the foot of a massive glacier of the same name. To take a look, ascend the right side of the stream for the one-hour side trip that offers views of the big glacier and of Fitz Roy. Once back on the main trail, continue north, and in 2 miles (3 km) the valley widens as the broad track follows the Río Blanco (on your right), with the beech forest off to the left. In 5 miles (8 km) the trail reaches the intersection with the Lago Eléctrico Trail, about two and a half hours from Campamento Poincenot. Turn left, west, and follow the trail another 3 miles (5 km) up through the beech trees and then alongside the Río Eléctrico to Piedra del Fraile, a small, rocky rise in the middle of the valley, 6 miles (9½ km) from Campamento Poincenot.

Piedra del Fraile, Stone of the Priest, was named in homage to Father D'Agostini, a Catholic priest who visited this area in the 1930s. This is the end of the road for hikers. Just beyond the park boundaries is a private campground and a very basic restaurant. Farther west along the track is Marconi Pass and, beyond that,

Hielo Sur, the Patagonian ice cap. The classic day hike from Piedra del Fraile is straight up to the south, ascending between two obvious streams to Paseo del Cuadrado, a mountain pass with killer views into the north side of the Fitz Roy group. This is what some people come for, but it's a tough half-day, 4½ mile (7¼ km) round-trip that finishes on a glacier, so it's not recommended except for those with appropriate skills. It's worth spending two nights at Piedra del Fraile, however, to do either that trip or the other day hike option: Visit the head of Laguna Eléctrico, a dramatic, windy, and sometimes desolate spot, by following the well-used track along its south side.

For the return to El Chalten, hike the 6 miles (9½ km) back to Campamento Poincenot, and then turn left on the trail leading to El Chalten. Hike 3 miles (5 km) to picturesque Laguna Capri for the final camp. Laguna Capri is one of the prettiest of all the lakes, with a view of the summit spires of Fitz Roy and a quiet, comfortable camp. In the morning, get up and walk the last 4½ (7¼ km) miles back to town, arriving at the extreme northern end of El Chalten in time for lunch and having well and truly hit the high points around Fitz Roy.

Information

PARQUE NACIONAL LOS GLACIARES
Zona Norte
El Chalten 9301, Pcia Santa Cruz
Patagonia, Argentina
54 2962 493004

For information on lodging and other facilities in El Chalten:
www.elchalten.com

Guide Services

FITZ ROY EXPEDICIONES
EV yT. Leg 9310
Lionel Terray 212
El Chalten 9301, Pcia Santa Cruz
Patagonia, Argentina
54 2962 493017 (phone & fax)
www.fitzroyexpediciones.com.ar

Camp below Fitz Roy at Campamento Poincenot; Lago de los Tres nestles behind the grassy ridge above camp.
PHOTO BY PETER POTTERFIELD.

TORRES DEL PAINE CIRCUIT
Parque Nacional
Torres del Paine

Chilean Patagonia

DISTANCE: 52 miles (84 km)
TIME: 7–9 days
PHYSICAL CHALLENGE: 1 2 3 4 5
PSYCHOLOGICAL CHALLENGE: 1 2 3 4 5
STAGING: Punta Arenas or Puerto Natales, Chile

The iconic Torres del Paine—the Towers of Paine—three massive slabs of pink granite turned on end, are not the only great peaks in this area of Chilean Patagonia. The Cuernos del Paine—the Horns of Paine—are equally dramatic, if totally different, the unevenly eroded summit caps of these two giants twisted into terrible dragon shapes. Big gestures wrought in stone define the landscape here, and this weeklong route encircles all of the great towers within Parque Nacional Torres del Paine.

In just over 50 miles (80 km), the Torres del Paine circuit unravels the mystery of these unique mountains tucked between the central spine of the Andes and the great Patagonian steppes that roll eastward to the Atlantic. Winding through ancient stands of beech forests, passing lakes tinged an unearthly milky turquoise, and following giant tongues of ice spilling off the Patagonian ice cap, the trail around these mountains reveals a world so unfamiliar that the sight of flightless birds as big as small ponies dashing around in flocks hardly seems surprising.

Odd animal denizens of Torres del Paine enhance the wonder of the place. Fleet and graceful guanacos, wild cousins to the llama, gather in small herds to share top billing with rheas, long-legged ostrichlike earthbound birds prone to rapid changes of direction. Giant condors soaring overhead on immense outstretched wings remind you that this place lies at a great remove. The juxtaposition of exotic wildlife and

LEFT: *The Torres del Paine circuit makes a complete loop around the major peaks in the photograph.* PHOTO BY JAMES MARTIN.

OPPOSITE: *The peaks of the Cuernos Towers rise above the glacier-fed waters of Lago Pehoe.* PHOTO BY GALEN ROWELL/MOUNTAIN LIGHT.

the mountains, lakes, and glaciers that distinguish the terrain makes this Chilean preserve constantly fascinating.

Although not particularly large in terms of area, the park remains a poster child for landscape rehabilitation on an epic scale. Not long ago, the park was a collection of *estancias* and smaller ranches, and the 1,000 square miles (2,400 square km) here endured draconian ecological damage when the beech forests were burned to create more pastureland. Intense overgrazing followed. But the Chileans moved to protect the area in 1959 with the creation of what was then Parque Nacional Lago Grey, in deference to the mighty Glaciar Grey that tumbles 17 miles (27 km) down into the park from the Patagonian ice cap farther west. Ironically, the park's reputation grew more quickly outside the country than in it, as climbers from Europe and North America, drawn irresistibly to the towers, quickly spread the word about this backcountry paradise. World Heritage Site status was bestowed in 1978.

Part of the draw is how these mountains of the Paine massif differ so dramatically from those of the central spine of the Andes. This land was formed by glaciers that ground away the Cuerno's soft rock. A layer of black sedimentary rock—which remained above the glaciers that once covered the lower mountains—forms the famous horns atop the elegant Cuernos. The same ice had an opposite effect on the Torres, polishing smooth the hard batholithic slabs. It is ironic that of these great mountains, only one rises above 10,000 feet, and just barely: the 10,007-foot (3,002 m) Paine Grande. The other four reach to between 8,000 and 9,000 feet (2,400 and 2,700 m) but show a lot of relief, proving that mountains don't have to be high to be impressive. The three towers of the Cumbré group, just southwest, are the highest of all, but lack equal spectacle.

The classic view of the Torres del Paine is from the north, from remote Lago Azul, or perhaps from the moraine at the feet of the towers, above Río Ascensio. The Cuernos are best viewed from the south, from Lago Grey, or from across Lago Pehoe, where the weird features of the summit horns all but obscure the Torres behind. But the only way to see all these towers from all sides is to walk the Torres del Paine

circuit, a week of constantly changing and constantly surprising terrain. You'll hike through forests, slip around in muddy bogs, cross streams without the benefit of bridges, climb rocky slopes to high passes, and see some of the most beautiful country in South America from an often trying trail.

Following the completion ten years ago of the new trail along the north shore of Lago Nordenskjold—the Sendero Paso Las Cuernos—much discussion has focused on the relative merits of the classic circuit route compared to those of the so-called W route. The latter became possible with the opening of Sendero Paso Las Cuernos, which connects Campamento Italiano with Hostería Las Torres. The difference between the two routes is this: The circuit route offers an excursion into the wild back side of the park, with no backtracking, and a look at everything. The W is basically three connected day hikes to the front-side highlights, with lots of backtracking. But there's no need, really, to choose one over the other, as one leg of the W, the Lago Grey hike, is the final section of the circuit route; another leg, the Valle de Francis, is an optional side trip off the circuit route. The third leg of the W route, the Río Ascensio Trail up to the moraine overlooking the Torres Del Paine at close range, is a day hike that is mandatory for every backcountry lover who comes to the park.

LOGISTICS & STRATEGY

A visit to Parque Nacional Torres del Paine can be routed through Chile or Argentina, and how you go determines how best to approach the park. Since Patagonia is pretty much at the end of the world, if you can take sufficient time it makes sense to see both highlights of the region—the Fitz Roy massif and the Torres del Paine massif—in one trip. If you're doing that, the easiest approach is through Buenos Aires and El Calafate (see Fitz Roy Grand Tour). From El Calafate, daily bus service can take you directly to the park, or to Puerto Natales, a gateway to the park farther south. The drive follows a dusty gravel track with exciting views of the towers from afar, through the uptight, militarized Argentine-Chilean border at Cerro Castillo. I completed that journey in a rental car in the late 1990s, but by 2002 the bus service was so good that it is preferable to the expense and risk of a private vehicle.

If you're going to Patagonia specifically for Chile's Parque Nacional Torres del Paine, it makes more sense to fly to Santiago and then on to Punta Arenas, the closest airport to the park. Both Chilean and international guide services operate from Punta Arenas, but this is a backcountry trip that's easy to do on your own. A good staging area is a few

This, the best view of the Torres del Paine, requires a half-day detour off the circuit, up the Río Ascensio. PHOTO BY JAMES MARTIN.

hours north of Punta Arenas: Puerto Natales, a cosmopolitan small town on the shores of Seno Ultima Esperanzo (Last Hope Sound). Whether you're coming from Punta, Puerto Natales, or Calafate, bring a week's supply of backcountry food with you, as only a limited selection is available within the park.

From Puerto Natales, a three-hour bus ride covers the 70 miles (113 km) up to the park administration center at Lago del Toro, 22 miles (35 km) from the park entrance at Laguna Amarga. Buses leave every couple of hours during the season. The 50-mile (80 km) circuit hike can be started from Laguna Amarga, but it's best to first get acquainted with the park by traveling the final 20 miles (32 km) past the pricey Hotel Explora and the moderate Hostería Pehoe down to Lago del Toro. The limited number of services available in the park can be found in this small cluster of buildings, a former *estancia*: an informal hotel (Posada Río Serrano), a pleasant bar specializing Pisco sours, an inexpensive

OPPOSITE: *The southern loop of the circuit follows the shore of Lago Grey, full of icebergs calved off nearby Glaciar Grey.* PHOTO BY JAMES MARTIN.

hostel, a small grocery, even a *mechanico* (who replaced the chewing gum we used to patch the hole in our gas tank with something more permanent).

Lodging options within the park include the hotel at Río Serrano, three hosterías (about $150 per night), the chic, expensive Hotel Explora, and a number of hostels and campgrounds adjacent to the hosterías. Since you'll be backpacking for a week, you might as well indulge yourself with the comforts of the hosterías at Lago Grey, Lago Pehoe, or Hostería Las Torres, the last being the best situated for hikers. All the hosterías are comfortable, but not fancy, and have good restaurants. Advance reservations are required during the busy summer months.

Getting around the park used to be quite difficult without a vehicle, but now a shuttle bus frequently plies the road (unpaved) between the administration building and the park entrance. Rather than start the hike from the entrance station at Laguna Amarga, take the shuttle instead to the Hostería del Torres, 4½ miles (7 km) farther down a rough road. In addition to the informal hotel, a campground, hostel, and restaurant make this a comfortable place to hang out before the circuit trek. The day hike from here up the Río Ascensio to the end of the trail on the moraine offers a classic view right into the towers from the best vantage point in the park. There is a good trail all the way, and while it is famously steep at first, the Grind soon relents and rewards with close-up views of the towers. This is the first leg of the W route. A good way to prepare for the circuit hike is to stay at the hostería (or the hostel or campground nearby), do the day hike up to the towers, then start out the following day on the 50-mile (80 km) trek.

The Torres del Paine circuit is best done counterclockwise, starting from either the entrance station, the ranger station at Laguna Amarga, or the Hostería Las Torres. The routes from both starting points meet up in about four hours on the banks of the Río Paine and do not differ substantially in terms of scenery. While the trail is well traveled enough to present few route-finding problems, the going can be challenging. The trail itself appears virtually unmaintained in places. Frequently muddy, blocked by tiring deadfall, and spiced by fords and marginal bridges, the route requires more time and energy than you might think by looking at a map. Long days of summer, however, mean that even on the difficult stages there is plenty of opportunity to enjoy the scenery, which is the whole point.

Refugios—huts, or the ruins of them—found along the route are not all usable. Some are in such disrepair that they provide little shelter; others are sound but unsavory. Excep-

tions include Refugio Pehoe and the new Refugio de Los Cuernos. For the back side of the circuit route the wise hiker will consider the refugios landmarks for the campamentos, and so not be disappointed. Bring a tent, a good one, and plan on using it every night. This is Patagonia, deservedly notorious for wet, windy weather.

Not a high route by Andean standards, the circuit seldom climbs above 1,500 feet (500 m), but a 4,000-foot (1,200 m) pass and typically stormy weather demand rain gear and warm clothing. You have to be prepared for everything from hot summer sun to snow. Cold streams are forded in the course of this hike; carry sandals or other waterproof shoes to avoid the discomfort of wet boots.

ABOVE: *Graceful guanacos, wild cousins to the llama, enhance the wonder of Chile's Patagonian park.* PHOTO BY GALEN ROWELL/MOUNTAIN LIGHT.

OPPOSITE: *A field of lupine sprawls across the windswept Patagonian plain, with the Torres del Paine visible in the distance.* PHOTO BY GALEN ROWELL/MOUNTAIN LIGHT.

HAZARDS

With no bears, no bugs and no snakes, there's not much to worry about down here except for breaking your ankle or otherwise doing yourself in by injury. The biggest risk factor is without a doubt the fickle Patagonian weather. Hikers must come prepared to deal with everything from hot sun to cold and wet, even snow at the high pass in summer. Boil, filter, or treat water from streams, especially near the popular camps.

SEASON

Parque Nacional Torres del Paine is so far south that the austral summer is the only time to go. The peak of the tourist season is January and February, but December and March can also see hikable weather. You can get lucky in November and April, but at the ends of the season you're risking inclement conditions.

ROUTE

You can start from either the Laguna Amarga entrance station or the Hostería Las Torres. The trails converge near the Río Paine before reaching the first camp. From the hostería, the circuit trailhead is 1½ miles (2 km) north along the road. From the trailhead,

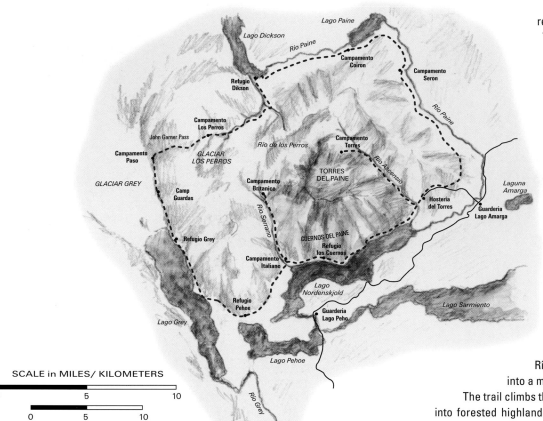

SCALE in MILES/ KILOMETERS

remind you this is Patagonia. The descent down to the lake at the head of the Río Paine valley is steep. The campground and refugio, the site of an old homestead, are right by the lake, about 6 miles (10 km) from Campamento Coiron. Surrounded by peaks and glaciers, this is a memorable place to overnight and one of the highlights of the circuit. Some people choose to spend a rest day here to get psyched for the hard work to come.

From the lake, the trail soon joins the Río de Los Perros and travels into a much wilder part of the park. The trail climbs the river valley as it ascends into forested highlands where it enters a windy, mossy grove of beech trees. The route continues ascending through the forest to the head of the drainage, entering an open meadow area with views in all directions if weather permits. The trail continues ascending beside the river, crossing side streams on log bridges as it climbs through the forest. Five miles (8 km) from camp, the route reaches welcome (if somewhat inadequate) bridges across the fast-flowing main channel of the Río de Los Perros. To the left, look for the Glaciar Los Perros as it flows down its north-facing mountainside. Once across the river, the route climbs steadily and then traverses rocky slopes below the glacier to hidden Campamento Los Perros, 7 miles (11 km) from Lago Dickson. The camp appears suddenly in a small forest grove above the small but picturesque lake full of little icebergs at the foot of the glacier.

The next day's 4½-mile (7 km) section is one of the most physically strenuous of the route, and one of the most impressive. It crosses a high pass (with strong potential for bad weather) and descends toward the mighty Glaciar Grey, a highlight of the route. From camp, follow the river along a muddy, difficult section of forest trail with cold but easy river crossings as you climb up toward the head of the valley. Once above tree line, the route, now marked by cairns, ascends scree and rocky terrain, toward the pass, climbing to 4,068 feet (1,241 m). The pass, which some maps label John Gardner, others Gadner, is the highest point on the circuit, marked by ragged orange flags. If the weather is clear, enjoy the views down the stunning expanse of ice that is Glaciar Grey, filling its constricting valley, the mountains behind a fitting backdrop. The glacier is actually a huge tongue of the Patagonian ice cap reaching down into the park. From the pass, hike down the rocky slope on a number of switchbacks before diving down into another muddy, difficult, and slippery section of forest trail to Campamento Paso, just a few hundred yards from the edge of Glaciar Grey.

The route to Refugio Grey traverses the slope just above the glacier, slowly coming around to icy blue Lago Grey with its

head north onto the Torres del Paine Circuit Trail. Climb steeply, up alongside the Río Paine, then down into a broad expanse of rolling meadow and through a gate. The trail stays fairly close to the river as it travels through the broad valley and open meadows with early-season wildflowers until arriving at Campamento Serón, on some maps called El Serón or Puesto Serón, five to six hours and 10 miles (16 km) from the hostería. Trail maintenance leaves something to be desired, but the going is relatively easy and fast on this first section of the route.

Despite the fact that the second day covers a lot of mileage, it actually is one of the circuit's easier days. The trail starts out in the broad river valley, crossing streams and passing by small lakes before climbing on rocky ground above the broad meadows and open grasslands. Follow the orange markers, climbing up into highlands as the trail turns southwest above Lago Paine. Pass a small, horseshoe-shaped lake and switchback up through the small pass. From here, the route traverses high ground above Lago Paine, down on your right, and offers an expansive view of peaks on the border with Argentina behind the lake. Once beyond the western end of the lake, the trail descends down into the broad river valley, reaching Campamento Coiron, 5½ miles (9 km) from El Serón in time for lunch near the lakeshore. The camp here makes for a scenic place for a midday break, with quintessentially Patagonian views of the mountains across the lake if the weather is clear.

From Coiron, the route follows the river for 2 miles (3 km) and then traverses a muddy section through a bog. Take care on some dicey log crossings here, and ascend up and over the small ridge (an old moraine) with a view of Lago Dickson, its glacier, and the mountains around it. The character subtly shifts right here at this ridge as the mountains and glaciers and a sense of wilderness massive chunks of floating ice. The trail here is narrow and erratic, with the potential for falls in some places. Ladders ascending short, steep sections of cliff are another potential hazard, as climbing them with a full pack can be a challenge. Eventually the trail descends back into a scenic beech forest, but one littered with deadfall. The trail eventually emerges back into more open meadows as it descends toward Refugio Grey, and the adjacent camp, 6 miles (9 km) from Campamento Paso. This is a popular spot, one of the most scenic overnight backpacking destinations in the park.

The next day, follow the shore of Lago Grey, at times clambering up and over old moraines. Side trails marked by cairns lead down to the snout, where the glacier calves into the lake. The route descends for approximately 3 miles (5 km) before cutting up and east over the ridge separating Lago Grey from Lago Pehoe. The trail climbs up onto the flat ridgetop, past an alpine lake of striking blue before coming around the corner (expect big winds here) to the turquoise expanse of Lago Peho. Follow the valley down to Refugio Peho and the guard station at the end of the route, 7½ miles (12 km) from Refugio Grey. The camp here, on the broad plain above the beautiful lake, makes a pretty but potentially windy camp.

From Refugio Pehoe, there are many options to complete the route. Most hikers, having had enough time on the trail, simply catch the passenger ferry for the half-hour ride back to the Guarderia Lago Peho. From there, you can catch the shuttle bus back to other areas of the park, or wait for the buses to Puerto Natales, Punta Arenas, or Calafate.

An on-foot option is to walk back to the Hostería Las Torres on the recently completed Sendero Paso Las Cuernos along the north shore of Lago Nordenskjold, and by the new refugio there. To try the new route, make the 6-mile (10 km) hike to Campamento Italiano, at the mouth of the famous Valle de Francis, which leads into the heart of Cuernos del Paine. (From Campamento Italiano, you can make an exciting day hike up to the site of Campamento Britanico for an up-close look at the hanging glaciers in the Cuernos. This is the middle leg of the W route.) From Campamento Italiano, it's 4½ miles (7 km) to the Campamento Los Cuernos and the new refugio on the north shore of Lago Nordenskjold. From there, it's 7½ miles (12 km) back to Hostería Las Torres. This relatively new route ascends over steep, rocky hills and crosses fast-flowing streams, often without benefit of bridges. But it's a fitting conclusion to this magnificent route—closing the circle on one of the Americas' great circuit hikes.

Information

PARQUE NACIONAL TORRES DEL PAINE
Administration and visitors center: 56-61-691931

The park itself does not give out a postal address. Inquiries should be sent to the main administration offices:
CONAF (Corporación Nacional Forestal)
Av. Gral Bulnes 285
Santiago, Chile
51-02-696-6677
www.conaf.cl

Park Accommodations: www.torresdelpaine.org/accommodation.html

HOSTERIA DEL TORRES
Sector Salto Chico
Parque Nacional Torres del Paine
56-61-226054
www.lastorres.com

HOSTERIA PEHOE
Lake Pehoe
Torres del Paine National Park
56-61-244506
www.pehoe.cl

HOSTERIA LAGO GREY
Lago Grey
Torres del Paine National Park
56-61-410220

Guide Services

Mountain Travel Sobek
1266 66th Street
Emeryville, CA 94508 USA
(510) 594-6000, 1-888-687-6235
www.mtsobek.com

The waterfall of Salto Grande flows out of Lago Nordenskold along the eastern leg of the circuit. PHOTO BY BETH WALD.

Three

EUROPE

KUNGSLEDEN
Northern Section
Lapland, Arctic Sweden

DISTANCE: 65 miles (104 km) one-way
TIME: 5–7 days
PHYSICAL CHALLENGE: 1 2 3 **4** 5
PSYCHOLOGICAL CHALLENGE: 1 2 **3** 4 5
STAGING: Kiruna, Sweden

In extreme northern Sweden, well inside the Arctic Circle, lies the last genuine wilderness in Western Europe. This is Lapland, and through it runs Kungsleden, a 275-mile-long (440 km) route that cuts through the heart of this expansive landscape of big Arctic valleys, birch forests, hidden glaciers, powerful rivers, and the highest mountains in Sweden. The sheer scale of Kungsleden and the country it traverses comes home when, after a 16-mile (26 km) day, you realize you're not halfway down the undulating, glacier-carved valley you dropped into that morning. Low-angled light from the Arctic sun paints the features with a flattering glow and masks the great distances. For me, the experience was exhilarating, the Arctic landscape so big and open I felt I could walk for days and not run out of room.

Kungsleden is often translated, incorrectly, as the King's Trail, when in fact it should be the King of Trails, an apt name for a hiking route that travels through four national parks and a nature reserve, in total an area larger than some European countries. The trail begins at Abisko, in the north, and continues south to Hemavan. Hiking the entire route takes a month or more, but the northernmost section recommended here covers many of the Kungsleden's highlights in just 65 miles (104 km) and a week on the trail. This section starts at Abisko and finishes at the Sami (these are the ethnic Laplanders) settlement of Nikkaluokta, located at the end of a minor highway.

In addition to one of the most impressive valleys in Lapland, the Tjäktjavagge, this weeklong route takes in Kebnekaise, Sweden's highest peak at 6,932 feet (2,113 m), and the highest point on the entire Kungsleden, Tjäktjapasset, a pass at 3,750 feet (1,140 m). This part of Kungsleden has the additional advantage of being relatively easy to get to, thanks to the small mining city of Kiruna, home to one of the largest iron mines in the world, as well as the tony Ice Hotel. Consequently, tiny Kiruna has good air connections to Stockholm, and bus transportation to both ends of this route.

Despite the terrain's wildness, there's a civility to the hike that reflects the Swedish sensibility. Sturdy suspension bridges span the deeper, more dangerous rivers, and comfortable lodges, called huts, are strategically placed to allow hiking with just a minimum of equipment. Near either end of the route—at Abisko and Kebnekaise—are two of Sweden's more elaborate mountain "stations," where hot showers and real restaurants provide an appropriately comfortable beginning and end to a grand wilderness experience.

PRECEDING SPREAD: *The Swedish Arctic.* PHOTO BY PETER POTTERFIELD.

LEFT: *The timbered gate at the start of Kungsleden at Abisko.*

OPPOSITE: *Wild Arctic rivers flow near the high point of the route below Tjäktjapasset.* PHOTOS BY PETER POTTERFIELD.

The Lapporten, an iconic Swedish landform that serves as the gateway to the wilds of Lapland; the buildings of Abisko mountain station are visible to the left. PHOTO BY PETER POTTERFIELD.

In some ways, hiking across this wild Arctic terrain recalls a more innocent time for American and European backcountry travelers. The landscape up here is so pristine that you can drink the water, untreated, out of any stream, a luxury long ago abandoned in most other places. And with no restrictions on tent camping for most of the route, this spectacular wilderness is a backpacker's paradise. Pitch your tent on a ridge top, or by the lakeside, or beside that low-elevation glacier, and no ranger will write you up. There simply aren't enough people here to create a problem with impact.

Backcountry management in Sweden is unique, a joint venture between the government, responsible for the national parks, and a large, voluntary hiking organization called the Swedish Touring Federation, universally known as the STF. The STF maintains most of Kungsleden, staffs the huts, and operates the comfortable mountain stations. Through the volunteer organization, hikers from other countries can request information about Kungsleden in Japanese, English, and several European languages.

Parts of this route traverse the traditional herding areas of the native Sami people, a fact evidenced by the odd reindeer fence encountered, or the occasional cluster of small red Sami structures tucked away in a hollow. The rare glimpse of this ancient way of life, revered and protected by the Swedes, does not sully the experience. This Arctic wilderness is big enough for everyone. People tell me Kungsleden gets quite busy in the middle of summer, but when I was there one glorious September, I walked 31 miles (50 km) in two days without seeing a soul on the trail. It was a wilderness excursion that rekindled my passion for remote places.

LOGISTICS & STRATEGY

The 65-mile-long (104 km) northern section of Kungsleden starts at Abisko Mountain Station (*Fjallstation* is the Swedish word) and ends in the tiny Sami village of Nikkaluokta. Both places are accessed from the small mining city of Kiruna, which has an airport with twice-daily air connections on SAS to Stockholm. Abisko is on Highway E-10 just 8 miles (14 km) from Norway and an hour and a half northwest by bus from Kiruna; Nikkaluokta is at the end of a minor highway, number 870, just over an hour west of Kiruna by bus.

You could hike the route in either direction, but virtually everybody starts in Abisko and hikes south to Nikkaluokta.

The high, narrow valley that holds the lake Alesjaure affords views all the way back to the Giron, the distinctive black peak in the distance.
PHOTO BY PETER POTTERFIELD.

Doing the hike that way puts the sun on your face as you travel, no small consideration in the Arctic. Fit hikers could do the route in four or five days, but most take a more leisurely six or seven. Since the route goes by Kebnakaise, some experienced backcountry travelers take a day to hike to the top, weather permitting.

Schedule extra days at the end of your hike to allow for unexpected delays, rest days, self-indulgent side hikes, or bad weather. That way, if you finish the hike on time, you can use the extra days to hang in laid-back Kiruna or do some sightseeing in civilized Stockholm before the international flight home.

The usual strategy for foreign visitors doing Kungsleden is to start by flying from Stockholm to Kiruna. This small, pleasant (despite the monstrous iron ore mine looming nearby) city is well inside the Arctic Circle, and makes a good staging area. Leave your bag with a change of clothes at your hotel before taking the bus from either the downtown bus depot or the airport to Abisko. The Abisko Mountain Station is one of the few in Sweden located on a road, so it boasts outstanding creature comforts. This large, well-run station has accommodations ranging from private rooms to dormitory-style lodging to separate chalets, and an excellent restaurant with wine and spirits. The cost per night is 200–900 Skr. The station is the place to buy maps, last minute groceries, even a limited selection of backcountry gear should you need it. A big breakfast buffet ensures you'll hit the trail well fueled, a good thing.

Abisko Mountain Station is within Abisko National Park, and the first day's hike will be entirely within the boundaries of the park. There are a limited number of designated camps within the park, so most people end the first day at the hut at Abiskojaure, 9½ miles (15 km) from Abisko. Here, you can stay in the hut or pitch a tent in the adjacent camping area. The park boundary is just beyond the huts at Abiskojaure. From that point on, the northern section of Kungsleden is a backpacker's field of dreams: You can pitch a tent virtually anywhere you please within this vast Arctic landscape. Huts are strategically located about a day's walk apart—anywhere from 7½ to 14 miles (12–22 km). Hikers can stay in the huts for fees ranging from 195 to 400 Skr, or camp in tents, or do a little of both.

There are four huts and two larger mountain stations along this route, all run by the 330,000-member strong Swedish Touring Federation (STF). From Abisko Mountain Station, it's 9 miles (15 km) by trail to Abiskojaure, 14 miles (22 km) to Alesjaure (a new and exceptionally comfortable hut), 8 miles (13 km) to Tjäktja, 7½ miles (12 km) to Sälka, 7½ miles (12 km) to Singi, and 8½ miles (14 km) to Kebnekaise Mountain Station and its welcome hot showers and restaurant. The settlement of Nikkaluokta is another 12 miles (19 km), but a boat is available to take you about half that distance by river. You'll find simple lodgings and a restaurant there, right where the bus picks you up for the ride back to Kiruna.

The huts along the trail are clean and comfortable, with wood-burning stoves for heat and gas stoves for cooking. The kitchens are equipped with pots, utensils, and dishes; a few even sell basic provisions. If using the huts, the hiker need not carry tent, sleeping pad, stove, pot, or utensils, resulting in huge weight savings. A light pack means you can travel faster, even do double stages in places should you be so inclined. But beware that the huts can be crowded in midsummer, and noisy. I hiked Kungsleden in September, outrageously late for an Arctic Circle adventure. I found the huts nearly empty, mostly quiet, and populated by a few invariably interesting and friendly hikers from all over Europe, but mostly from Sweden. The French and Germans I met said they were hiking Kungsleden to escape the crowds and teleferiques of the Alps. The people I encountered were frankly astonished at my presence, so rarely do North Americans come here.

The advantage of packing your own tent for Kungsleden is that you can set up next to raging rivers, or in hidden valleys, or on mountaintops, or on the open tundra. This freedom is enough to make North American campers giddy. Having a tent also frees one from the tyranny of a schedule: There's no reason to hike to the next hut, just make camp when and where the impulse strikes. I think the best way to go is to do a little of both: Travel with bivy bag and stove to enjoy the freedom to camp anywhere when the weather is right, but relish the comfort and camaraderie of the huts when it's not.

Variations on this route are many. Most of the side valleys have tracks or trails that offer room for exploration. This northern section of Kungsleden has the advantage of air access through Kiruna, but is only a quarter of the entire route. If you've got the time and inclination, keep walking south, beyond Kebnekaise, where three more weeklong sections, each with its own unique landscape, follow: Kebnekaise to Saltoluokta covers 32 miles (52 km) across broad mountain plateaus, with steeply incised valleys at Teusajaure and Kaitumjaure, as it traverses Stora Sjöfallet National Park. The five- to seven-day hike ends in Vakkotavare. Saltoluokta to Kvikkjokk covers 45 miles (73 km) in four to six days, passing through virgin forest, expansive heaths, and lakes where travel by boat is required. Ammarnäs to Hemavan, Kungsleden's southernmost section, covers 48 miles (78 km) across open plains dotted with large lakes.

HAZARDS

There are few hazards endemic to hiking the Kungsleden. The route is well marked, the dangerous rivers are bridged, and the huts have emergency radios. Weather can be a problem: Cold, stormy conditions that far north demand appropriate clothing and shelter, and snow can hinder progress early or late in the season. The altitude is not extreme, with the highest point of the entire Kungsleden encountered the third or fourth day at Tjäktjapasset, more than 3,700 feet (1,140 m) feet high. But in the Arctic, it doesn't take a lot of

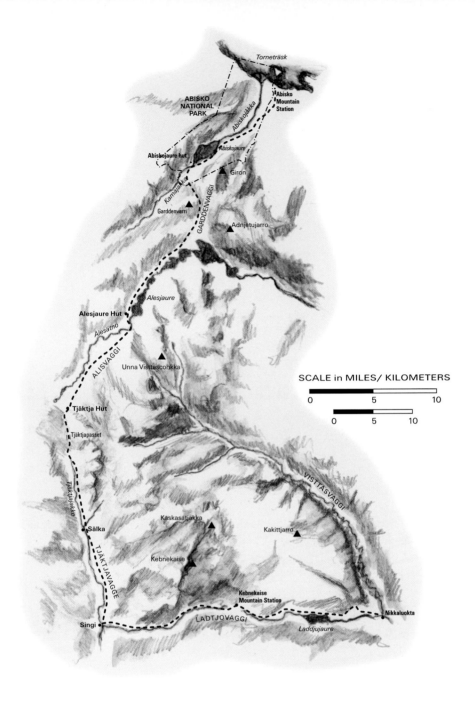

Torneträsk

ABISKO NATIONAL PARK

Abisko Mountain Station

Abiskojåkka

Abiskojaure hut   *Abiskojaure*

Kamajåkka   ▲ Giron

Garddenvarri ▲

GARDDENVAGGI

▲ Adnjetujarro

Alesjaure

Alesjaure Hut

Alesätno

ALISVAGGI

▲ Unna Visttascohkka

Tjäktja Hut

▮ Tjäktjapasset

Tjäktjajåkke

■ Sälka

TJÄKTJAVAGGE

VISTTASVAGGI

Kaskasatjakka ▲

Kakittjarro ▲

Kebnekaise ▲

Kebnekaise Mountain Station

■ Singi

LADTJOVAGGI   *Laddjujaure*

Nikkaluokta

SCALE in MILES/ KILOMETERS

0   5   10

0   5   10

---

elevation to put you into a different climate zone, so take appropriate measures. The locals say there are brown bears lurking somewhere in this wilderness, mostly in the forested areas, but sightings are rare.

SEASON

The huts are open from mid-June to mid-September, the period when the trail is sufficiently snow-free to be hiked. The busiest time by far is July 15 to August 15, when midsummer conditions attract the vast majority of Kungsleden's hikers. June means uncrowded trails and huts, all under the famous midnight sun, but a wet track and snowy passes.

OPPOSITE: *Hendry, the warden of the Alesjaure hut, and his Arctic domain.* PHOTO BY PETER POTTERFIELD.

September means fewer people and fall color, but an early season snowstorm could leave you stuck.

ROUTE

Abisko Mountain Station is on the shores of Torneträsk, a vast Arctic lake, the sixth-largest in Sweden. Highlights include a view into the famous mountain formation of Lapporten, the storied gateway to Lapland, good food, and a scale to weigh your pack before departing on the weeklong trek to Nikkaluokta. From the front door of the station, walk south across the highway to the elaborate wooden gateway that marks the Kungsleden's northern terminus. The mountain station is the center of activity for Abisko National Park, so the first few miles of the trail are broad and easy, busy with day hikers and other short timers. The rocky trail meanders through the dense forest of low birch trees stunted by the Arctic climate, staying close to and just east of the Abisko River (Abiskojåkka). The forest grows denser as the trail penetrates deeper into the mountains. Glaciers are visible in side valleys just a thousand feet above,

Early-morning September sunlight paints the tundra of the Swedish Arctic a tawny amber below the huts at Salka. The photographer's shadow is his only companion. PHOTO BY PETER POTTERFIELD.

and the view here is dominated by Giron, farther south, at 5,087 feet (1,551 m) a local landmark. In three or four hours, a white STF flag marking the spot of Abiskojaure hut becomes visible above the thick forest. You have to hike slightly south of the huts before coming upon the bridge that crosses the swiftly flowing Kamajakka and leads to the cluster of buildings, 9 miles (15 km) from Abisko, about four or five hours on the trail. Tent camping is restricted to just a few places within the national park, one of which is a grassy area adjacent to the huts.

From Abiskojaure, the route recrosses the suspension bridge over the Kamajakka and turns to the southeast, leaving Abisko National Park. From here, there are no restrictions on tent camping. The mood and terrain both get perceptibly wilder as one leaves the park and the trail gradually ascends out of the trees to climb up into Garddenvaggi, a narrow valley between the peaks of Giron and Garddenvarri. Cairns and painted rocks mark the way as the trail arrives at a high point, with good views back to Abiskojaure. Curving south along the flank of Garddenvarri, the trail reaches a long,

broad valley filled with a number of lakes but dominated by the 6½-mile-long (10 km) Alesjaura. The trail goes through a makeshift gate in an eight-foot-high reindeer fence, evidence that this part of the valley is used by the Sami for herding these animals. The route follows the west shore of the lakes all day, the buildings of the Alesjaure huts gradually coming into view on a distant rise at the southern end of the big lake. The stage between Abiskojaure and Alesjaure is the longest of the hike, 14 miles (22 km). Expect to take seven to nine hours on this stage. The cabins at Abiskojaure are new and exceptionally comfortable, but it's the setting that makes the place memorable. The lake fills the big valley from the huts north to its terminus, where the black triangle of the Giron guards the horizon.

From Alesjaure, the route crosses a substantial suspension bridge over the Alesätno, on the east side of the buildings, and starts up Alisvaggi, another broad, glacier-carved Arctic valley. The trail climbs gradually over several small rises, becoming more barren and alpine as Kungsleden ascends toward the hut at Tjäk-

toward Tjäktja, or south, down into Tjäktjavagge, one of the most impressive Arctic valleys in Lapland. High peaks line both sides of the broad, U-shaped valley, and in its center, a fast stream of deep blue water meanders through. The trail switchbacks about 650 feet (200 m) from the pass down into the head of Tjäktjavagge, and follows the valley floor for 4½ more miles (7 km) to the Sälka hut. The hut is invisible from the north, hidden behind a small ridge coming in from the left. Sälka is 7½ miles (12 km) from Tjäktja, making for a 15½-mile (25 km) day if you do the double stage from Alesjaure.

From Sälka, it's another short stage, 7½ miles (12 km), south down the vast Tjäktjavagge to the next hut at Singi. The route follows similar terrain, with increased ups and downs as the valley broadens. Singi is the point at which the hike leaves Kungsleden proper and turns east into a valley known as Ladtjovaggi for the 8½-mile (14 km) journey to Kebnekaise Mountain Station. Some hikers choose to do a double stage between Sälka and Kebnekaise by taking a shortcut that shaves about 2 miles (3 km) off the route that goes through Singi. Hot showers and a restaurant make the sprawling complex at Kebnekaise a comfortable base camp for day hiking or an attempt on Kebnekaise summit.

From Kebnekaise, a final 12 miles (19 km) of trail lead through the forest to the road end at Nikkaluokta. If you've had enough walking by then, a boat can cover half the distance. Scheduled water taxis take on passengers at a lake called Laddjujaure and run up the river to Nikkaluokta. A restaurant and simple cabins make for a comfortable overnight stop here, near the Sami reindeer corrals, or, if you arrive before the last bus departs at 4:50 P.M., you can be back in Kiruna by dinnertime.

Information

SVENSKA TURISTFÖRENINGEN
Box 25
101 20 Stockholm Sweden
46 (0)8 463 21 00
www.svenskaturistforeningen.se/STF_INT/st.asp

RIGHT: *The impressive Tjäktjavagge is one of the largest Arctic valleys in Lapland.* PHOTO BY PETER POTTERFIELD.

tja, 8 miles (13 km) from Alesjaure. Soon the hut comes into view, dwarfed by 4,635-foot (1,413 m) Muorahiscohkka rising just behind it. This is wild country, the valley open tundra cut by big rivers, with high, rounded, rocky peaks bordering either side under an expansive Arctic sky. The Tjäktja hut lies on the other side of a deep gorge that holds a roaring river, crossed by another elaborate suspension bridge. But since this small hut is only four hours from Alesjaure, some hikers choose to do a double stage and continue on across the pass known as Tjäktjapasset, the highest point on the entire Kungsleden. From the pass the route drops down into the long, open valley of Tjäktjavagge and then on for another 4½ miles (7 km) to the hut at Sälka.

From the hut at Tjäktja, the route ascends via an extremely rough and rocky trail marked by painted rocks to the head of the now barren valley. In 3 miles (5 km), the way steepens for a few hundred yards as it works to top out at 3,736-foot (1,140 m) Tjäktjapasset, where a small "rescue" hut offers safe haven in bad weather. From the pass, one can look back north, into Alisvaggi,

TOUR DE LA VANOISE GLACIERS
Parc National de la Vanoise

French Alps, France

DISTANCE: **31-mile (50 km) loop**
TIME: **4–5 days**
PHYSICAL CHALLENGE: **1 2 3 4 5**
PSYCHOLOGICAL CHALLENGE: **1 2 3 4 5**
STAGING: **Pralognan-la-Vanoise, France**

Parc National de la Vanoise, the oldest of the relatively young French national parks, protects one of the largest, and one of the last, mountain wilderness areas in the country. Here on the relatively untrodden slopes of what's called the Graian Alps the adventurous hiker can find more than 100 peaks at 10,000 feet (3,000 m). The hike recommended here makes a long, high loop through this surprisingly wild and rugged landscape, but does so with a touch of civility: in a classic hut-to-hut alpine tour that connects two of France's venerable hiking routes.

The French have one of the most enviable, well-developed trail systems of any country. A vast network of national trails called *sentiers de grande randonnée* (everybody calls them GRs for short) crisscrosses the entire nation. These

ABOVE: *The original Refuge du Fond d'Aussois.*
PHOTO BY JUDY ARMSTRONG.

RIGHT: Grand Randonnee *route marker with alpine wildflowers.*
PHOTO BY JUDY ARMSTRONG.

OPPOSITE: *A section of trail between the Refuge du Fond d'Aussois and Refuge de l'Arpont is protected by chains.*
PHOTO BY JUDY ARMSTRONG.

routes wind for an impressive 38,000 miles (61,000 km), often connecting with lesser trails, to form a network that makes it possible to walk almost anywhere in the country. This being Europe, we're not talking wilderness here. Most of the trails run from village to town to city through farmland and rural countryside, not backcountry.

But some routes amount to European versions of the Appalachian or Pacific Crest Trails. The GR 5 runs from Holland to the Mediterranean, near Nice, more than 500 miles (800 km). Along the way the storied *Grande Randonnée* traverses the heart of the French Alps, including the mountains of Parc National de la Vanoise. The Tour de la Vanoise Glaciers uses sections of the GR 5 in combination with the GR 55 to make a 31-mile (50 km) loop through this region of high peaks, hanging glaciers, deep gorges, and vast alpine slopes.

This is about as wild as it gets in the Alps. Parc National de la Vanoise adjoins Gran Paradiso national park in Italy, and together the two preserves form the largest protected natural area in Western Europe. Here in Vanoise, a 51-mile-long (82 km) plateau of pristine peaks and glacier, the alpine ibex still lives, almost certainly saved from extinction by its protection here. The mountains of Vanoise are set between the Pennine Alps to the north and the Dauphine Alps to the south. The area, not nearly so well known to foreign visitors as nearby Mont Blanc, is virtually surrounded by some of France's most famous ski areas, including Val d'Isere and Albertville, site of the 1992 Olympic Winter Games.

Just south of Mont Blanc and its busy tourist hub of Chamonix, the trails through the Vanoise mountains let you see some of the Alp's most spectacular scenery while running into a lot fewer people than you would on the more popular mountain trails farther north. Despite its mountainous character, the terrain here is well suited to hiking, with high, open routes threading along the plateau across open meadows and rocky slopes, weaving gracefully between the peaks (some more than 12,000 feet, 7,500 m) and glaciers. Long-established huts, which supply bedding and meals (even picnic lunches in some cases), mean that the hike can be done in superlight fashion. There's no better introduction to the spectacular landscape of the Alps.

LOGISTICS & STRATEGY

The closest city with good air connections to Parc National de la Vanoise is Geneva, Switzerland, but the area is easily accessible by car or train from most places in the alpine region of France, Italy, and Switzerland. The traditional start of this route is Pralognan-la-Vanoise, on the northern slope of the Vanoise massif. The village is reached by taking the A-43 motorway from Geneva to Albertville, and the Route de Tarentaise (N-90) to Moutiers (17 miles, 27 km, from Albertville). From Moutiers take D-915 to Pralognan-la-Vanoise (16 miles, 26 km, from Moutiers). (If you're not driving, take the train to Moutiers, and from there, catch one of five buses that leaves each day for Pralognan-

la-Vanoise.) The route is a closed loop, however, and so can be accessed from the village of Aussois, should you choose to approach it from the south.

Pralognan-la-Vanoise is a comfortable and picturesque resort village, very near the center of one of the highest and most remote sections of the Alps. The drive up from Moutiers is beautiful, taking you from lowland hills into the high mountains, with steep drop-offs on one side, 12,000-foot (7,500 m) peaks on the other. The elevation of the village is just below 5,000 feet (about 1,450 m), and from here more than 150 miles (250 km) of alpine trails can be easily accessed. Most of these trails are connected to the GR 55, which passes just a few kilometers from town.

The laid-back nature of Pralognans and its proximity to accessible Moutiers make it the favorite approach and staging area for this tour of Vanoise glaciers. This is an old village, unlike some of the modern tourist towns of the Alps, one that has long been a traditional center for mountaineering and alpine hiking. The village is tucked away at the head of its valley, with Mont Bocho leaning in from the east, Aiguille de Août high on the ridge to the west. Check out the town's tourist office when you arrive. This efficient clearinghouse can provide you everything from the latest weather forecast to information on lodgings and restaurants to where to buy food, fuel, and other necessities. A national park ranger station in Pralognan offers in the high season (July and August) slide shows of trails and climbs in the vicinity. Pralognan is a tourist town, for sure, but a pleasant and easygoing one. A night or two here can be well spent confirming hut reservations and making preparations for the hike, or even doing one or two of the half-dozen good day hikes from town.

The tour of the Vanoise glaciers, traditionally, goes from Pralognan counterclockwise a hard first day to Refuge du Fond d'Aussois, then to the Refuge de l'Arpont, and to the Refuge de la Vanoise, and back to Pralognan. It is usually done in four days, with each of the three nights spent in the refuges. Meals and bedding are provided at the huts, meaning that this 30-mile (50 km) route through the heart of the Graian Alps can be done in extremely lightweight style. Strong hikers can complete the route in three days by hiking back to Pralognan on the final day rather than spending the third night in a hut, but a final night at the popular Refuge de la Vanoise is the icing on the cake, one you wouldn't want to miss. Only 4 miles (6 km) from Pralognan, this hut is a popular day hike, and so may be full if you haven't made reservations. This part of the route features some of the most rugged scenery of the circuit, so it's worthwhile to spend a couple of days savoring the mountains and

OPPOSITE: The mighty four-tier cascade below the Refuge de la Vanoise. PHOTO BY JUDY ARMSTRONG.

RIGHT: The ibex, or bouquetin, still roams the mountains of Parc National de la Vanoise. PHOTO BY COLONEL MARIO, SCOPE IMAGES.

glaciers around Aiguille de la Vanoise on the return to Pralognan.

Some of the huts in the park are private enterprises, some are run by the alpine club of France, and some by the national park. All are open to the public, but it's a good idea to make advance reservations. You can probably get away with making your hut reservations on arrival, but it's possible that a large party may result in oversold situations. If you wish, reservations can be made before you leave home through the central reservations office in Pralognan.

Like all of the Alps, the mountain valleys and meadows of Parc National de la Vanoise are crisscrossed by trails. These trails allow for innumerable variations to the hike described here, although none is likely to be more scenic. Two of the more popular long routes from Pralognan include hiking the GR 5 all the way to Chamonix, a seven-day, 48-mile (75 km) trip, or hiking into the Gran Paradiso national park of northwestern Italy via a number of routes, some as short as a couple of days.

HAZARDS

While this route penetrates some of the most remote backcountry in the Alps, this is Europe, so the hiker is seldom more than half a day from a hut or a road or a village. With no carnivorous wild animals to contend with, the only substantial threat to the hikers, besides injury or medical emergency, is weather. The Col d'Aussois approaches 10,000 feet (3,050 m), so hikers should be prepared for storms and snow, even in summer, and short stretches of snow-covered trail.

SEASON

Parc National de la Vanoise is high in the French Alps, so there's no cheating on season. After an average winter, these trails won't be sufficiently snow-free for hiking until early July, and you can expect snow in the higher passes as late as August. Snow can fall any time in September, although the first half of the month often sees good, if chilly, weather.

ROUTE

On the first day of the tour, try to catch a ride or take a taxi from Pralognan-la-Vanoise for the drive up the narrow paved road to the GR 55 trailhead. The hike begins at the end of the road, at a bridge known as the Pont de la Pêche, where there is a parking lot. You could walk from Pralognan, but that means an additional 4 miles (6 km) and 1,000 feet (300 m) of elevation. This day is going to be hard enough without adding to your efforts. This first day, in fact, is where you gain most of the elevation on the route; once up over the Col d'Aussois, you remain high on the plateau for much of the tour, with only moderate up-and-down on the following days.

Cross the Pont de la Pêche, at 5,800 feet (1,770 m), and begin the long traverse on the GR 55 next to the river. Follow the wide, well-graded trail southeast toward the Col d'Aussois. After about an hour and a half, you'll come to a trail intersection. Here, the GR 55 continues straight, to the east. Turn left, southward, off the GR 55

and cross the bridge, following signs toward Ritort and Col d'Aussois. You're now on a connecting trail between GR 55 and GR 5. The trail passes stone buildings to the left and works up via switchbacks to a prominent rise at 7,000 feet (2,160 m), a good place for lunch. Here, you'll have views down valley to glaciers and peaks in the distance, just a taste of what you're in for during the days to come. Above the rise, the trail's steepness relents for a bit. Pass an intersection where the trail to Pointe Ariande joins from the left. Bear right, or southeast, as the route becomes more rugged, now marked by cairns. Working up to the Col d'Aussois is strenuous as the tour ascends to the highest point on the entire four-day hike, 9,500 feet (2,900 m), four to five hours from the trailhead. Cross a bridge just before the final steep, muddy climb to the col. In early season, the trail may be snow-bound, so take care. The prominent peak to your right, the unimaginatively named Pointe

OPPOSITE: *The remote valley of l'Arcelin, on the return to Pralognan from the Refuge de la Vanoise.* PHOTO BY JUDY ARMSTRONG.

de l'Observatorie, is well worth the half-hour climb, and is the usual destination for those doing a day hike from Pralognan.

At the col, take care as you start the descent toward the south over awkward rocky outcrops. A number of small paths branching off to the right can lead you astray, so try to stay left, following the main trail, which is marked with painted rocks (some are red and white, but some are yellow). The trail from the pass winds down to the large boulder-strewn flat below, which has several trails leading through it. Once down on the level plain the correct route is easier to find, leading down and right, and finally up and over the hill to the Refuge du Fond d'Aussois at 7,620 feet (2,325 m), nestled in its small valley. This is the traditional first stop of the circuit, about 8½ miles (14 km) from the trailhead. You could continue for another hour or so to the Refuge du Plan Sec, to shorten the second day, but most hikers have had enough by now.

From the Refuge du Fond d'Aussois, take the trail south down the valley as it crosses a stream and passes some stone buildings. Just above the Plan d'Amont, a manmade reservoir, approximately 3 miles (5 km) from the Refuge du Fond d'Aussois, you'll come to the intersection with the GR 5, one of the longest trails in France. It begins in Holland, traverses the Alps, and continues all the way to the Mediterranean. You'll follow the GR 5 most of the way around the southern leg of the circuit. Take the left fork, following signs to Refuge de la Dent Parrachee; but when the turnoff comes for the refuge, don't bear left toward the refuge, but keep going straight to the GR 5.

The route from the intersection stays quite high, between 7,000 and 8,000 feet (2,200–2,400 m) as it undulates through scenic, open high country, with glaciers and waterfalls and high peaks all around. Within 1 mile (2 km) the GR 5 intersects with a trail leading to the left toward the Refuge du Plan Sec. Continue on the main trail, the GR 5, keeping left and following signs for Refuge de l'Arpont. The route follows an exposed section here, protected by a

chain, and then traverses into a small gorge. At several trail intersections in the next mile or so, bear generally northeast, following signs toward Refuge de l'Arpont. Traverse far above the village of Aussois and ascend via a series of switchbacks to an open bowl. This makes a good lunch stop, with some of the best views so far of the surrounding peaks.

Reach the pastures of La Loza, at 7,870 feet (2,400 m), via a switchback trail followed by a long traverse. You'll pass abandoned stone buildings and outstanding views of the rocky peak of La Dent Parrachee. Beyond Montafia, at 7,200 feet (2,200 m), you pass large waterfalls and substantial mountain streams as you head toward the Refuge de l'Arpont, still about an hour away. This is the most scenic section of the day's route. The trail passes a farmhouse offering local cheeses and accommodations before crossing several bridges over fast-flowing streams and climbing up to the stone hut of the Refuge de l'Arpont, set above 7,500 feet (2,309 m), about 12 miles (19 km) from the Refuge du Fond d'Aussois. A short but strenuous hike above the hut up to the lake offers views of the Glacier de l'Arpont.

The tour of the Vanoise glaciers saves the best for last. The third and most scenic day of the route leaves the Refuge de l'Arpont on a trail marked for Refuge Felix Faure (the old name for Refuge de la Vanoise) and continues east on the GR 5. This section holds some of the most spectacular scenery in the Graian Alps, and may be the best hike in the park. About 4 miles (6 km) from the hut you cross two fast-flowing streams and get a view of the Glaciers de la Vanoise, and two of the highest peaks in the area, Le Grand Motte and Le Grande Casse. Where the trail crosses a ridge, take some time to enjoy this vantage at almost 7,500 feet (2,300 m), with three classic alpine valleys spread out below.

About four hours from the Refuge de l'Arpont you reach a trail junction. The GR 5 turns right, toward Termington; continue straight, or north, on what the French call a *sentier balcon*, a steep

side-hill traverse, toward the GR 55. Watch for Chamois, the small native deer, for the next few miles as you hike past glacial lakes and tarns below four peaks above 9,800 feet (2,990 m), draped with glaciers pouring out meltwater streams in high summer. If you're here in early season, watch for wildflower displays in the meadows.

At the intersection with the GR 55, bear left and continue ascending toward a low pass. The trail can be difficult to find on the rocky slope, so look for cairns as you go up and over the pass into a sprawling basin. The trail is mostly level here as it follows the valley down past an old stone house. Stay on the GR 55, following signs toward Pralognan or Refuge Felix Faure, passing an old World War II pillbox. Continue past a small lake tinged by glacial sediment through open, rocky slopes up toward the col and the Refuge de la Vanoise, which, confusingly, is sometimes called the Refuge Felix Faure. The large hut is perched quite high in a meadow at almost 8,500 feet (2,600 m), at the foot of a large glacier hanging off the peak looming above.

I recommend spending a night here, enjoying short hikes from the hut to lakes and meadows, and stunning views of this classic alpine scenery. Only 4 miles (6 km) from Pralognan, this hut is a popular day hike, and may be full if you haven't made reservations in advance. The trailhead is less than three hours beyond, however, so you can continue on the trail for a return to Pralognan-la-Vanoise in time for dinner if you wish. From the hut, the quickest way back is to turn onto the GR 55 toward Les Fontanettes, 1½ miles (2½ km) from Pralognan, where there is a telephone for calling a cab. The more scenic route is to head west from the refuge on a trail that goes to the south of the Aiguille de la Vanoise and finish the hike on this higher side trail as it meanders through meadows, offering better views of the glaciers and peaks of Vanoise.

Information

PARC NATIONAL DE LA VANOISE
135 rue Docteur Julliand
B.P. 705
73007 Chambiry Cedex France
33-4-79-62-30-54
www.vanoise.com
E-mail: parc.national@vanoise.com

Pralognan-la-Vanoise Ranger Station:
33-04-79-08-71-49, 33-04-79-08-79-08

Huts and Accommodations

The Tourist Office in Pralognan-la-Vanoise can help make reservations at all the huts:
33-04-79-08-79-08
www.pralognan.com
Refuge de la Vanoise: 33-04-79-08-25-23
Refuge du Fond d'Aussois: 33-04-79-20-39-83
Refuge de l'Arpont: 33-04-79-20-51-51

Guide Services

Bureau des Guides et Accompagnateurs
Le Grand Couloir
73710 Pralognan-la-Vanoise France
04-79-08-71-21, 04-79-08-77-25 (fax)
E-mail : guidepralo@wanadoo.fr

ABOVE LEFT: *Snow covered in July, the trail near the Refuge de la Vanoise is overlooked by the Glacier de l'Arcelin.* PHOTO BY JUDY ARMSTRONG.

ABOVE RIGHT: *Gaining elevation on the GR 5, between Refuge du Fond d'Aussois and Refuge de l'Arpont.* PHOTO BY JUDY ARMSTRONG.

RIGHT: *Crossing the Lac des Vaches, below the glaciers of La Grande Casse.* PHOTO BY JUDY ARMSTRONG.

WEST HIGHLAND WAY
Scottish Highlands
Scotland, United Kingdom

DISTANCE: 95 miles (153 km) one-way
TIME: 7–9 days
PHYSICAL CHALLENGE: 1 2 3 4 5
PSYCHOLOGICAL CHALLENGE: 1 2 3 4 5
STAGING: Glasgow, Scotland

Certainly the premier long-distance hike in Scotland, the West Highland Way officially opened for traffic in 1980 under the auspices of the country's first national park. Although only 25 years old in its present incarnation, the West Highland Way follows historic routes as it traverses from the lowlands around Glasgow to the wilds of the Scottish Highlands. The classic walk passes through some of Scotland's most spectacular scenery as it follows ancient drove roads Highlanders traditionally used to get their cattle and sheep to market, old military roads built in the 1700s during the Jacobite uprising, former coach roads, and even the abandoned rights-of-way of old railway lines.

Over the course of its 95-mile (153 km) length, the route links Scotland's largest city to Fort William, the principle urban area of the Western Highlands. Don't be fooled by the urban beginnings near Glasgow; the trail is a veritable tour of Scottish superlatives. Hiking the length of the route takes you past the wild shores of Loch Lomond, Scotland's largest, through the wilds of Rannoch Moor, Scotland's biggest, and eventually 4,077-foot (1,243 m) Ben Nevis, Scotland's tallest. You'll see more sheep and cattle than wildlife, but keep an eye pealed for wild goats and red deer, and Golden Eagles wheeling above the moors.

Much of the trail is roughly parallel to either a road or a railway line, or both, but there are wilder stretches of open moor and high hills in the far north. Those memorable sections of Scottish Highland hill walking can be enhanced by taking an extra day in certain sections to climb some of the

The sun rises on Beinn Dorain in cloud as the West Highland Way skirts Beinn Odhar, between Tyndrum and Glen Coe.

PHOTO BY TINA NORRIS.

CLASSIC HIKES *of the* WORLD ❖ EUROPE

higher mountains nearby. But even the route's more civilized sections have tremendous appeal, taking you to classic Highland villages, such as Bridge of Orchy, the 200-year-old inns in the valley of Glen Falloch, even a cave where Scottish outlaw Rob Roy once hid his captives. You get a bit of wilderness travel on this weeklong route, but much more besides.

The West Highland Way is becoming an international attraction as well, drawing each year more than 10,000 visitors from outside Scotland. At almost 100 miles, the route is long enough for most, but if you've got more time the West Highland Way can be combined with the Great Glen Way, opened in 2002, to form a 170-mile (274 km) walking route from Glasgow to Inverness. An even newer long-distance route opened in 2003, the Rob Roy Way, goes from Drymen to Pit Lochy, and proves that the Scots are enthusiastic walkers

Getting accustomed to the local idiom and walking tradition takes a wee while, but that's part of the fun. Some Scottish terms we've all heard before, *glen* for valley, *loch* for lake, *moor* for heather slope, *burn* for creek, *fell* for hill. Others are more esoteric: Much of the Way follows "military roads," but these were built in the 1700s for wagons and horses, and better resemble a wide, stony path. Some terms

are nearly unfathomable. *Munro* means mountain over 3,000 feet (900 m) high, and was coined after the guy who found all of them. As for the pronunciation of villages, towns, and landmarks, there's no rhyme or reason, you just find out when you get there.

LOGISTICS & STRATEGY

Staging for the West Highland Way is usually done from Glasgow, the largest city in Scotland. Since you'll be on the trail for a week at least, it makes sense to live well in Glasgow and to see the sights for a few days, if you've got the time. One can approach the Way and avoid Glasgow altogether: The night train from London arrives at the train station at Milngavie, about 7 miles (11 km) from the city center, at the very beginning of the Way, in time for an early morning start. When vacation time is short, that's an efficient way to start the trail.

Almost everybody hikes the route from south to north, for a variety or reasons. The terrain works better that way, giving you a chance to warm up on easier ground before reaching the challenges of the mountains. This tradition of starting in Glasgow and finishing in Fort William takes you from the Lowlands to the Highlands, a pleasingly dramatic progression, and keeps the wind mostly at your back.

The West Highland Way is long enough that you've got to spend about a week on the trail, give or take a few days. Some people spend six nights, others spend eight. Like hiking in much of Europe, no matter how quickly or slowly you plan to walk, you can do the route in a way that puts you in a comfortable hotel or similar lodging every night. If you prefer, you can choose lower-cost accommodations in hostels, bunkhouses, or camp shelters (stone huts sometimes called "bothies"). Pubs, cafés, and hotels along the route make arranging for meals pretty easy, including even lunch stops on most route stages. In a few cases, you'll need to pack a lunch.

Almost everybody chooses indoor accommodations somewhere in the extensive range of available options, but there are places where it's possible to camp. Regrettably, there's no wild camping permitted along the way—you can't just hike up a side valley and pitch a tent to experience the wildness of the Scottish moors. But there are plenty of places to camp out, whether it's to save money or to enjoy being outdoors. So-called free campsites, on public land, have no facilities at all. Some of these have limits on how long you can stay, but that's not a problem as you're just stopping overnight anyway. There are three of these designated backpacking sites: in Garadhban Forest north of Dry-

men, Ardeas near Rowardennan, and Inversnaid Boathouse, north of the Inversnaid Hotel. Private campsites can be found at most of the traditional overnight locations, and in fact at some rather surprising locations, such as on the lawn of the local pub. Both traditional and surprising frequently come with rest rooms and showers.

However you do decide to travel along the Way, there will be logistical problems—where to stay, how to reserve accommodations, how do you deal with your luggage, and so on. If you decide to hike in the busy seasons, spring and fall, your problems will multiply unless you reserve early. The official Web site for the West Highland Way, published by the national park that administers the route, includes a comprehensive list of accommodations of every sort, including camping places. Despite the plethora of up-to-date information, if you're coming from a foreign country it is difficult to make accurate judgments about a place you know so little about. But this being civilized Britain, that's no problem. You can hire services providers to help arrange all the details—reserving accommodations, arranging transportation, and transferring luggage—so you can relax and enjoy the Way, hiking with only a day pack with your camera, clothes, food, and water. Bring some pound notes on the hike, because some of the smaller country establishments won't take credit cards.

Renting a car on arrival in the UK is tempting, and convenient, but it has its drawbacks: Where, for instance, do you leave the vehicle for the week you're on the Way? A good idea is to leave it not at the start or finish, but some-

ABOVE: *Walkers between Inversnaid and Doune on the eastern shore of Loch Lomond.*

OPPOSITE: *Storied Blackrock Cottage on the plateau known as Black Mount, a section of the Way that traverses one of the wildest and largest moors on the route.*

RIGHT: *Hikers descend the rough section of track between Inversnaid and Inverarnan, near the site of Rob Roy's cave.*
PHOTOS BY TINA NORRIS.

where about midway on the route, parked at an accommodation you've reserved for your arrival there. This will give you a midpoint cache of clean clothes, a place to dump your dirty ones, and may obviate the need for a baggage-transfer service. You can use public transportation to get to the start of the hike and to return to your car from the end.

Probably the most compelling reason to rent a car is a situation in which not everyone in the group is hiking the trail. A rental car makes it possible for some members of the party to tour the Scottish Highlands by vehicle, meeting up each evening with the hiking members at prearranged lodgings. This is a feature unique to the West Highland Way: If your spouse or partner is on a genealogy quest, or is an avid golfer, or history buff, you can both do what you love and still have dinner together every night.

Most of the traditional stages of the Way are between 9 and 15 miles (15–24 km). That sounds like a lot of distance until you spend some time on the route. The going is mostly pretty easy compared to wilderness hiking, as the Way follows old military roads, drovers' tracks, country lanes, and abandoned railway rights-of-way. All of these sections have excellent tracks on easy grades, and you can really put some miles behind you, particularly if you're hiking with only a day pack. There are some rugged sections of trail east of Loch Lomond, and in the national park between Inveroran and Kinlochleven, but those are not typical.

Hiking in Scotland is a thing unto itself, following the old tradition of hill walking. The combination of civilized comforts and wild landscape is appealing. Those who are drawn to the West Highland Way from other countries would do well to observe the rules for hikers in Scotland, both legislated and traditional. All are mere common sense: Close all gates, be careful with fire, don't pollute water supplies, leave livestock alone, and my favorite, be quiet. The latter even extends to the use of cell phones on the trail.

HAZARDS

Scottish weather is undoubtedly the chief danger to West Highland Way hikers. In winter, exposure to rain, cold, and snow far from shelter still results in fatalities from exposure and hypothermia on the highest parts of the Way. Even spring through summer, the weather can rapidly turn dangerous, so bring appropriate clothing and make prudence the better part of valor should conditions turn nasty.

Incidents of giardia contamination have been reported, so campers should purify water from streams. Most hikers who stay in village accommodations start out each morning with a day's worth of water, obviating the problem.

Reports of injuries to hikers from encounters with Highland cattle are not unheard of. These furry beasts, a common sight along the route, look like something out of a fairy tale but have long, sharp horns, so it's best to keep your distance.

SEASON

The national park that administers the Way says the most popular times for hiking the route are April to May and September to early October. The trail can be traveled most of the year, weather permitting, but winters in the mountains of northern Scotland can be dangerous, and winter days are short. April, May, June have long days and weather that's usually drier than midsummer. September and October have the bonus of autumn color. Accommodations are generally available spring and fall if you reserve far enough in advance. But if you go in midsummer, they might not be, as the Scottish Highlands are full of tourists.

ABOVE: *A solitary rowan tree stands guard as the West Highland Way begins its descent to the Inveroran Hotel, with Black Mount in the background.* PHOTO BY TINA NORRIS.

LEFT: *Walkers follow the old military road above the Devil's Staircase, heading for Kinlochleven in typical Scottish weather.* PHOTO BY TINA NORRIS.

ROUTE

Over the decades, standard stages, not unlike those on the Everest trek, have become traditional. They may be helpful when describing the route, but it is not necessary to follow them as prescribed, as there are many other options.

Most people think the West Highland Way starts in Glasgow, but the official start of the route is about 7 miles (11 km) to the northwest, in Milngavie. (Beware that Milngavie is pronounced *mullguy*. Don't ask me why; it's another mystery of Scotland.) Here, at the north end of the train station, the trail begins its 95-mile (153 km) journey northward to Fort William.

Milngavie to Drymen. Follow the signs for Drymen and Strath Blane out of Milngavie and through the suburbs along the Allander Water (a river) and out onto rolling moorland. This first day of the route meanders across open country, through the Mugdock Wood, and up to a low ridge at Carbeth, where you cross a road (B 821) running between Carbeth Inn and Blanefield. Here the trail enters a Lowland valley called the Strathblane, between the Kilpatrick Hills and the Campsie Fells, marked by the odd volcanic plug of Dumgoyne. The first glimpses of the Scottish Highlands come into view, a preview of what's to come. The walking is easy and fast through farmland crossing under the B 834 road, all the way to Drymen, a large village with all the necessary amenities. Beware that Drymen is the last such cosmopolitan place until you reach Crianlarich. This stage is 12 miles (19 km).

Drymen to Rowardennan. Soon after leaving Drymen, the Way joins a forestry track and begins climbing Conic Hill. Watch closely for posts (waymarkers) along the route as the trail leads through Garadhban Forest, then up the hill. From the top, the views extend back toward Milngavie and Glasgow, over to sprawling Loch Lomond, and north to the Highlands. From the hill, the Way descends to Balmaha, where the path picks up the eastern shore of Loch Lomond and proceeds through open oak forests to the lakeside village of Rowardennan, with its many accommodations and forestry office. Some people like to schedule an extra day at Rowardennan for an ascent of Ben Lomond, 3,195 feet (975 m). This peak is the southernmost of the Scottish Munros, a sure sign you're getting into the Highlands. This stage is 14 miles (23 km).

Rowardennan to Inverarnan. From Rowardennan the Way continues along the east bank of Loch Lomond to the head of the lake, sometimes right down on the shore, sometimes up on the flanks of Ben Lomond. Once beyond the hotel at Inversnaid, the Way gets uncharacteristically rugged as it climbs and falls over wooded

SCALE in MILES/ KILOMETERS

0   10   20

0   10   20

heart of the Highlands. The route passes a waterfall, the Falls of Falloch, and follows the east side of the River Falloch through stands of alder and birch up to Derrydaroch, almost halfway. Here the Way crosses to the west side of the river and follows an old military road to Crianlarich, the first significant town since Drymen. Crianlarich represents the Way's halfway point, and most people turn off here to enjoy the village despite the short distance from Inverarnan (7 miles, 11 km). Others drop down into the valley of Strath Fillan and go all the way to Tyndrum, another 6 or 7 miles (9 ½–11 km).

Crianlarich to Tyndrum. If you stopped in Crianlarich, you've got another short day to Tyndrum. The route stays west of the River Fillan as it follows open heather slopes, crosses a creek, and enters the Strath Fillan, a pretty Lowland valley surrounded by craggy hills and moorland. The Way shares the valley with roads and railway tracks, then crosses a major highway (A 82) twice before joining up with the River Cononish and finishing up the day between two railway lines as it drops into the old mining town of Tyndrum, the last good place to restock before Kinlochleven. Ben Lui (3,708 feet, 1,130 m) is a popular day climb out of Tyndrum. This stage is 7 miles (11 km).

Tyndrum to Inveroran. From Tyndrum, it's another relatively short stage to Inveroran. The Way crosses the A 82 again and follows a military road with good views of Beinn Odhar (2,948 feet, 899 m) before ascending to a low pass out of Strath Fillan. When you start down into Auch Gleann the impressive sight of Beinn Dorain, at 3,529 feet (1,076 m), really gets your attention among the other more distant peaks farther north. Once into Auch Gleann, a former royal hunting ground, the Way contours the mountain's flanks into picturesque Bridge of Orchy. There are good views back into the famed Glen Orchy as the easy roadway leads down into the classic Highland village and its namesake bridge, situated on the edge of the vast moorland. There is a hotel and train station here, but many hikers continue on to the hotel at Inveroran, about 3 miles (5 km) distant. From the Bridge of Orchy, the trail at last leaves the highway and strikes out on an old military road through the forests of Mam Carraigh. From the top of the hill, there are good views of the Highlands before the trail descends toward the 200-year-old hotel at Inveroran, a classic base camp for serious Scottish hill walkers, but there aren't a lot of rooms. This stage is 9 miles (14 km).

Inveroran to Kingshouse. This may be the wildest and most enjoyable section of the entire route; if not, the section that follows is. For me, these two stages are the reason to come here. From the hotel at Inveroran, the trail follows the flats around the head of the lake, Loch Tulla, and then ascends through the remnants of Scotland's ancient Caledonia Forest, now part of a forest plantation. The Way climbs up onto a high plateau called Black Mount as it skirts the edge of Rannoch Moor, one of the wildest in Scotland. It is boggy, dotted with ponds, and surrounded by mountains so high there is a ski area. This is a wilderness area, and in bad weather, experience is necessary to navigate this section of the trail safely, as it's high and exposed. The locals tell you to turn back at the River Ba if the weather looks threatening. This relatively remote section has no pubs or services from Inveroran to Kingshouse, and on a gray windy day it can be a bleak place. The trail reaches the day's high point, about 1,500 feet (460 m), and then continues to Blackrock Cottage (a mountaineering hut), where the route descends back down toward the A 82. Across the highway is the Kingshouse Hotel, one of the oldest inns in Scotland, situated in historically rich Glen Coe, 9 miles (15 km) from Inverovan.

slopes just above the lake. This is about the toughest walking on the entire route. A little beyond the waterfall at Inversnaid, watch out for the cave that reputedly was a hiding place for the famous Scottish outlaw, Rob Roy. The route passes Ardleish, where a ferry can take you to the village Ardlui, if that's where you want to spend the night, and reaches the north end of the lake, where a small rise offers a good vantage point to look back down the loch, and north to the Highlands to come. The village of Inverarnan, at the head of Glen Falloch, is home to several historic inns and is the traditional stopping place for this leg of the Way, 14 miles (23 km) from Rowardennan.

Inverarnan to Crianlarich. From Inverarnan the trail follows the valley of Glen Falloch for some welcome easier going between the craggy peaks. This section is a scenic one, with glimpses to 3,000-foot (1,000 m) mountains, as the Way winds up and over the low pass to Crianlarich, where you really feel like you're getting into the

Kingshouse to Kinlochleven. From the old inn, the trail stays east of the A 82, following an old military road before climbing sharply northward up the steep slope of Rannoch Moor to the highest point of the West Highland Way. The final part of the steep climb out of Glen Coe is made via switchbacks up to the top of the Devil's Staircase, at 1,850 feet (564 m). The Devil's Staircase, something of a misnomer, is actually a pretty good trail, some of it built as early as the mid-18th century as a part of the military road system. Stop here if weather permits to take in the view across the wild expanse of Rannoch Moor, and northward to Ben Nevis. From the top, the route gradually descends as it contours around a prominent ridge, then descends steeply down past an old aluminum plant into Kinlochleven and its array of shops, pubs, and accommodations. Cross the river to reach town, 9 miles (15 km) from Kingshouse.

Kinlochleven to Fort William. The last leg of the Way follows an old military road through a small, forested valley. Note there are no places at all on this section to buy food or drink, so you have to start out with everything you'll need for the day. At first the trail rises gently but soon begins to ascend steeply on switchbacks to emerge from the trees into open moorland. The Way climbs easily from here up to the Lairigmor, or Great Pass, a col between the higher peaks on either side. This can be an uncomfortable spot on a rainy day. In good weather, the views are dominated by the peaks of the Ridge of Mamores to the north, all of them over 3,000 feet (900 m). From the Lairigmor, descend gradually until the Way leaves the old military road and drops down onto the wooded slopes of pretty Glen Nevis. Follow Glen Nevis on a forested trail and eventually by public road into Fort William, the main city in the Western Highlands, 14 miles (23 km) from Kinlochleven. The place comes as something of a shock after the wilds of the past few days, but it turns out to be comfortable. Many hikers take a day or two here to climb Ben Nevis, which, weather permitting, makes an appropriate finale to the West Highland Way.

Information

THE NATIONAL PARK
Gateway Centre
Loch Lomond Shores
Ben Lomond Way
Balloch G83 8QL Scotland
01389-722-199
www.westhighlandway.com

Guide Services

CONTOURS WALKING HOLIDAYS
Smithy House, Stainton
Penrith CA11 0ES Scotland
01768-867-539, 01768-892-171 (fax)

MACS ADVENTURE
1435 Dumbarton Road
Glasgow G14 9XR Scotland
0141-434-0795 (phone & fax)

MAKE TRACKS WALKING HOLIDAYS
26 Forbes Road
Edinburgh EH10 4ED Scotland
0131-229-6844, 0131-229-6808 (fax)

TRANSCOTLAND
5 Dunkeld Road
Aberfeldy, Perthshire PH15 2EB Scotland
01887-820848, 01887-820148 (fax)
www.transcotland.com

Accommodation Booking Services

EASYWAYS
Room 32
Haypark Business Centre
Marchmont Avenue
Polmont, Falkirk FK2 0NZ Scotland
1324-714132
E-mail: info@easyways.com

AMS WEST HIGHLAND WAY SERVICES
Audrey Paterson
26 Lansdowne Drive, Carrickstone
Glasgow G68 0JB Scotland
01236-722795

Many North American hikers find the section of trail running over Rannoch Moor between Tyndrum and Glen Coe the most scenic stretch of the Way.
PHOTO BY TINA NORRIS.

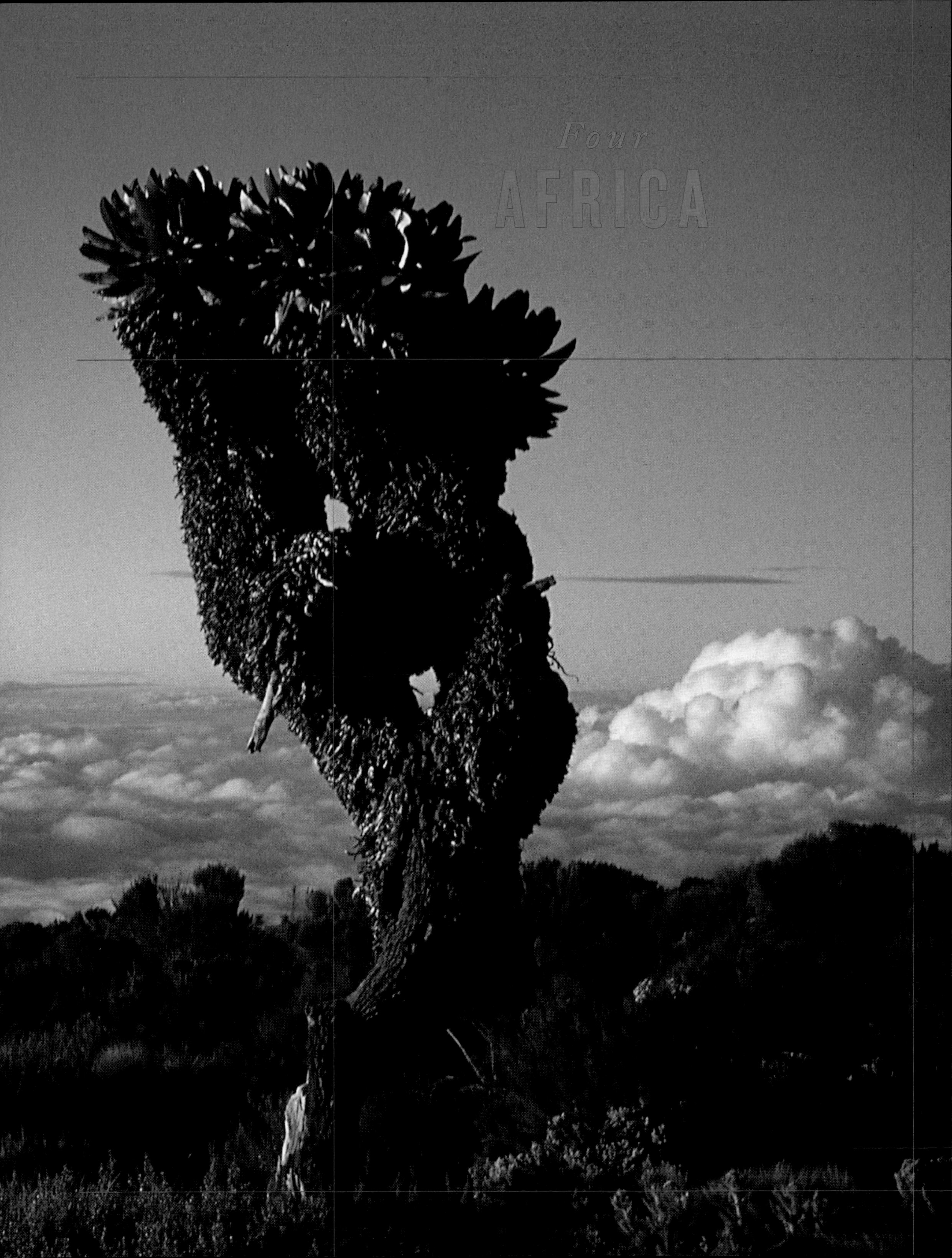

Four

AFRICA

MOUNT KILIMANJARO
Machame-Mweka Route

Tanzania, East Africa

DISTANCE: 42 miles (68 km) round-trip
TIME: 6–8 days
PHYSICAL CHALLENGE: 1 2 3 4 5
PSYCHOLOGICAL CHALLENGE: 1 2 3 4 5
STAGING: Nairobi, Kenya, or Arusha, Tanzania

Crowned by its famous snows, Africa's legendary Mount Kilimanjaro—at 19,340 feet (5,895 m)—is among the highest freestanding mountains anywhere. One of the most impressive sights in all of Africa, the volcano looms high above the plains of Tanzania, reigning over the renowned game preserves that sprawl at its feet. A classic mountain peak rising above a fascinating and diverse region of natural wonders, Kilimanjaro attracts trekkers and climbers and nature enthusiasts with a magnetic power.

It's no wonder. The trek on "Kili" goes not to a base camp, nor around the mountain, but right to its summit, the highest in Africa. Because the weeklong journey to the top of this great peak is nontechnical—it truly is a "walk-up"—Kilimanjaro is that rarest of high mountains: It offers to any fit hiker, not just the skilled climber, both the rewards and the misery that come from an attempt on its glacier-clad summit. More than any other hiking route in the world, the hike up Kilimanjaro has the potential to touch people in

significant ways, even to change lives. Kili is Everest for Everyman, a journey of self-discovery. Part of the allure is that Kililmanjaro is one of the so-called seven summits, the highest peaks on each of the seven continents.

Kilimanjaro exacts a significant price for the thrill of reaching the top. Summit day on this route is one of the hardest, longest days you'll ever spend in the mountains. A prerequisite for a successful experience here is to be in good physical condition and to be psychologically prepared. On Kilimanjaro, altitude is the great equalizer. The summit is the highest point reached by any hike in this book, almost 2,000 feet (610 m) higher even than Everest base camp. Surrounded by the flat, sprawling expanse of the East African plains, the great height is exhilarating, but the potential for serious altitude sickness very real. For the hiker, Kili represents a pinnacle of aspirations. For climbers, it is perhaps the most underestimated of all the seven summits. For anyone, Kilimanjaro is a high-altitude venture that demands much, but gives even more in return.

This massive mountain is composed of three extinct volcanoes. Kibo is the true summit; its top is called Uhuru Peak; Mawenzi is lower at 16,893 feet (5,149 m); and Shira, whose crater was filled in by lava from Kibo's eruption, the lowest at 12,998 feet (3,962 m). The great bulk of Kili shows a staggering 16,000 feet (4,900 m) of relief above the rolling plain. The first documented climb of Kilimanjaro came in 1889, by the German Hans Meyer.

As appealing as Kilimanjaro's lofty, solitary summit is, the natural world that surrounds it challenges with some of the richest wildlife habitat in Africa. The culture, too, is exotic to visitors from North America and Europe. Swahili is the lingua franca of Tanzania and the surrounding countryside, but around the mountain the unique dialects of the Chagga tribes add a colorful local flavor. Almost no one comes to Tanzania to climb Kili without taking some time to see the game parks nearby. In fact, most guided treks end with a safari. Seven days on the mountain followed by four days gawking at the wildlife in Ngorongoro Crater and the Serengeti can combine to make an adventure to Kilimanjaro the most amazing two weeks in your life.

LOGISTICS & STRATEGY

While Kilimanjaro presents a daunting physical challenge, one needs no previous climbing experience nor technical climbing skills to attempt the strenuous trek to the top. The ascent is made by hiking on a trail of variable quality, but minimal cross-country travel or scrambling is required. A small amount of snow is usually encountered near the summit, but not in sufficient quantities to require the use of crampons or an ice ax.

Up through the jungles of the lower Machame route on a typically rainy day. PHOTO BY JAKE NORTON/MOUNTAINWORLD PHOTOGRAPHY.

OPPOSITE: *Hiking through the Karanga Valley, high on Kilimanjaro.* PHOTO BY JAKE NORTON/MOUNTAINWORLD PHOTOGRAPHY.

Good conditioning is the primary requirement for a climb up Kilimanjaro. The demanding, weeklong route to the top mandates that those who make the attempt be capable of traveling for 10-mile (16 km) days that gain 3,000 feet (900 m) while carrying a pack of 20 pounds (9 kg) or more. On the summit day you climb from around 15,100 feet (4,700 m) at the Barafu camp to the 19,340-foot (5,895 m) summit. But it doesn't stop there. You must then descend almost 9,000 feet (2,744 m) to a lower camp at a safer altitude.

There are at least a half dozen hiking routes to Kilimanjaro's summit. Every climber on the mountain is required by Kilimanjaro National Park to have a Tanzanian guide, so there are no truly "independent" hikers. The traditional route, popular decades ago, was the Marangu, or Coca-Cola route. The usual strategy was to arrive at the park, hire a local guide, and ascend in five days. By staying in the Mandara, Harombo, Mawenzi, and Kibo huts, which are very basic and often quite crowded, the hiker could travel fairly light. The major concern was the guide's expertise in terms of altitude and related problems, and the quality of the food. Still, it remains possible for budget-minded hikers to attempt Kili in this way for about a thousand dollars.

These days, many Western climbers sign on long before leaving home with a trek offered by one of the reputable guide services with international connections now operating on Kilimanjaro. This, for most, is a better alternative, for Kilimanjaro is an extreme adventure in the heart of Africa best experienced with an adventure-travel company that can protect your safety, health, and comfort. The logistical problems of hiring porters, arranging transportation, and finding suitable food and lodgings are problematic for most travelers, which is why guided trips have become the standard. A further bonus is that virtually all the guided hikes to Kilimanjaro conclude with a three- or four-day safari.

Most Western guide services now hike up the mountain via the Machame route, a varied and scenic trail through five distinct eco-zones to Kili's frigid summit. The descent is almost always made via the Mweka route, which offers a fast, direct way down to safer altitudes. The best guide services will have a Western guide as well as a local Tanzanian guide and will camp out every night of the trip, staying some distance from the huts. With dining tents, a kitchen staff, and dozens of porters, the hike up Kili with a professional guide service can be more comfortable than you might imagine. Since Chagga porters, who live at the base of Kili and who are eager for the well-paid work, carry most of the gear, you need carry only a day pack with camera gear, personal items, and extra clothes.

The old tradition of climbing the mountain in five days has been rethought. For the past several years, the new standard has become six or even seven days. The latter has become common among the best guides services as it became obvious that two short, low-mileage days before the summit attempt greatly facilitated acclimatization and dramatically improved the success rate for the climb.

That's why leading guide services, instead of trekking from Barranco Valley to the Barafu camp, now make a midpoint camp on the way up. The extra day often gives hikers a critical edge when it comes to facing the trials of summit day.

This attention to altitude is why it makes sense to spend upwards of $5,000 on a guided trek. Experienced guides know how best to facilitate acclimatization, can supervise the use of drugs such as Diamox to minimize the effects of hypoxia, and can recognize when altitude sickness is turning serious—and take appropriate action. The other reason for using a guide service with a proven record is comfort. Before and after the trek, lodgings, transfers, and safaris are taken care of; during the trek, comfortable camps and good food can make an important difference in the quality of the experience.

When choosing a guide service, use common sense. Are your questions answered in a timely fashion, with courtesy? Is the company responsive to your concerns? Ask about the chief guide and his or her experience; inquire as to the quality of the lodgings before and after the trek. Most important, ask questions about safety record, liability insurance, and measures for dealing with altitude problems. Finally, ask about the guide/client ratio and team size, to find a group with whom you'll feel comfortable spending a week living together in close quarters.

Staging is the final consideration. Some operators have their clients come and go via Nairobi, Kenya, others via Kilimanjaro International Airport, near Arusha, Tanzania. Both have advantages. From Europe, many national airlines have flights to Nairobi, offering more options and, frequently, lower fares. At present, only one airline has connections from Europe to Arusha, so using that option can be more expensive, but it can be more convenient, saving a day or even two. The staging city depends on the guide service you choose, so that will be another factor in your decision.

You'll need the usual equipment on Kili, but here are a few tips. Trekking poles can make a huge difference on this hike, particularly on the first day, which can be quite muddy, and on summit day, with its steep descent. The upper reaches of Kilimanjaro will be colder than you think, so make sure you have a down jacket, or something comparable, in addition to appropriate waterproof, breathable shells. More than any hike in this book, the trek on Kili has the potential to expose your gear to downpours. Because most of your gear will be carried by a porter, it makes sense to bring a rugged, truly waterproof duffle to keep your sleeping bag and other gear dry.

HAZARDS

Altitude is the primary concern when hiking on Kilimanjaro, as a trip to the top will take you to the realm of 20,000 feet (6,096 m). Drugs such as Diamox can help, but most important is the presence of a guide who will recognize when mountain sickness has turned from predictable discomfort to a more serious condition. The best cure for high-altitude afflictions, such as pulmonary edema or cerebral edema, is to descend quickly.

SEASON

There are two seasons on Kilimanjaro: the summer season, between June and August, and the winter season, from December to February. Both seasons avoid the rainiest times of year. Some old hands on Kili say they prefer the summer season for slightly better weather, others say they like to go in winter when the game migrations in the Serengeti are in full swing.

SHIRA PLATEAU
Shira Camp
Western Breach
Uhuru Peak
Lava Tower
Stella Point
Machame Camp
Great Barranco Valley
HEIM GLACIERS
KERSTEN
DECKEN
Barranco Hut
Karanga Valley
Barafu Hut
Mweka Camp
Machame Gate
Mweka Village

SCALE in MILES/ KILOMETERS
0   5   10
0   5   10

ROUTE

The first day begins with a jeep ride from your lodging near Arusha through cultivated fields and low forests of ferns to the Machame gate at Kilimanjaro National Park. There at the ranger booth, trip leaders pay entrance fees and climbing fees, a process that takes one to two hours. Chagga porters and your camp staff use this time to sort loads for the trek to come. When the business is done, the walking begins from the ranger booth at 7,000 feet (1,490 m).

The hike up to the Machame camp is a long day on a trail that in places is unexpectedly steep, second only to the summit day in terms of strenuous work. At this elevation, the weather is often wet, and that can make for a muddy trail that exacerbates the physical demands of the hike. Use your trekking poles here; they can be extremely helpful. You'll likely start out in shorts, but keep your rain gear and fleece handy in the event the weather turns wet. The route maintains a steep grade as it ascends through the rain forest (watch for monkeys) a total of 7 miles (11 km) to the Machame camp at 9,800 feet (2,980 m) after six or seven hours on the trail. On arrival, the porters and kitchen staff set up a camp here. After the jet lag from the long journey just a few days earlier and the exertion required getting there, arrival at Machame is a welcome cessation to some hard labor.

The second day of the Kili route is an improvement in every way, taking you out of the trees and into more open country, where at last the views open up in a stimulating way. The trail meanders a little bit as it traverses toward Shira camp, gaining about 2,300 feet (700 m) as it winds through what is called the heath and moorland eco-zone. Open grassy terrain is littered with boulders, and you start seeing odd flora: giant lobelia and *senecios*, exotic giant groundsels. Toward the end of the day, the trail turns west into a river gorge and ascends across the Shira Plateau and down slightly to reach Shira camp at 12,300 feet (3,840 m), 5½ miles (9 km) from Machame camp, after five to six hours on the trail.

At Shira, the camp staff will erect tents some distance from the Shira cave. There's good camping here, an excellent water supply, and views down to Arusha and the surrounding mountains. This is where altitude problems can become manifest, and where the usual symptoms of altitude sickness—nausea, headache—must be watched to ensure they don't progress to more serious maladies. Difficulty breathing, or reasoning, can indicate the development of high-altitude pulmonary edema, or high-altitude cerebral edema, so be watchful.

High mileage and another 2,500 feet (760 m) of elevation gain mark the third day on Kili. The trail leaves Shira camp and turns eastward through an arid landscape, an expansive, open plain ascending imperceptibly. This rolling terrain entails little steep uphill going, but it is the kind of elevation gain that can sneak up on you. You'll be feeling the altitude but enjoying the views of the East African plains now far below. More lobelia and giant groundsel dot the landscape, making dramatic photographic subjects against the upper mountain. The trail eventually winds through boulder fields and passes a feature called the Lava Tower, a huge volcanic plug with a pretty good fourth-class scrambling route up the back side—if you've got the energy. The Lava Tower marks the high point of the day, at 14,700 feet (4,482 m), and a lunch stop, after which the trail begins to lose altitude. The old glacier ice and the huge rock wall of the Western Breach come into view before the route drops down to the Great Barranco Valley at 12,800 feet (3,900 m), approximately 7 miles (11 km) from Shira camp, a six or seven hour's walk.

Critical in terms of acclimatization, the fourth day is one where the difference between a six-day ascent and a seven-day ascent becomes apparent. A six-day climb means today you've got to go

OPPOSITE: *On the summit ridge between Uhuru Peak and Point Stella.* PHOTO BY JAKE NORTON/MOUNTAINWORLD PHOTOGRAPHY.

View of the southern icefield from the summit ridge of Kilimanjaro. PHOTO BY MARC SCHLOSSMAN/PANOS PICTURES.

all the way to the Barafu hut. By adding one day to the ascent you make this fourth day very short, stopping for the night in the Karanga Valley, almost 2,000 feet (610 m) below the Barafu. From the Barranco camp, the trail ascends up and over the imposing, 1,000-foot (300 m) Barranco Wall (a few scrambling moves are required here) at 15,100 feet (4,600 m), up to a large plateau cut by several valleys. Continue over rocky ground and low ridges into the Karanga Valley at 14,300 feet (4,000 m). With this strategy, you climb high to get over the Barranco Wall but sleep lower, the best technique for acclimatization. Another bonus is that you're in camp by 1 or 2 P.M., with some time to rest. From this interim camp, you can look up to the icefalls of the Heim, Kersten, and Decken glaciers, receding but still beautiful. The route passes below the famous Breach Wall, the largest ice and rock face in Africa. Karanga Valley is four to five hours from the Barranco Valley.

The fifth day of this seven-day ascent climbs through nondescript high desert. Winding through the austere landscape, arid and dotted with boulders, the trail offers views up toward the summit and across the desert plains to the pinnacles of Mawenzi Peak. Camp this night is near the Barafu hut, at 15,100 feet (4,700 m), about five hours from Karanga Valley, and about 6 miles (10 km) from the Barranco hut. For those with guided groups who camped the previous night in the Karanga Valley or elsewhere on that plateau, tonight's camp is established about an hour farther and therefore an hour closer to the summit the following day. The area at Barafu and above is not comfortable. You're camping on rocks in an exposed, cold, and often windy place. There's no water, either—guided parties have to bring water from the Karanga Valley.

Summit day on Kili is infamously brutal and long. It begins with an alpine start, as early as midnight or 1 A.M. The route is as benign as can be expected for a peak almost 20,000 feet (6,100 m) high, but it has its difficult sections. The trail begins with a steep rocky climb of about 400 feet (120 m), then works up, with frequent switch-

backs, toward the summit, with a little scrambling. Expect subfreezing temperatures on this early morning ascent in the dark. Frequent breaks to catch your breath and drink water will help on this seven- or eight-hour climb. Side trails up high can be confusing, so take care, you'll still be climbing by headlamp. The route follows a steep slope up to the crater rim, at Stella Point, about 19,000 feet (5,800 m), then traverses northwest around the rim to the main summit, Uhuru Peak, 19,340 feet (5,895 m), about 4 miles (6 km) from high camp. The famous summit sign is here, and the summit register, along with a stiff breeze that makes the temperature seem even colder.

The idea is to reach the summit just about dawn, between 6 and 8 A.M. As the sun rises over Africa, you've got the best seat in the house. Views to the north take in the twin summits of Mount Kenya, Africa's second highest peak at 17,056 feet (5,200 m), much lower than you are. From the top, the rock pinnacles along the crater's rim and the summit glaciers seem very close.

The return to Barafu goes more quickly on the descent. Expect to be on the summit by 8 A.M., and down at high camp by 11 A.M. You'll already be pretty fatigued, and the day is only half over. Use this opportunity to revitalize with some hot food and drink from your kitchen staff before the second phase of summit day, the descent down the Mweka trail to Mweka camp, far below at 10,000 feet (3,000 m).

The descent to Mweka is what makes summit day such a brutal ordeal, what old hands call the longest day of your life, but it's essential now to get down to lower altitude. Exhaustion and hypoxia are going to render you impaired, so take care on the descent, because the track down can be slippery, particularly up high. Trekking poles can make a real difference here. It's more than 7½ miles (12 km) down a gravelly trail as you traverse the upper section of the Mweka route. Since you got up at midnight or before, it's not easy to remain focused on where you're putting your feet, but you don't want to twist an ankle here. Knowing that the hard part is almost over can keep you going, and the farther you go, the better you feel as the atmosphere's oxygen content begins to increase noticeably. Don't be surprised if it's dark by the time you get to Mweka camp, on the edge of the forest. After a meal, maybe a beer from the hut, it's time to get some well-deserved sleep in the luxuriously thicker air.

The final day on Kilimanjaro is a four- to five-hour descent through the forest and out to the park gate near Mweka village, 6½ miles (10 km) from Mweka camp. The lower section recently has been rerouted and regraded; it used to be steep and dangerous, but is much better now. By 1 P.M. most people arrive at the gate, where they get their certificates, and perhaps cold drinks or souvenirs from the merchants. From there it's back into the bus for the drive back to Arusha for a celebratory dinner. Most guide services finish the trip with a few days of safari at nearby Ngorongoro Crater and Serengeti National Parks. To conclude a remarkable few weeks, think about finishing off the trip with a little snorkeling and swimming on the beautiful beaches of nearby Zanzibar. After all, when will you be back in Africa again?

View of Mawenzi from Uhuru Peak, the summit of Kilimanjaro.
PHOTO BY MARC SCHLOSSMAN/PANOS PICTURES.

Information

GUIDE SERVICES
Alpine Ascents International
121 Mercer Street
Seattle, WA 98109 USA
(206) 378-1927
www.alpineascents.com

GEOGRAPHIC EXPEDITIONS
2627 Lombard Street
San Francisco, CA 94123 USA
(415) 922-0448, 1-800-777-8183
www.geoex.com

INTERNATIONAL MOUNTAIN GUIDES
P.O. Box 246
Ashford, WA 98304 USA
(360) 569-2609
www.mountainguides.com

High camp on the Mweka descent route.
PHOTO BY JAKE NORTON/MOUNTAINWORLD PHOTOGRAPHY.

BALTORO GLACIER TO K2 BASE CAMP
Karakoram Range

Baltistan, Pakistan

DISTANCE: 108 miles (174 km) round-trip from Askole
TIME: 12–16 days from Skardu
PHYSICAL CHALLENGE: 1 2 3 4 **5**
PSYCHOLOGICAL CHALLENGE: 1 2 3 4 **5**
STAGING: Islamabad, Pakistan

The angular, monstrous mass of K2 may be a bit lower than Mount Everest, but the spectacular peak presents the more striking sight when it rises suddenly in all its glory from the amphitheater of Concordia. The second-highest peak in the world, but by consensus the more difficult to climb, 28,253-foot (8,611 m) K2 lies in Pakistan's Karakoram Range, almost a thousand miles west of Mount Everest. Described by Italian climber Fosco Mariani as the world's greatest "museum of shape and form," the Karakoram Range is an unbelievably rugged landscape, a place where 60 peaks rise above 23,000 feet (7,000 m). Penetrating more than 43 miles (70 km) into the heart of this mountain realm, the Baltoro Glacier offers a way in to K2 and this amazing range, resulting in the most visually stunning trekking route in the Himalaya.

The 54-mile (87 km) hike to K2 base camp traverses through Islamic villages before pushing up into the austere Braldu Valley. In just two days of hiking, the route reaches the glacial moraines that lead onto the Baltoro's vast river of ice, the only feasible route through these mountains. At first barely recognizable as a glacier, covered as it is in boulders, rocks, and dirt, the Baltoro winds ever upward between the most imposing rock faces and ice walls in the world. Eventually, this one-of-a-kind route rises to 15,500-foot (4,726 m) Concordia, the confluence of two major glaciers at the foot of K2 itself, the place the late Galen Rowell described as the "throne room of the mountain gods." A final day's walk takes you to K2 base camp at 16,500 feet (5,100 m).

From the start of the walking at Askole, each day reveals new peaks along the Baltoro corridor: Paiyu or "Salt" Peak, Cathedral Towers, Great Trango Tower, Mitre Peak, Masherbrum, Mustagh Tower. Fittingly, it seems, the 26,000-foot (8,000 m) giants remain hidden until the end—Broad Peak, Gasherbrum I and II, and finally, on the last day, K2 itself. The struggle to describe the awesome power of the sudden unveiling of K2 has challenged writers from Alistair Crowley to Reinhold Messner.

It takes a week of hiking up the Baltoro Glacier route to reach Concordia, the confluence of the Baltoro and Godwin Austen glaciers. In every direction, dramatic mountains rise to ultimate heights. K2 leaps out from the north in all its massive grandeur. To the northeast, Broad Peak's imposing three summits resemble a giant's roller coaster. Gasherbrum IV looms 10,000 feet (3,000 m) above the glacier to the east. Chogolisa's elegant crest rises in the southeast. Mitre Peak looks like a twisted skewer piercing the southern sky. Concordia's view is a perfect reward for those who make it this far on the challenging Baltoro, and sunset here a great visual feast as the Karakoram giants go gold with alpenglow.

The indigenous Balti people are to the Karakoram what the Sherpa are to the Nepal Himalaya; the Balti porters and guides make the trek possible. Arriving in Baltistan, in northeast Pakistan, 800 years ago from Tibet, the Baltis share a common ancestry, even a common language, with the Sherpas. But the similarities stop there. During the Moghul insurgence of the 1500s, Islam replaced Buddhism in northern Pakistan. Visitors to Baltistan quickly see that it is different from Nepal. There are no teahouses, no alcohol,

PRECEDING PAGE: *Breakfast in Dingboche, Nepal.*
PHOTO BY PETER POTTERFIELD.

OPPOSITE: *Gasherbrum IV and Hidden Peak above the Baltoro Glacier in Pakistan's Karakoram Range.*
PHOTO BY GALEN ROWELL/MOUNTAIN LIGHT.

Porters, trekkers, and the incredible scenery of the Baltoro Glacier trek. PHOTO BY ED VIESTURS.

not even a permanent settlement beyond day two of the trek. But the warmth and camaraderie that develop between the Baltis and the trekkers is real, part of a long tradition of travel along the Baltoro. Among the first Europeans to come to the Karakoram was the Duke of Abruzzi, who in 1910 made a credible attempt on K2 that got within several thousand feet of the summit. Many of the camps along the Baltoro used by modern trekking parties today, right down to the tent platforms, were first established by the Duke of Abruzzi in the early part of the 20th century.

What has changed in the past ten years is a new wrinkle to the return leg of this famous journey. Prior to the mid-

'90s, once K2 base camp was reached, everybody just turned around and retraced their steps. But since then, most trip operators now offer an option to return via the 18,000 foot (5,500 m) Gondogoro La, a route pioneered by a Balti named Ali Janjungpa that makes a huge loop out of the trek. For this return route, trekkers head south from Concordia, climb up and over the perennial snows of this high pass—one of the great vantage points accessible to nonclimbers in all the Himalaya—and descend into the Hushe Valley. The strenuous option completes an unsurpassed circuit through one of Asia's great mountain landscapes.

must now weigh the situation before making the decision to embark on the journey to K2.

The trek to K2 base camp requires from 12 to 15 days on the trail, plus six or seven overnights in Islamabad, Skardu, and Askole as you come and go. About the same amount of time is required even when returning via Gondogoro La, because the return to Skardu over the pass goes a little quicker. In total, the trek requires about three weeks in Pakistan.

Any trek in the Baltoro region begins with an international flight to Islamabad, Pakistan's capital city. The airport, modernized, secure, familiar-seeming to international travelers, is a far cry from the bustling madhouse it was just a decade ago. And while the city, a relatively new, planned urban area laid out on a perfect grid and designed to feature Islamic architecture, is a safe and easy place to visit, it is not a culturally interesting one. Many adventurous trekkers take the time to venture a few miles to the Sudder and Raja bazaars in nearby Rawalpindi for the sights and sounds and genuine ethnic flavor of Pakistan, punctuated by the evening "Hazzan," the haunting Islamic call to prayer.

Just about every trekker (and climber) who comes to the Baltoro arrives as part of a previously arranged party with a Pakistani or Western trek operator. While it is possible to arrive in Pakistan on your own, getting a trekking permit and hiring local guides can be difficult if you don't already have good connections in the country. The Baltoro trek is best experienced with a top-quality guide service, on which your safety and comfort will depend, so choose with care. Thorough research will show the trek will cost $1,500 to $4,000 from Islamabad. Since your outfitter will have arranged in advance for your trekking permits, lodgings, and transportation to and from the airport, you'll need to spend just one night in the capital. In the morning, it's back to the airport for, if you're lucky, one of the most outrageous sightseeing flights you'll ever take.

The first stage of the Baltoro journey is a flight to the high mountain region of Baltistan in northeast Pakistan. Predictably, weather in this area is problematic for flying. With good conditions, the 50-minute flight comes with killer views of both Nanga Parbat and K2, and leaves a day free in Skardu for sightseeing and to recover from the shock of the scenery. The PIA pilots fly at 28,000 feet (8,500 m) and barely 1 mile (1½ km) west of the solitary bulk of Nanga Parbat. This, the Naked Mountain, standing alone above the plain, is so close to the windows it seems you could see if someone were on the summit. (Be sure to request a right-side window seat for the flight.) Coming into the Skardu bowl, the pilots have to make a dramatic descending turn into the airport. It's a memorable flight, punctuated by an alarming landing.

The excitement of arrival by airplane is definitely preferable to the alternative. Bad weather means that instead of a flight with views to savor you're in for a 24-hour epic in a dilapidated but colorful Bedford bus as it grinds 290 miles

LOGISTICS & STRATEGY

Geopolitical realities of the current millennium have left their mark on adventure tourism in Pakistan, as they have in other countries in proximity to areas of unrest. The years 1999 through 2001 saw record numbers of trekkers head off to the Karakoram region, underscoring that in the previous ten years northern Pakistan ranked among the safest destinations for foreign visitors in the Himalaya. By 2003, however, there was a steep decline in the number of trekking and climbing permits issued for the Baltoro. The number of climbers returning to the Karakoram recovered to about 60 percent of the previous record highs, according the independent Central Asia Institute, but the trekking business still lags a bit even if it is now on the upswing. Each trekker

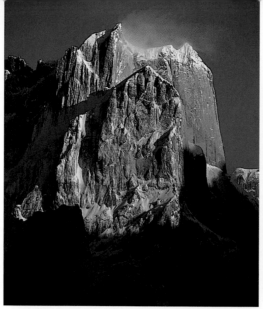

LEFT: *K2 from the Godwin Austen Glacier, Karakoram Himalaya, Pakistan.* CENTER: *Great Trango Tower, Karakoram.* RIGHT: *Sunset on Gasherbrum IV, elevation 26,180 feet (7,980 m).* PHOTOS BY GALEN ROWELL/MOUNTAIN LIGHT.

(470 km) over the tortuous Karakoram Highway along the Indus River. With Urdu love songs on a boom box as background music and the smell of thick diesel fumes drifting in the windows, this exhausting road trip, which includes one night in Chilas, will rob you of the rest day in Skardu.

The next stage of the journey, getting to the village of Askole, is a sometimes terrifying all-day jeep ride. At times the rough road shows only inches of clearance between the tires of your four-wheel-drive vehicle and the drop-off down to the roaring river. The trip has been made in six hours, but twice that is not uncommon. Once within the Braldu Valley, you're in the land of the Balti people, at the threshold of the Karakoram. Villages in the Shigar have changed little in five hundred years: farms with fields of barely, wheat, and vegetables surrounded by stone walls; stands of poplar, willows, and apricot trees. The landscape becomes more barren once within the sheer valley of the Braldu itself, and you arrive in Askole.

It is here in Askole where you finally hit the trail. The route from Askole follows the Braldu Valley for two more days, crossing wild torrents in a primitive cable car. At Paiyu, where the route finally joins the Baltoro Glacier, most parties take a rest day. This is where the Balti porters slaughter the goats and cows that will be their meat supply (the meat ration is mandated by Pakistani law), and cook their unleavened bread, *qurba*, as little firewood is to be found beyond.

Paiyu marks a kind of dividing line. Up to this point, the walking is relatively easy, and altitude not yet a serious problem. Instead, it is the heat that saps energy on the six-hour stages under the Karakoram sun. By Urdukas, you get high enough that things start to cool down, but there at 14,000 feet (4,200 m), the altitude begins to take its toll. The hiking itself becomes more arduous, adding to the stress of each day's elevation gain. The route from Urdukas to Goro II can be trying. From Goro II, it's only one more day (with little elevation gain) to Concordia, and the day trip up to K2.

From Concordia, everybody used to simply retrace the route back to Skardu for the flight to Islamabad. With the recent opening of Gondogoro La, a return trip can now be made by crossing the pass and returning via the Hushe Valley, ending eventually with another jeep drive back at Skardu. Approximately one-third of Baltoro trekkers choose this return route. Depending on conditions, the trek over the pass can create challenges for porters and clients, and may necessitate waiting several days for sufficiently stable weather to cross. Going back via the pass takes no more days than returning down the Baltoro.

The 54-mile (87 km) Baltoro Glacier trek (Askole to K2) into the central Karakoram is not for everyone. The difficulties of hiking on a rubble-strewn glacier, when combined with effects of high altitude, can render some sections of the upper trek nothing short of grueling. Every imaginable kind of weather is probable, from scorching heat and stinging sandstorms down low to snow and blizzards at the upper end. This unforgettable journey requires good physical fitness and an adventuresome attitude.

Because of the disputed boundary between India and Pakistan, you'll see signs of the Pakistani military presence all along the trek. The route, in fact, follows a military telephone line all the way up the Baltoro. Most all the camps used by trekking parties have a small army post nearby, staffed by two or three soldiers and commanded by a *halwadhar*. If you wish to speak with the soldiers, it is polite to ask first for the *halwadhar*, or commander.

HAZARDS

Altitude is the most serious danger to hikers bound for K2. Most trekkers on the Baltoro will experience the symptoms of mild altitude sickness; trekkers returning via Gondogoro

La can encounter the same altitude problems as those who venture to Everest base camp.

Strenuous travel in hot weather can take a physical toll during the lower part of the hike, but the stages are sufficiently short that most people don't suffer unduly. On the upper Baltoro, the going is rough enough that broken bones have occurred: watch where you step, especially when altitude and fatigue combine to take you off guard.

SEASON

The route is done in July and August.

ROUTE

After the short, scenic flight (or long, grinding bus ride) from Islamabad, you arrive in Skardu, the capital of Baltistan. This small city sits at the edge of a floodplain near the confluence of the Indus and Shigar Rivers. A trip out to Kachura Lake on the edge of the valley is a good way to spend a free day. Everyone spends the night in Skardu, many at the famous K2 Motel.

The next stage, from Skardu to Askole, is an eight-hour test of nerves on a careening and precarious jeep trail. Passengers are squeezed into the vehicle of choice for the Karakoram, the ubiquitous 4WD Toyota. The rough road leads along the Shigar and Braldu Valleys to the end of the road at Askole. Once in the Braldu Valley, the road crosses the river several times over suspension bridges. Depending on when you go, it's likely the road may have washed out in a place or two, requiring you and your fellow trekkers to transfer gear on foot across the wash out to a vehicle on the other side. Eight hours is an average time, but this tough ride can take up to twelve. Arrival near Askole in midafternoon is typical, and here the first camp is made at approximately 9,800 feet (3,000 m). Some people camp in the big field about 300 feet (90 m) below the village, some near the village school.

The walking begins at Askole, where the trail leads out through irrigated fields between the mountains as the valley opens out to where the Biafo Glacier enters from the north. The glacier actually advanced a mile or so in 1996, so now the route crosses the 1½-mile-wide (2 km) Biafo, weaving through glacial erratics and crevasses toward Jhola. Beyond the Biafo, the trail crosses the Dumardo River bridge, if the water is not too high to prevent its use, as it is almost all summer. If the bridge is out, or not above the water, the only way across is the cable car, essentially a wooden box on a wire cable. This can add a couple of hours to the journey, as the rig can handle only about 20 people per hour. The camp is near Jhola, just across the river, at about 10,500 feet (3,200 m).

From Jhola camp the route follows a stretch of sandy river beach, rising and falling according to the level of erosion and water levels of Braldu River. The trail continues towards Paiyu, climbing to a vantage point where, weather permitting, you get your first look of the Baltoro Glacier itself, a glimpse over to the Masherbrum group (or at least its magnificent snow plume), and, much farther away, the Cathedral Towers. This can be a tough day. The weather is often hot and dry under the Karakoram sun. As the route nears Paiyu, small glacial streams flow down from the north, creating difficult crossings in high summer. Most outfitters build in a rest day at Paiyu, near 11,800 feet (3,600 m), for acclimatization and rejuvenation.

From Paiyu, the trail approaches the actual snout of the Baltoro Glacier. As you work up the moraines, a 200-foot-wide abyss of blue ice belches water, rocks, and debris as it drains most of the Karakoram Range. The route climbs up onto the glacier, which leads 38 miles (62 km) up the valley. Walking on the glacier can be problematic, littered as it is with rock and stones and small but cold meltwater streams that must be forded. The route ascends on a long, steady, diagonal climb past Liliwa, eventually reaching the southern edge of the Baltoro at Khobotse, at approximately 13,000 feet (4,000 m), in five to six hours.

From Khobotse, a short stage follows the crest of a lateral moraine that affords the first views of Paiyu Peak, Uli Biaho, Trango Towers, the Cathedral group, and other landmarks of this classic mountain landscape. The hike enters the threshold of the storied Karakoram Range, and the scenery is fantastic. Look for ibex on the grassy slopes nearby above the glacier. You may share the trail itself with mule trains carrying supplies up to the army camps above Concordia. Helicopters overhead provide a reminder of your proximity to the disputed territory of Kashmir to the east and south.

The stage ends after just three hours at Urdukas, at approximately 13,800 feet (4,200 m), a spectacularly scenic campsite,

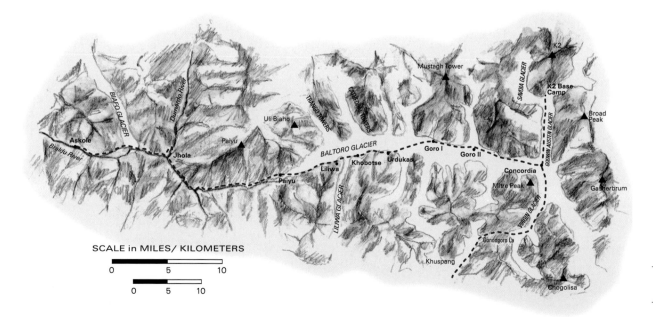

SCALE in MILES/ KILOMETERS

0   5   10

0   5   10

grassy and comfortable, but over-used and polluted. A massive 150-foot-high (45 m) boulder split in two marks Urdukas, which means split rock. Look to the northeast for killer views of Uli Biaho and west for sunset on the southwest face (the Alex Lowe route) of Trango Tower. Up valley, the views are to Broad Peak and Gasherbrum IV.

People come here for the views of Karakoram's 26,000-foot (8,000 m) peaks, and the stage between Urdukas and Concordia is the climax of the hike. But it also is the most arduous walking of the entire trip. While there is nothing technical, and the route here is well worn by trekkers, mule trains, and soldiers, the altitude and the grade begin to take a toll. Some trekkers remain in, or retreat to, Urdukas. The morning you leave, porters gather for a big Allah Akbhar chant, pumping their fists, getting psyched up for the next few days on the main section of the Baltoro.

The stage leaves Urdukas, climbs up on the side of the glacier, and crosses a crevassed section on the glacier's flank as it cuts over to the medial moraine on its south side. The route follows the south side of the glacier to the army outpost and helicopter pad at Goro I, opposite the Yermanendo Glacier. The second half of the walk today features stunning views of Mustagh Tower as the route follows the military telephone wire up the glacier to Goro II at 15,500 feet (4,700 m). Some people will finish the route in the average time of five hours from Urdukas, but others will straggle in after dark, the 1,600-foot (500 m) elevation gain taking a toll. The camp is situated on rough stones and ice near the middle of the glacier, where meltwater is available.

Concordia, the intersection of the Baltoro and Godwin Austen Glaciers, is generally reached on the sixth day. The hike from Goro II entails little elevation gain, a big relief after the strenuous walking of the past two days. Everybody will be craning his or her neck for a glimpse of K2, which remains stubbornly hidden behind Marble Peak, but suddenly revealing itself within just a few minutes. The route follows the north side of the medial moraine up to the apex, the high point of ice, where the Baltoro, Godwin Austen, and Virgin Glaciers come together in such a dramatic way that Martin Conway named the spot after La Place de Concorde in Paris. Concordia, still about 15,500 feet (4,700 m), is roughly six hours from Goro II. Once here, the mythic power of Concordia becomes apparent. To the north, up the Godwin Austen, the scene is dominated by the angular, masculine form of K2, truly the archetypal mountain. In myth, K2 is known as Chogori, the "husband," in contrast with the more feminine shape of nearby Chogolisa, the "wife." But the pair is somewhat overshadowed by Gasherbrum IV, so close as to be overpowering, reflecting the sunset off its western flank.

Some outfitters spend a night at K2 base camp. Others make it a day trip from Concordia. The views of K2 are actually better from Concordia, the Abruzzi Ridge route clearly visible. Most people who reach Concordia continue up to K2 base camp for views up the Savoia Glacier to Windy Camp and Advance base camp on the Abruzzi Ridge route. North American trekkers often make the trip to visit the Gilky Memorial, a tribute to the climbers killed during the American attempt in 1953. Base camp is at 16,500 feet (5,100 m).

From Concordia, everybody used to simply retrace the route back to Skardu for the flight to Islamabad. With the recent opening of Gondogoro La, a high mountain pass at 18,000 feet (5,500 m), a return trip can now be made by crossing the pass and returning via the Hushe Valley, ending eventually back at Skardu. Note that this is a strenuous route, but one offered by many guide services, and

something that perhaps about a third of the Baltoro trekkers undertake. Depending on conditions, the route over the pass can create challenges for porters, and may necessitate waiting several days for weather stable enough to cross.

The return via the Gondogoro La crosses the Vigne Glacier, with superb views of Chogolisa and Miter Peak, to camp below the pass at approximately 15,700 feet (4,800 m) at Ali Camp (named for the feisty, 5-foot-tall (1½ m) Balti porter who pioneered the route in 1986). When weather permits, trekkers make an alpine start, near midnight, descend a short 50° slope, and attempt to cross the glacier and climb to the top of the pass before the sun gets high in the sky. The descent down the other side into the Hushe Valley can be as difficult as the ascent, with tough going over the rocky, unstable slopes. Camp the first night in the Hushe Valley, at a place called Khuspang, also serves as base camp for Gondogoro Peak, a trekker's peak. To the west is the 4,000-foot (1,200 m) face of Laila Peak, perhaps the most striking, jagged summit in any range. A five-hour walk down a moraine descends to a lovely campsite at Dalzampa (literally "field of flowers"), at 14,000 feet (4,300 m). In late summer wildflowers fill the nearby meadows. Some trekking parties continue farther to Siapscho.

The following day the route descends moraines past wild roses and tamarisk into the Charksa Valley. The trek concludes on an easy trail through cultivated fields to a camp outside the village of Hushe, a very cool place full of particularly amiable Baltis. From here jeeps are taken back to Skardu and the flight (or vehicle) back to Islamabad. Big landslides at Khanday in 2001 have made it necessary for trekkers to walk across the rubble; Toyotas wait on the other side. Expect the return to Skardu to take eight hours or so.

Information

Guide Services

Mountain Travel Sobek
1266 66th Street
Emeryville, CA 94508 USA
(510) 594-6000, 1-888-687-6235
www.mtsobek.com

ADVENTURE TOURS
P.O. Box 1780
Islamabad, Pakistan
0092-51-2260820, 0092-51-2264251 (fax)
www.atp.com.pk

NAZIR SABIR TOURS
P.O. Box 1442
Islamabad, Pakistan
0092-51-2252553, 0092-51-2250293 (fax)
www.nazirsabir.com

JASMINE TOURS
G.P.O. Box 859
Rawalpindi, Pakistan

OPPOSITE: *Trekking in the Karakoram Range, Pakistan.*
PHOTO BY GALEN ROWELL/MOUNTAIN LIGHT.

EVEREST BASE CAMP TREK
Lukla to Mount Everest
Nepal Himalaya

DISTANCE: 74 miles (119 km) round-trip
TIME: 16–20 days
PHYSICAL CHALLENGE: 1 2 3 4 **5**
PSYCHOLOGICAL CHALLENGE: 1 2 3 4 **5**
STAGING: Kathmandu, Nepal

An adventure in the human arena as much as in the natural one, the 35-mile (56½ km) walk to Mount Everest may be the premier mountain journey of our time. Days of often-strenuous hiking into the very heart of the Himalaya alternate with acclimatization days of enforced quiet and reflection. The combination of opposites makes for an appropriate pilgrimage to the highest peak on the planet. Everest is a worthy destination, but the day-by-day magic worked by the Khumbu region of Nepal and its Sherpa people is what makes the way so memorable.

This hike is no wilderness experience, but a deep immersion in an outrageous landscape and its exotic culture, spiced with a polyglot international scene of climbers and trekkers unlike any other. The fact that the excursion comes with surprising creature comforts and human warmth—the Sherpa are capable hosts, and take some of the effort out of the hard traveling—completes the irresistible package. You see not only unrivaled topography but also a different way of life.

Despite its big payoff, the long, slow trek to the actual ice-and-rock flanks of Everest can take a toll psychologi-

cally as well as physically. Hiking through the Khumbu, a region named for the glacier that tumbles down the southern flank of the mountain, isn't so much about distance covered as altitude gained. The higher one goes the greater the potential for unexpectedly debilitating effects from lack of oxygen, cold, accumulated trail miles, and even cultural disorientation. An off day here and there should be expected, as should the occasional distraught trekker suffering from elevation gain or intestinal problems. But high altitude is part of the game here in the upper Khumbu, and it has an interesting side effect: Acclimating to the altitude adds days to the trek, mandatory down time that allows for introspection and an enhanced receptivity to the surrounding strangeness. It's an element that makes this excursion so much more than a hike.

And while many people come this way (who can resist a chance to see the highest mountain?) everybody's trek turns out to be subtly different. The surreal vistas, the windswept monasteries, the strange travelers encountered, even the ravages of altitude, apply in markedly personal ways, rendering each trekker's Everest experience unique. That explains why, having done it once, so many come all the way back for another dose.

Human beings have been plying this very route on foot for centuries, so there's nothing artificial about it. What has

Yaks and dzopkyos (yak-cow crossbreeds) outside the dining tent at camp, a few days' travel below Mount Everest. PHOTO BY PETER POTTERFIELD.

OPPOSITE: *Houses cling to the steep bowl at Namche Bazaar, while surrounding peaks emerge from the clouds.* PHOTO BY BETH WALD.

Trekkers and porters on the high route from Dingboche to Lobuche, the peak of Kangtega behind. PHOTO BY PETER POTTERFIELD.

first took note of the region's grinding poverty, lack of education, and nonexistent medical care. The trekking industry has brought relative affluence to some in the Khumbu, a situation that works to the benefit of all: The Sherpa are better off economically, the traveler better off for having been there.

The memories one brings home from the Khumbu are indelible, and diverse. Mine include that place on the trail below Lobuche where you can see three of the highest mountains on earth in a glance, and the ornate interior of the Thyangboche monastery as the rinpoche offered prayers for enlightenment, for my enlightenment. I remember the infectious smile of a laughing Sherpani as she delivered "bed tea," one of the great luxuries in the world. And always there was Everest, coyly hiding behind Nuptse, only to emerge unexpectedly in a staggering display to remind me why I came.

LOGISTICS & STRATEGY

The Everest experience begins in Kathmandu and calls for approximately three weeks in Nepal to get to the mountain and back again. Scheduling extra days in Kathmandu on the return from the mountains accommodates unavoidable delays along the way—most likely the flight out of Lukla—and helps ensure being on time for the international flight home.

Most hikers going to Everest sign up for an organized trek through an international outfitter months before arriving in Nepal. Established guiding companies take care of the details, from Kathmandu hotels and domestic flights to trekking permits and park fees. On the trek itself, the operators provide guides, meals, lodgings, camps, and, frequently, Western guides. Clients with organized treks will both camp in tents and stay in lodges, depending on weather and location, while the outfitter's kitchen staff provides all meals. Lodges along the route grow ever more comfortable every year, and there are no better practitioners of tent camping than the Sherpas. The trekking industry in Nepal has matured to the point that once on the trail, you can expect to eat well and live comfortably. All that remains is to enjoy the experience.

Independent trekkers may choose to acquire on arrival in Kathmandu the services of a Sherpa guide, a less-expensive alternative to an organized trek. The Sherpa guides show the way, offer expertise with acclimatization, and help carry at least a portion of the trekkers' gear (or arrange for porters where necessary). The guides can prepare meals and find camping locations, or arrange for meals and lodgings in local teahouses. Budget-conscious travelers may prefer to go through the Khumbu on their own, carrying their gear, staying and eating in lodges all the way from Lukla to Gorak

changed in the four decades since Briton Jimmy Roberts, a former Ghurka army officer, invented trekking in Nepal, is that the stream of Westerners has evolved from trickle to steady flow. The challenge now is to preserve the landscape in the face of larger numbers of pilgrims. Sagarmatha National Park, formed in 1976 and named a World Heritage Site in 1979, has proved an important step. Woodcutting is no longer allowed in the park, mitigating a devastating trend toward deforestation, and stringent enforcement of trash removal has led to a continual improvement in the areas around the mountain. The lot of the Sherpa has improved significantly since the early 1950s, when Western climbers

OPPOSITE: *Weathered stupas draped in prayer flags occupy the ridge tops between Dingboche and Pheriche in the upper Khumbu.* PHOTO BY PETER POTTERFIELD.

Shep. All these modes of travel in the Khumbu support Nepal's indigenous trekking industry and are culturally appropriate. The choice comes down to a matter of personal preference.

The traditional route to Mount Everest begins in Lukla, where Sir Edmund Hillary built the first airstrip in the Khumbu region. From there it proceeds through the famous villages of Namche Bazaar and Thyangboche, then higher through Pheriche and Lobuche, and eventually to Gorak Shep and Everest base camp. This is how Hillary and the British came in 1953, and Jim Whittaker and the Americans in 1963, and most climbers and trekkers since.

The 35-mile (56½ km) journey to the mountain gains more than 10,000 feet (3,000 m). Because a very slow pace is required to properly acclimate to increasing altitude, the journey takes about ten days. One must spend two nights at most overnight locations, utilizing those days for rest or short side trips, to allow bodies and blood to adjust to the lack of oxygen. Move faster than that and potentially lethal altitude sickness can bring a bad end to your trek.

How far to go? Namche Bazaar and Thyangboche are the cultural highlights of the trip, and some tourists happily turn around after a visit to the monastery at 12,000-foot (3,600 m) Thyangboche. Most serious hikers will go farther, but increasing cold and high-altitude malaise can sap motivation at the upper end of this journey to Everest. A common tactic for independent hikers is to make a final overnight stop at Lobuche, and finish the trek with a day hike to Gorak Shep and its famous viewpoint hill, Kala Pattar. The view of Everest from this rocky hill at 18,200 feet (5,500 m) is generally regarded as a reason to come here. By contrast, Everest cannot be seen at all from base camp, save for the Khumbu Icefall, but its historic allure draws mountain lovers anyway. Most organized treks do it like this:

camp near the rough lodges at Gorak Shep for two nights, climb to Kala Pattar (perhaps multiple times, for a sunset and a sunrise), and day hike the final 3 miles (5 km) for a look at base camp and the Khumbu Icefall.

The trip down takes only three days. With altitude no longer a consideration, and with increasing vigor in the ever-thickening atmosphere, trekkers just bomb downhill with as few as two overnight stops before arriving at Lukla. With luck and a well-timed arrival, you can be back in Kathmandu in time for dinner. But beware that if the weather socks in around the hilltop strip, as it often does, neither airplane nor helicopter can get in. You can be stuck for days waiting for a flight out; you can be stuck so long you miss the international flight home. Lukla can be an uptight place; a few days cloud-bound here can erase the tranquility hard won over the past two weeks.

Returning to Lukla by the same route you went up is no drawback to this trip. Trekkers by then are better acclimated and more psychologically at home in the strange milieu. Strangers on the way up are friends on the way down, so the return journey can be relaxed and conducive to sharper insights and increased appreciation for the landscape.

If you just *have* to come down by a different route, it will cost you in time and effort. The single major alternative is to cross from the Khumbu drainage into the Dudh Kosi drainage via a 17,782-foot (5,419 m) pass known as the Cho La, and return via Gokyo. This seldom-done variation is physically demanding and calls for advance planning, but it is feasible. This option leaves the main trail at Lobuche on the descent, crosses over the Cho La in two days (weather permitting at the pass) to reach Gokyo, and from there back to Namche Bazaar. A highlight of this variation is the side trip to Gokyo-Ri, a vantage point that rivals that of Kala Pattar.

HAZARDS

Altitude is undoubtedly the most serious danger to hikers bound for Everest. Most visitors to the Khumbu will experience some symptoms of mild altitude sickness, but don't go without familiarizing yourself with more serious high-altitude edemas, cerebral and pulmonary, which can be fatal. Take care with food and drink purchased along the way; a gastrointestinal illness can make for an uncomfortable trek. Yaks, surprisingly, represent a danger as well. A trekker on the wrong side of the trail can be nudged into the abyss by a loaded pack animal. It happens every year: Pass yaks on the upslope side of the trail.

SEASON

Trekking season comes to Everest twice a year: pre-monsoon, in April, May, and June, and post-monsoon, September, October, and November. Too much snow in the winter and too much rain in the summer limit trekking in those seasons.

ROUTE

From the chaos of Kathmandu's domestic air terminal, Twin Otter aircraft in various livery (Royal Nepal, Nepal Air) take trekkers to the short, steeply sloping airstrip at Lukla. Large treks, or those attached to mountaineering expeditions, sometimes charter one of the Russian MI-8 helicopters, well suited to Third World travel, to fly members and equipment up in a single load. Weather in these hills is changeable, and flights can be cancelled or even aborted en route; generally, morning flights have a better chance for success. Touchdown on the tiny hilltop strip will be a landing you'll never forget.

From the 9,400-foot-high (2,900 m) airstrip, the route follows the busy trail—everything for the Khumbu comes through Lukla—north through the village and then sharply downhill through cultivated fields. The first teahouses are reached within the hour at the village of Choplung. Bear right on the main trail and continue toward Namche Bazaar. The village of Ghat is notable for its soaring prayer flags and huge boulders painted with the Buddhist mantra, *Om Mani Padme Hum* (Hail to the Jewel in the Lotus), a pleasant reminder that you're not in Kansas anymore. Pass all religious structures, whether stupas, chortens, or mani walls, on the left.

From this low point at 8,500 feet (2,590 m), the trail begins to climb gradually toward Phakding at 8,700 feet (2,650 m), where the trail crosses the Dudh Kosi on a long suspension bridge. This village, approximately three hours down the trail, has lodges and a good campsite on the west side of the river and is often the first overnight stop for those starting from Lukla. Parties arriving earlier in the day may continue on to Mondzo, at 9,300 feet (2,830 m) and about 7 miles (11 km) from the airstrip. At the entrance to Sagarmatha National Park, Mondzo is crowded with lodges. Here, with a somewhat off-putting air of heavy authority, park officials and Nepalese soldiers check your trekking permit, confirm you (or your outfitter) have paid the entrance fee, and perhaps ding you for additional fees should you be carrying a video camera or other device deemed taxable.

From the entrance station, the trail climbs steeply through a dark, narrow canyon, the Dudh Kosi Gorge, before switchbacking up the big "Namche" hill to Namche Bazaar, at 11,300 feet (3,440 m). Namche Bazaar, the heart of the Sherpa universe, is a destination in itself, holding comforts and delights in ample compensation for the effort to get there. The first views of Everest, acclimatization side trips to the villages Khunde and Khumjung, or Thame, tea at the Everest View Hotel, are some of what make acclimatization days in Namche so much fun.

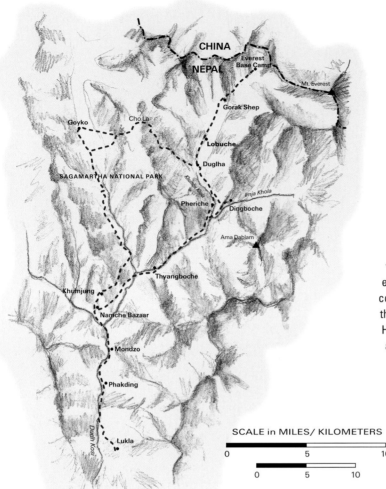

CHINA

NEPAL

Everest
Base Camp

Mt. Everest

Gorak Shep

Goyko   Cho La

Lobuche

Duglha

SAGARMATHA NATIONAL PARK

Imja Khola

Pheriche   Dingboche

Ama Dablam

Thyangboche

Khumjung

Namche Bazaar

Mondzo

Phakding

Dudh Kosi

Lukla

SCALE in MILES/ KILOMETERS

0   5   10

0   5   10

Above Thyangboche, the trek takes on a more serious feel as the route penetrates deeper into the high Himalaya. Both the villages and the landscape become more austere, and the issue of altitude becomes paramount. From Thyangboche, the stage leads to either Pheriche, in the Khumbu Khola drainage at 14,000 feet (4,270 m), or Dingboche, in the Imja Khola drainage at 14,250 feet (4,350 m). I prefer the route through Dingboche on the climb up, as the high route from Dingboche to Duglha, the following stage, is one of the trek's most stunning sections. Then, on the return trip, the route from Duglha to Pheriche is new ground and the somewhat greater creature comforts (including the Himalayan Rescue Association clinic) at Pheriche are better savored. Either route works, however, so it's a matter of personal preference. Both villages are exposed and windy, and in cold, snowy weather can seem somewhat bleak. By this point, there's no mistaking that one is high in the Himalaya. The air is thin, lassitude can sap energy, and rest days are welcomed. This is where a comfortable lodge or a good Sherpa camp staff can begin to make all the difference. A pair of ancient stupas, spooky and mystical, perched on the hill between Dingboche and Pheriche, is a moving destination for an acclimatization hike.

From Dingboche, the high route follows trails leading northwest over the hills separating Pheriche and Dingboche, and follows the ridge crest beyond the hamlet of Dusa, with unreal views of Ama Dablam and Kantega. From Pheriche, the route follows the east side of the Khumbu Khola and climbs northward to join the high route from Dingboche in approximately two hours, with good views of Cholatse and Taboche. The trail crosses a moraine before descending to the Khumbu Khola and crossing a small bridge to the primitive lodges at Duglha, just above 15,000 feet (4,570 m). The trail ascends the steep moraines of Khumbu Glacier to arrive on a ridge marked by stone monuments to climbers and Sherpas who lost their lives on or near Everest. It's a sobering place that reminds one of the harshness of these high mountains. The trail levels out as it rounds a corner to reveal the beautiful shape of Pumori before arriving at the cluster of lodges at Lobuche, at 16,150 feet (4,290 m). This rough village is a choke point on the trail; everyone has to come through Lobuche, so it can be crowded and polluted. New lodges in recent years have made this stop more appealing, but even so, most parties spend only one night despite the need to acclimate.

For some, Lobuche is the end of the road. Most trekkers make the day trip up to Gorak Shep for an ascent of Kala Pattar, the best viewpoint of Everest since Thyangboche, and one of the best vantage points available in the Khumbu. The route from Lobuche follows the valley alongside the Khumbu Glacier, but the ice is buried under sand and gravel. The way to Gorak Shep can be tricky as it ascends steep moraines and weaves between morainal features, crossing the stream of the Kangri Glacier, and then down to the primitive stone huts of Gorak Shep. Everest cannot be seen from the sandy bowl. For a view, follow one of two tracks, obvious through the sand, to the twin summits of Kala Pattar. From the top,

Above Namche Bazaar, the stage to Thyangboche is one of the highlights of the trek, as it climbs out of the protected bowl, past the police checkpoint, and runs high above the Dudh Kosi. Within an hour, stunning views of Everest and Ama Dablam open up, with the monastery at Thyangboche just visible in its low saddle far ahead. The route passes several small settlements and lodges before descending toward the village of Trashingo and the beginning of the steep down-climb to the Dudh Kosi. The trail crosses the river at 10,650 feet (3,250 m), the lowest point on the route through the upper Khumbu, and the confluence of the Dudh Kosi and the Imja Khola. (The Dudh Kosi drainages lead up to Gokyo and Cho Oyu, the Imja Khola up to Everest.) Just across the river the trail passes the water-powered prayer wheels at Phunki Tenga and begins the steep climb up to Thyangboche at 12,600 feet (3,840 m). The 2,000-foot (610 m) ascent is a famous feature of the Everest route, climbing gradually up through the forest on switchbacks before reaching a traditional arch painted in Buddhist icons, and finally the village itself, situated beside the famous monastery, a spiritual center for the Khumbu as Namche is a commercial center. Acclimatization days spent here afford time to visit the monastery, perhaps even meet the rinpoche, the head lama.

OPPOSITE: *Pheriche, the last Sherpa village on the way to Everest, has many comforts and even a clinic.* PHOTO BY PETER POTTERFIELD.

Trekkers are greeted in camp with the Sherpa's favorite beverage, sweet milk tea. PHOTO BY PETER POTTERFIELD.

Information

Guide Services

ALPINE ASCENTS INTERNATIONAL
121 Mercer Street
Seattle, WA 98109 USA
(206) 378-1927
www.alpineascents.com

MOUNTAIN TRAVEL SOBEK
1266 66th Street
Emeryville, CA 94508 USA
(510) 594-6000, 1-888-687-6235, (510) 594-6001 (fax)
www.mtsobek.com

ADVENTURE CONSULTANTS LIMITED
58 McDougall St.
P.O. Box 97
Lake Wanaka, New Zealand
64-3-443-871
www.adventure.co.nz

INTERNATIONAL MOUNTAIN GUIDES
P.O. Box 246
Ashford, WA 98304 USA
(360) 569-2609
www.mountainguides.com

Everest's north and west ridges, even the South Col, are clearly seen, but the dramatic shape of Nuptse steals the show.

A few organized treks schedule a night at base camp, but most make the journey a day hike from a camp at Gorak Shep. The trail begins north of the stone Huts, and can be difficult to find and follow. During the spring, pre-monsoon climbing season, there's usually enough traffic to point the way. If not, climb over moraines onto the Khumbu Glacier beyond the stone memorials, and follow it for 2 or 3 miles (3—5 km) to base camp. The mountain remains hidden, but the intimidating chaos of the Khumbu Icefall let's you know you've arrived.

OPPOSITE: *A yak wrangler guides his loaded beasts over the suspension bridge across the Dudh Kosi before starting the steep ascent up to Namche Bazaar.* PHOTO BY PETER POTTERFIELD.

Ironically, Mount Everest cannot be seen from Everest base camp, at approximately 18,000 feet (5,486 m) at the foot of the Khumbu Icefall. PHOTO BY CHARLES CORFIELD.

OVERLEAF: *Trekkers depart Namche Bazaar for Mount Everest, still a week away, hidden in the distance by massive Nuptse and its customary cloud cover.* PHOTO BY PETER POTTERFIELD.

ROYAL TREK
Annapurna Region
Nepal

DISTANCE: 24 miles (39 km) one-way
TIME: 4 days
PHYSICAL CHALLENGE: 1 2 **3** 4 5
PSYCHOLOGICAL CHALLENGE: 1 **2** 3 4 5
STAGING: Pokhara, Nepal

Not everyone can take two or three weeks to do one of the iconic Himalayan treks, such as the walk to Mount Everest Base Camp, but that doesn't mean there isn't a way to enjoy the intense pleasures of trekking in Nepal. Less than a week is all that's required for one of the most culturally diverse and scenic ridge walks in this Himalayan kingdom, set in the pretty foothills east of the city of Pokhara. In the course of just four days and three nights the Royal Trek reveals picturesque villages of Garung, Chetri, and Newari peoples, lush cultivated terraces and rice fields, and epic views into some of the most impressive of all Himalayan peaks, including the Annapurna Range, Machhupachhare, and even Dhaulagiri.

This short but almost unbelievably rewarding trek got its name after the Prince of Wales passed this way in December 1980. In fact, the route was specifically designed for Prince Charles and his huge entourage, and has grown popular in the decades since. But the trek has another, perhaps

LEFT: *A chorten, a religious monument, along the Royal Trek, with Annapurna South and Machhapuchhare behind.*
PHOTO BY KEITH GUNNAR.

ABOVE: *The Annapurna Range and Machhapuchhare, the "Fish Tail" peak, at dawn.*
PHOTO BY KEITH GUNNAR.

more legitimate royal connection: It follows paths once taken by Nepal's royalty as they traveled south to winter in India; King Mahendra's royal family used it as recently as 1960. Mick Jagger is among the luminaries who have walked these ridgetops.

This journey through the Nepal Midlands—the foothills between the Annapurna Range and the low-elevation jun-gles to the south—follows an off-the-beaten-track route through an area still largely untouched by the modern world. The trail contours around the Pokhara Valley's lush rim and meanders along prominent ridges through hilltop villages such as Kalikathan, Syaklung, and Chisopani. This is the other side of Nepal: Go higher in the mountains and you enter the realm of the Sherpa, but here you see the

Gurang, the Chetri, and Newari, the peoples of the foothills, whose rich Hindu culture has been little changed for centuries. Trails on this gentle side of Nepal are trod only by the local farmers and villagers going about their daily business.

Early on, as the trek unfolds, you encounter the first *chautaara*, a low wall or stone bench, constructed at just the right height to allow porters to rest their loads as they take a break. These modest structures are always built under huge pipal trees, usually paired with a banyan tree, both often more than a hundred years old. The broad leaves and spreading branches extend for 20 or 30 feet (6–10 m), offering welcome shade to travelers. Because it was under a banyan tree that Buddha attained enlightenment more than 2,000 years ago, these trees and the shaded resting spots underneath are an important spiritual element in Nepalese culture in these hills, a place where everyone walks everywhere because there are no roads. The *chautaaras* encountered along the way are just one of the glimpses into the local customs that makes this trek so much fun.

The route, though relatively short, has much to recommend it, including the fact that you are unlikely to

encounter other trekkers. You don't have to be in Nepal during the traditional pre-monsoon and post-monsoon trekking seasons, as this trek is low enough to be done fall, winter, or spring, anytime but the rainy summer. One surprising aspect I grew to relish is that there are no teahouse accommodations anywhere along the route, because there are insufficient tourists to support them. So you spend every night in a comfortable camp, under the expert care of your Sherpa staff, dining al fresco when weather permits, enjoying the fresh Himalayan mountain air, the sunsets and sunrises, and the stars at night.

OPPOSITE: *Machhapuchhare and the Annapurna Range, viewed from the ridgelines of the Royal Trek.* PHOTO BY KEITH GUNNAR.

ABOVE: *Trekkers pause at a* chautaara, *or spiritual resting place, built along the trails of the Royal Trek.* PHOTO BY PETER POTTERFIELD.

BELOW: *An eighty-year-old rice farmer pauses on the trail near his village.* PHOTO BY GORDON WILTSIE.

Perhaps the biggest advantage is that altitude presents no problems here as the highest point, at Kalikathan, is only about 6,000 feet (1,830 m) above sea level. So on this, a route sometimes called the Skyline Trek, there are no worries about blood-sat levels or cerebral edema. Instead, there is just the pleasure of walking day after day through a human-scale landscape of small villages and friendly locals, with the famous Himalaya framing the scene to the north.

Terraced rice paddies in the valley of the Madi Khola are a deep green in the wet summer months. PHOTO BY GORDON WILTSIE.

LOGISTICS & STRATEGY

Staging for the Royal Trek is best done from Pokhara, a city set in a place of real natural beauty on the shores of Phewa Lake, the largest in Nepal. The city is dominated by the blue waters of the lake, and by Machhupachhare, the famous Fish Tail Mountain, almost 23,000 feet (7,000 m) high, a peak that looms over the entire valley. Pokhara is Nepal's second-most popular destination city, attracting visitors from all over the world as well as those from neighboring countries, notably India. All this activity makes the place an unabashed tourist town, but one that is comfortable and relatively inexpensive.

Coming from Kathmandu, or returning from a trek to the Khumbu, the creature comforts of Pokhara at first seem too good to be true. Compared to the bustle, noise, and pollution of the capital city, Pokhara seems quiet, scenic, and conducive to reflection. And compared with the harsh cold and altitude of the Khumbu region, the warm, low-elevation atmosphere in this valley and its lakes seems almost tropical. The city is in constant evolution; new lodgings and restaurants open every week, so take recommendations with a grain of salt. In the mid 1980s, on my first visit, virtually the only decent hotel in town was the venerable Fish Tail Lodge, but now there are dozens. So Pokhara becomes part of the charm of the Royal Trek, an exotic yet relaxing interlude away from the madness of Kathmandu, and the perfect launch pad for a trek that reflects the laid-back character of Pokhara itself.

Part of the Royal Trek's appeal is that the usual difficulties of Himalayan trekking just don't apply. For the Everest trek, for example, just getting to the tiny airstrip at Lukla can present real difficulties, as weather often forces the Twin Otters to turn back, and the distance from Kathmandu makes it impractical to trek there. Getting to Pokhara presents few problems for air travel. And the flight from Kathmandu to Pokhara concludes with one of the most scenic moments a mountain lover could ask for: a broadside of the Nepal Himalaya, including the black pyramid of Mount Everest, seen at eye level.

Some travelers prefer to take the bus from Kathmandu to Pokhara in order to see a little of the countryside from the busy highway. I'd rather spend the five or six hours of driving time relaxing by the lakeside in Pokhara, so without question I recommend flying. And that raises another issue: To do the Royal Trek, you'll definitely want to engage the services of a trekking company. Your outfitter will likely arrange transportation from Kathmandu to Pokhara, your trekking permit, and your accommodations in Pokhara. Some trekking outfits do charter a minibus for the leg to Pokhara, a more comfortable option than the regular buses.

Backpacking the Royal Trek on your own isn't an option. Unlike the more popular routes around Annapurna or to Everest, the route followed by the Royal Trek has no teahouses or lodges to provide meals or accommodations. The lack of such infrastructure presents no problems, and in fact actually enhances the quality of the experience. Your Sherpa guides ensure you'll be comfortable and well fed, and also

The Royal Trek offers opportunity for close interaction with farm and village life. PHOTO BY GORDON WILTSIE.

that you travel with respect for the locals by observing custom and camping in the right places. Porters carry most of the gear, leaving you with only a day pack. The kitchen staff provides luxuries such as "bed tea"—your favorite beverage brought to the tent flap upon awakening. The Sherpa crew provides dining tents, tables, and chairs, as well as excellent food, allowing you to merely hike along, enjoying the view.

Many of the major trekking companies from the United States or the United Kingdom offer the Royal Trek, but this is a route than can be done just as well with some of the Nepalese trekking outfitters based both in Kathmandu or Pokhara. The Web is a good resource to find out which trekking companies get the best reviews from their customers. Make sure, too, that your operator has chosen hotels and modes of transportation in keeping with your preferences.

Although the Royal Trek remained virtually unchanged for a quarter century, economic progress in the Pokhara region has finally brought development to the area. The trek now encounters a road at two places. The route follows a unique ridgeline around the valley, the so-called skyline, so there are few variations that might be taken.

HAZARDS

So benign is the four-day Royal Trek, and free of overt dangers, that it is suitable even for children as young as twelve or so. Short of a trail accident, there isn't much that can go wrong.

SEASON

Most companies offer the Royal Trek from October to May, but the weather is driest and coolest from November through March. June through September is the monsoon season, a time of year that's too rainy to even think about trekking.

ROUTE

The first day of the trek begins from your Pokhara lodgings after breakfast. From town, it is about 3 miles (5 km) by minibus to the Bijayapur Khola, where a Nepalese army camp is located just east of the river. From here, your Sherpa staff will lead you down a broad trail that winds through the rice fields and soon crosses the river, which in summer can present a minor obstacle. Not far from the river, you pass the first of many resting places under large banyan trees called *chautaaras*. These resting places with their handy benches are built—often by the village wealthy at the suggestion of a priest—for the many porters and other walkers who ply these trails, and you'll see a dozen of them on the Royal Trek.

Across the river, the trail climbs gently onto a ridgetop through Brahmin and Chetri villages towards Kalikathan. The children along this part of the trail are particularly bold and come tearing out to see the visitors, asking for candy. A lunch stop is made at one of the villages, sometimes at a schoolhouse, depending on what time you started. The intimate insight into village life is one of the unique features that make this trek so memorable. From the lunch stop it's another hour or two of pleasant walking on mostly level ridges to the village of Kalikathan, at about 6,000 feet (1,830 m), the highest point of the entire trek. The total walking time the first day is five or six hours, and finishes on high, grassy, flat ridges. These campsites

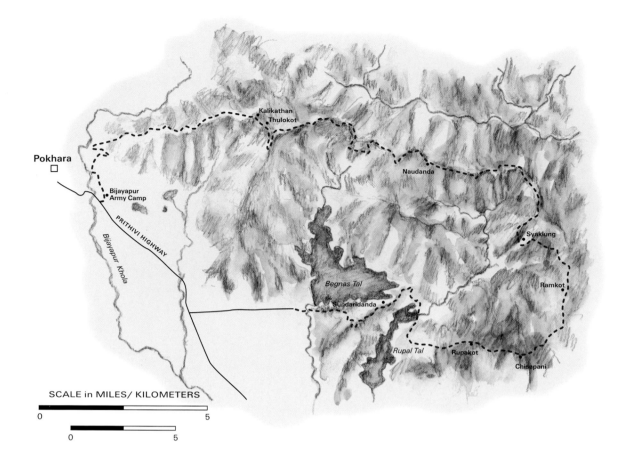

SCALE in MILES/ KILOMETERS

0   5

0   5

are extremely pleasant, bright and airy, with good views into the Himalaya. The Annapurnas utterly dominate the view to the north, but there are also good views of Machhupachhare and Lamjung Himal. If the weather is clear, the spectacular Himalayan views stretch from Dhaulagiri to the west and to Manaslu to the east, both rare 26,000-foot (8,000 m) peaks. For the effort it takes to get here, this campsite at Kalikathan rates high in terms of scenic payoff.

After breakfast served al fresco on the ridgetop at Kalikathan, the route winds through farmland, thinly forested sections, and several small villages. The route mostly stays on the broad ridge, offering occasional views north to the higher peaks in the Anna-purna Range. Southward views are dominated by a lake, Begnas Tal, in the valley on right hand side and the Nepal lowlands beyond. It's a beautiful route for trekking as the trail continues along the forested ridge through picturesque villages and farming country, mostly millet and maize fields tended by Garung farmers. The path goes through Thulokot to Mati Thana, where there are a few shops offering tea and soft drinks. The route then reaches the village Naudanda and continues along the ridge to Lipini before making the short but steep (this stretch gets your attention) climb through forest to Syaklung, at about 5,000 feet (1,520 m), with its distinctive white-and-ochre painted houses. Syaklung is famous, widely referred to simply as the Garung Village. This is one of the main areas from which Gurkha soldiers have been recruited into the British Army. Soldiers' pensions were for years the biggest source of foreign exchange in Nepal until eclipsed in the 1980s by the income from the trekking industry.

The final full day of the trip involves the greatest elevation loss, and gain, of the entire trek. From Syaklung, the Himalayan skyline continues to change in perspective as the route comes around the corner for some of the clearest views yet of Annapurna II, Lamjung Himal, and Himalchuli. The route passes through a classic

Nepalese rhododendron forest to the traditional lunch stop at Ramkot. After lunch, the trail drops steeply down the south side of the hill for almost 1,200 feet (370 m) to a spectacular banyan tree and its magnificent *chautaara,* several teashops, and a police post at Chautari. This is an important trail junction; routes lead west to Begnas Tal and east to the Marsyangdi Khola. The Royal Trek route climbs up out of the valley toward Chisopani, winding around the

back of the hill and gaining more than 1,800 feet (550 m) up to the village. A short distance above Chisopani is a high knoll and a small temple. This is Chisopani Danda, meaning Chisopani ridgetop, at 5,600 feet (1,710 m), a wonderful spot, with spectacular mountain and foothill views stretching far to the eastern horizon. The camp here has unobstructed views northward to Annapurna II, Lamjung Himal, Manaslu, and Himalchuli. Chisopani Danda is a place you want to have clear weather, as it rivals Kalikathan as the best viewpoint on the trek. If conditions are clear, look hard for a glimpse of Dhaulagiri to the west of Annapurna.

The final, half day on the trail takes you from the very scenic Chisopani Danda back to where the bus awaits to take you back to town. Follow along the gentle ridge for an hour or so, then descend quite steeply via a series of stone steps into a small valley and across a stream that feeds the lake known as Rupa Tal. Continue for a short distance through the rice field before starting back uphill. Then make a final ascent of about 600 feet (180 m) up to the ridge that separates the two large lakes in the region, Begnas Tal and Rupa Tal, on a wide path with heavy local foot traffic as the residents go about their daily business. From the ridge, descend to the road into the Begnas Bazaar, where you meet the minibus for the ride back to Pokhara.

Information

Guide Services

REI ADVENTURES
P.O. Box 1938
Sumner WA 98390 USA
(253) 437-1100, 1-800-622-2236, (253) 395-8160 (fax)
www.rei.com/adventures

SHERPA SHANGRI-LA TREKS & EXPEDITIONS
G.P.O. 6802, Kapan 03
Kathmandu, Nepal
977-1-44-90-984, 977-1-44-88-317 (fax)
www.shangrilatrek.com

MOUNTAIN TRAVEL SOBEK
1266 66th Street
Emeryville, CA 94608 USA
(510) 594-6000, 1-888-687-6235,
(510) 594-6001 (fax)
www.mtsobek.com

ABOVE: *From the villages near Syaklung, views of the Himalaya include peaks from Annapurna on the left and Lamjung Himal on the right.* PHOTO BY KEITH GUNNAR.

OPPOSITE: *Trekkers finish another alfresco meal prepared by their Sherpa camp staff.* PHOTO BY PETER POTTERFIELD.

Six

PACIFIC

KALALAU TRAIL
Na Pali Coast

Kauai, Hawaii, United States

DISTANCE: 22 miles (35 km) round-trip
TIME: 3–6 days
PHYSICAL CHALLENGE: 1 2 3 4 **5**
PSYCHOLOGICAL CHALLENGE: 1 2 3 **4** 5
STAGING: Kauai, Hawaii

The 11-mile (17.7 km) long Kalalau Trail provides the only land access to Kauai's spectacular Na Pali Coast and the hidden beaches along the way. The rugged trail, dangerously steep and eroded in places, traverses five deep, distinct valleys before ending at a final one, Kalalau. The trail contours around the heavily vegetated cliffs, or fluted ridges—*pali* in Hawaiian, hence Na Pali Coast— dropping to sea level only twice: at Hanakapi'ai Beach, a little more than 2 miles (3 km) from the trailhead, and at Kalalau Beach itself, a mile of golden sand and pounding surf at the mouth of a lush, expansive tropical valley. Here, further progress is absolutely obstructed by one magnifi-

cently sheer, fluted *pali*. But this valley and this beach are reason enough to come.

The juxtaposition of rugged coast and wild ocean is irresistible, but for a route through paradise, the Kalalau Trail exacts a high toll. This foot journey from lovely Ke'e Lagoon, at the trailhead, to the secluded valley of Kalalau cuts through the heart of the Na Pali Coast's rugged terrain. It's an intoxicating landscape but a tough walk, even an unnerving one in places. The route dates to ancient Hawaiians, who grew taro root on stone terraces constructed in the fertile valleys of the north shore. The present trail was originally built in the late 1800s for agricultural purposes, and improved slightly in the 1930s with an eye toward recreation.

Contemporary hikers might well wonder if the trail is maintained at all, given its marginal tread, or if there is some other, easier way into this unique paradise. As recently as 1996, there was: Commercial outfitters used to run people out in big rubber boats from the town of Hanalei. But with a recent ban on for-profit activity out of Hanalei Bay, if you want to see Kalalau, you've got to walk the trail.

The Kalalau Trail is a fitting route to be found on Kauai, a quirky place. This enchantingly beautiful island surprises

PRECEDING PAGE: *Kalalau Beach on the Na Pali Coast of Kauai.* PHOTO BY JAMES MARTIN.

LEFT: *An appalling number of people have died just wading at Hanakapi'ai Beach, so posted warnings there are strident.* PHOTO BY PETER POTTERFIELD.

OPPOSITE: *All the wind and water in the North Pacific bears down on the spectacular Na Pali Coast, on the north shore of Kauai.* PHOTO BY JAMES MARTIN.

The rugged, 11-mile (17.7 km) long Kalalau Trail climbs over and around the famous green palis, *or cliffs, of Kauai's north shore.*
PHOTO BY PETER POTTERFIELD..

with lethal, unexpected dangers, such as leptospirosis caused by an organism that lurks in much of the fresh water. The island harbors, too, a spirituality that is so palpable it's kind of scary, the sort of magic that can go either way. For Hawaiians both ancient and contemporary, Kauai is famous for this big medicine, called *mana* in the native tongue. The spiritual element is evident in the ancient terraces still visible in Kalalau Valley. The entire north end of the island, in fact, reverberates with a certain mysticism. The locals call that part of Kauai Ha'ena, an area famous for strong *mana*. A pair of sacred hula sites, called *heiau*, are just yards from the trailhead, and ancient legends are rooted in this very place. In one story, the goddess Pele hexed the place, and moved on to make her home on the Big Island, finding the fiery crater of Kilauea preferable to the wetness of Kauai.

The island can be gloriously sunny and beautiful, or depressingly gray and wet. The rainiest place in the world, by actual meteorological measurement, is just a few miles from Kalalau Valley, in the lush green mountains between Waimea Canyon and the north shore. The peak of Wai'ale'ale holds the record, at more than 600 inches (15 m)

in a year. That's a lot of rain, and a fact that goes a long way toward explaining the water-carved features of the ineffably beautiful Na Pali Coast. No wonder this is the land of 4,000-foot (1,200 m) waterfalls, a landscape flaunted in dozens of Hollywood films, from *Blue Hawaii* to *Jurassic Park*.

Two sharp, verdant peaks stand like sentinels at the start of the root-strewn, red-dirt trail that leads to Kalalau. Pohaku-O-Kane and Makana gather around their summits on even the hottest days a shroud of fog and mist that seems in keeping with the mystical nature of the north shore. What better place to begin a journey of discovery than this, the incomparable Ke'e Lagoon, often rated the most beautiful beach on the planet. In the first few miles, when the trail rounds the flank of the first impressive jungle-covered ridge and the canopy opens to reveal an endless expanse of blue Pacific bordered by a series of jutting headlands, you know you're in for something special. A thousand feet straight down the big surf booms and thunders, even cracks like howitzer fire as it crashes ashore. All the water in the North Pacific barrels down on this exposed north coast of Kauai, and at times the very ridges seemed to shudder underfoot with the onslaught. If you're up to the challenge, the hike to Kalalau is a sensory experience on many levels.

LOGISTICS & STRATEGY

The international airport on Kauai is at Lihue. Most hikers will fly there via Honolulu, although San Francisco and Los Angeles have direct flights to Lihue. A rental car is essential for touring the island.

The 11-mile (17.7 km) Kalalau Trail itself is on the wild north shore of Kauai, at the very end of the highway. Most of the tourist accommodations are on the south coast of the island, around Poipu, or on the busy east side, around the largest town, Kapa'a. There are places to stay and good restaurants in the north, however, clustered around Hanalei and the tony resorts at Princeville. Conditions on the south and western shores of the island are often sunnier and hotter than on the more exposed, and more frequently rainy, north shore, a fact that figures in to your travel strategy.

In fact, it doesn't really matter where you stay. No place on the island is more than a few hours from the Kalalau Trail trailhead at Ke'e Lagoon. The rangers advise that hikers not leave a car at the trailhead, but virtually everybody does just that, because there are few alternatives. You could hire a taxi, but then how would you get back? Just make sure you leave valuables and extra luggage at your hotel before leaving your car at the trailhead at Ha'ena State Park.

Hiking permits are required on the Kalalau Trail beyond Hanakapi'ai Beach, about 2 miles (3 km) from the trailhead. The permits are a big deal, and often must be obtained

OPPOSITE: *Often called the most beautiful beach in the world, Ke'e Lagoon marks the starting point for the hiking route out to Kalalau Beach.* PHOTO BY PETER POTTERFIELD.

months in advance. A maximum of five nights per visit is allowed in Na Pali State Park (all of the Kalalau Trail lies within the park), and no more than one night can be spent at either Hanakapi'ai or Hanakoa (6 miles, 9½ km from the trailhead), the only two legal camps before the end of the trail at Kalalau Beach. All the camping areas are located on shaded beaches near freshwater streams, although you can camp farther out in the open at Kalalau.

There is more to Kauai than the Kalalau Trail, but because hiking permits must be obtained in advance, most hikers won't have the luxury of adjusting their hiking schedule on arrival to suit changing whims or weather. In general, the best strategy is to do the hike early in one's visit, and then spend the rest of your time on the island recovering through well-earned self-indulgence: swimming, snorkeling, reading, and eating and drinking well.

The most efficient approach is to spend as many days at Kalalau Beach as holiday time and your permit allow. Not only does that extract the maximum enjoyment from the significant work invested getting there, but the fact is the experience evolves, mellows, and improves the longer one stays in the valley. Kalalau is a beautiful place, one that deserves some contemplation and time for savoring.

Rain is a fact of life on Kauai, particularly on the north shore. The wettest place on earth is the mountain of Wai'ale'ale, just south of Kalalau Beach, where an average of 420 inches (11 m) of rain falls annually. You can plan on getting wet, but here in the tropics it's not a serious situation. Temperatures rarely dip to 60°F (15°C), even in winter, so hypothermia is not a consideration. You *will* need to bring a tent, or at least a tarp, to stay dry while in camp.

The trail itself is an exceptionally tough one, however, contouring around steep, heavily vegetated ridges at an elevation about 1,000 feet (300 m) above the pounding surf. As you move westward, toward Kalalau, you round each ridge, contour back south in this new valley to where it steepens, then work back out to the coast, and around the next cliff. It's a convoluted route that frequently doubles back on itself. That's why kayakers can take a straighter course from Ke'e Lagoon and get to Kalalau Beach in a two or three hours (in the right conditions), while hikers will require much longer—anywhere from four or five hours for a fit hiker traveling light to a day and a half for the unsuspecting pilgrim who hasn't done the research.

Experienced and capable backcountry travelers have been surprised and humbled by this walk, so come psycho-

Ha'ena State Park

Ha'ena Beach Park

Ke'e Beach

Tunnels Beach

Hanakapi'ai

Hanakoa Valley

Hanakoa Falls

Wainiha River

Kalalau Beach

Kalalau Valley

56

SCALE in MILES/ KILOMETERS

0   3   6

0   3   6

logically prepared. The heat is debilitating. It's one thing to go snorkeling at Tunnels Beach on the north end of Kauai, quite another to hump a big load on that rough trail under a tropical sun. The best advice is to follow one of two strategies: Start early, at first light, and put as many miles behind you as possible before the day heats up. The other strategy is to go slow, and plan on spending the first night in the campground at Hanakoa, 6 miles (9½ km) in. Before leaving, confirm with rangers that the campground is open; when I was there in April 2003, it was temporarily closed.

Most hikers plan on a day in and a day out, saving the full five nights of their permit for Kalalau. But taking a couple of days to get in with a full load of food isn't a bad idea. And on the way out, I've camped at Hanakapi'ai, a mere 2 miles (3 km) from the trailhead. Most people just grind on out to go grab a Bubba Burger in Hanalei, but I just wasn't ready to leave the weird embrace of the Na Pali Coast. There are, in fact, rumors of semipermanent residents here, beach hippies living in established camps at Kalalau for months, dodging rangers, subsisting on hidden gardens of vegetables and fruits, making the occasional foray out for supplies. After a few days at Kalalau, one can understand the motivation.

HAZARDS

For a walk in paradise, the Kalalau Trails harbors a surprising array of potentially lethal realities. Fresh water is often contaminated with leptospirosis, which can invade the body via small cuts when just crossing a creek and can cause a sometimes-fatal hepatitis-like sickness. Precautions are required when swimming in fresh water, and it is necessary to treat or filter all drinking water.

The elevation gain on the route is comparable to summit day on Mount Rainier, an honest 5,000 feet (1,500 m) of work; exacerbated by tropical heat and an equatorial sun,

this exertion can lead to exhaustion and sunstroke. The heat is extreme, and frankly surprising, so protect yourself by drinking plenty of water, starting early, and stopping if you start to wilt.

The trail itself is steep and exposed in places, and during wet weather it can become treacherous. Pay attention to how you go as the trail penetrates a remote area from which assistance in a medical emergency can be had only be sending a companion for help, or by signaling a passing helicopter or boat. Don't try to cross swollen streams, which can rise quickly to dangerous levels in heavy rain. The beaches along the route are exposed to dangerous surf conditions, and an appalling number of people are killed swimming or just wading in the surf. Heed the plentiful warning signs about surf dangers, or at least the makeshift memorials to the dead hikers who didn't. Travelers to Kalalau are warned to guard against tsunamis rolling in across the Pacific, fired off by some Ring-of-Fire earthquake, but there's little to be done about that except to check in with the rangers when you get to Kalalau.

SEASON

Unlike on other Hawaiian Islands, such as Maui, winters in Kauai can be wild and wet. For that reason, most visitors come in the summer season, from May through September, when the weather, generally, is drier and more settled. April and October see fewer hikers, and permits may be slightly easier to get, but weather is more problematic. Rain is a fact of life on the north shore of Kauai, and even in summer hikers on the Kalalau can expect showers.

ROUTE

The trailhead is located literally at the end of the road, the terminus of the Kuhio Highway (HI 56), about 41 miles (66 km) and two hours from the airport at Lihue. The road ends at a parking lot near Ke'e Lagoon, a popular beach of stunning beauty and views out toward the Na Pali Coast, located in Ha'ena State Park. The trail itself is in Na Pali State Park.

From the parking lot, the trail ascends immediately into the jungle slopes of the north shore's storied cliffs. The initial section is a popular one: Day-hikers go for the views that open up within the first mile (1½ km) or so of the fluted cliffs along the coast or continue on another tough mile to the sandy beach at Hanakapi'ai for a picnic lunch. You'll be hot and sweaty when you arrive, but heed the warning signs here about swimming or even wading in the surf. If you've got the time to spare, the waterfall at the head of Hanakapi'ai Valley can be reached in about an hour via the unmaintained 2-mile (3 km) trail leading south (upstream) through deadfall and rocky terrain. A shaded camping area near the beach allows travelers to stop overnight on the way in or out of the Kalalau Valley, and there's one more open campsite farther west, higher and with a better view. Beyond Hanakapi'ai, a hiking permit from the Department of Natural Resources is required, even if you're only day-hiking.

A steep and strenuous 800-foot (240 m) climb on the switch-backing red-dirt trail takes you out of the Hanakapi'ai Valley and back up the jungle slopes to the 1000-foot (300 m) contour, where you'll stay for most of the route. You won't hit the Pacific again until Kalalau. From the ridge west of Hanakapi'ai, the trail drops down into Ho'olulu, the first of several hanging valleys. From there it's across the stream and then up and over the next cliff, 5 miles (8 km) from the trailhead, into the valley of Waiahuakua. Both these small valleys are within the boundaries of the Hono O Na Pali Natural Area Reserve, a refuge for native plants. The trail beyond Hanakapi'ai is more narrow, which is not a route-finding issue but increasingly a matter of safety the farther you go. Take care where you walk.

The next valley, Hanakoa, at 6½ miles (10 km), is much bigger. The legal camping area here is found near the Hanakoa stream crossing, and is more elaborate than the one at Hanakapi'ai, sporting a cooking shelter and an outhouse. If you're camping here, take time to explore around the campsites, built on old agricultural terraces. Hawaiians once planted taro here, and coffee plants from more recent agrarian efforts can still be found nearby. This area offers the only legal overnight camping between Hanakapi'ai Beach and Kalalau Beach, and gets heavy use by hikers who expected to make Kalalau in one day but found themselves caught short by heat and fatigue. There is no beach here: Hanakoa is a classic hanging valley. The stream flows not across the beach but pours over sheer cliffs at the ocean's edge. A rough, poorly marked (and even dangerous) ½-mile (1 km) trail leads up the east fork of the stream to a spectacular view of Hanakoa Falls.

The trail climbs steeply out of Hanakoa Valley to the top of the next *pali* and one of the best viewpoints so far. From there you descend into more arid, open terrain. The trail contours along the coast well above the ocean, with precious little shade. The intense heat from the afternoon tropical sun can be wilting on this rough trail, so take care to stay hydrated. Backpacking in this kind of tropical heat was a new experience for me.

On the final ridges before Kalalau, exposed sections of trail feature attention-getting drop-offs. The route here, just where you are most fatigued, demands extreme care, particularly in wet weather when conditions can be patently dangerous. Hikers have been known to crawl on all fours over the steepest cliff crossings. From a ridge called Red Hill, tantalizing views of Kalalau Valley's fluted cliffs and the beach open up below, offering the promise of reward to wasted hikers who have come from Ke'e Lagoon in a single day.

Finally, just beyond mile 10 (km 16), the trail crosses Kalalau Stream and ends a mile (1½ km) later at the camping area just behind the idyllic strand of Kalalau Beach. A ranger station at the west end may or may not have a ranger in residence. A small waterfall flows down the cliff near the camping area. Camping in Kalalau is allowed in tent sites along the sandy beach, or farther back where some sites are shaded beneath the trees. A nearby meadow has several campsites as well. In high summer, sea caves just beyond the waterfall become popular natural camping shelters, but be careful: Winter surf frequently crashes into these caves, so check with the rangers before moving in.

The trail to the head of the valley is much better here than in the previous valleys, and an easy 2-mile (3 km) hike upstream leads to a pleasant pool. This is a big valley, one that offers days' worth of roaming. Exploration reveals not just remnants of agricultural terraces formerly planted with the staple crops of early Hawaiians but hidden groves of fruit trees such as guava and mango, rumored to provide a supplemental food supply for those who wish to extend their stay beyond the legal five days.

Swim in the Pacific only if surf conditions are benign, as you are in the middle of the ocean out here on the north shore. Take some time to recover from the hike in: Stroll along the strand, admire the sunlight on the towering green *palis*, explore the upper valley, and get to know your fellow hikers—there are likely to be some characters. A good spectator sport is to watch the kayakers try to paddle through the surf. No matter how you pass the time, your days at remote and hidden Kalalau Beach will be memorable, as will the hike out.

Information

DEPARTMENT OF LAND & NATURAL RESOURCES
DIVISION OF STATE PARKS
3060 Eiwa Street, Room 306
Lihue, Kauai, HI 96766 USA
(808) 274-3444
www.state.hi.us/dlnr/dsp/kauai.html

Na Pali State Park allows camping in only two places between Ke'e Beach and Kalalau Beach: Hanakoa Valley and Hanakapi'ai Beach.
PHOTO BY PETER POTTERFIELD.

ROUTEBURN TRACK
Mount Aspiring and Fiordland National Parks

South Island, New Zealand

DISTANCE: 28 miles (45 km)
TIME: 3–4 days
PHYSICAL CHALLENGE: 1 **2** 3 4 5
PSYCHOLOGICAL CHALLENGE: 1 **2** 3 4 5
STAGING: Queenstown or Te Anau, South Island, New Zealand

As we crossed the narrow, swaying suspension bridge at the end of three days on the Routeburn Track, I shared a novel moment with companions from three different countries. Realizing the end to an astounding backcountry excursion was near, we stopped to look at each other with a single, simultaneous impulse: to turn right around and do the whole thing again the other way.

The Routeburn Track is like that, a hike of rich variety and complex beauty that whets the appetite for more. This historic alpine route penetrates the glacier-carved landscapes of New Zealand's Southern Alps—rain forests, high basins, and mountain peaks. From classic U-shaped glacial valleys to snowy passes, the Routeburn traverses strikingly diverse mountain terrain while delivering botanical surprise,

exotic bird song, and scenic payoff on a big scale. I'd have to say the experience here surpasses that of even its superstar sibling, the neighboring Milford Track.

Slightly shorter than the Milford, and much less popular, the 28-mile (45 km) Routeburn Track connects Mount Aspiring and Fiordland National Parks on New Zealand's South Island via a high pass called Harris Saddle. The route is a venerable one steeped in local tradition. Nineteenth-century European settlers used the track to connect settlements on the Greenstone River with budding commercial centers on Lake Wakatipu. Long before that, as early as

The beech forest below Lake Mackenzie is a magical place for hikers. PHOTO BY PETER POTTERFIELD.

1500, the Maori used the track to reach the Dart River drainage and its treasure of jade—the precious greenstone, or *pounamu*.

While the route has been plied for centuries, today's track offers a different sort of treasure. By connecting a series of radically different eco-zones, the track covers an almost unbelievable assortment of natural wonders, given the three or four days it takes to complete. An ancient, tranquil grove of ribbonwood trees called the Orchard, with the feel of cultivated acreage among the surrounding wildness, gives way to the high-decibel wonder of Earland Falls. Earland's roaring torrent descends in streaming cascades and drifted spray as it drains Roberts Lake, 265 feet (80 m) above. Ocean Peak Corner, a highlight of the second day, is the start of the long grinding traverse up the Hollyford Face. From here you get a view all the way down valley to Martin's Bay on the Tasman Sea.

From the high vantage of the flat mountaintop known as Key Summit, the peaks of Mount Aspiring National Park surround an open meadow set high on a rare triple continental divide. Three epic valleys—the Hollyford, the Eglington, and the Greenstone—drain into the Tasman Sea (west), the Foveaux Strait on the Southern Ocean (south), and the South Pacific Ocean (east), respectively. The landscape is astonishing, spiced with views into the Darran Range, where Hillary trained for Everest.

The sum of these parts renders the Routeburn memorable, but the allure is sharpened by the oddness of the flora and fauna, left here way down under to evolve on its own. This is home to the Kea, an alpine parrot prone to comic behavior, swooping overhead, making a racket, hoping for a handout at lunch stops. At Lake Mackenzie, set in a hanging valley surrounded by granite boulders the size of buildings, dawn is heralded by the haunting chorus of the New Zealand bellbird, backed up by the tomtit, coming from somewhere in the weird dragon-leaf shrub.

The route in places reminded me of the rain forests of the Pacific Northwest, rising through an ancient forest draped in moss—except here the stuff in the trees is wispy goblin moss and the trees are twisted silver beech and red beech, not Douglas fir. Those flowers include the world's largest fuchsia, the *kotukutuku*, and Mount Cook lilies, the big buttercups you see on the Hollyford Face, the biggest on Earth. Things down here look slightly familiar but, on closer inspection, unmistakably are not, so the overall effect is to give the landscape a cockeyed look, as if one landed on a planet a lot like Earth, only different.

This wilderness is even more appealing because in New Zealand the seasons are reversed. One can go hiking—they call it tramping down here—in the dead of a Northern Hemisphere winter, an appropriately twisted schedule for a place so full of surprises. When you fill out the landing card on arrival, for instance, you find out that "dangerous goods" include your tramping boots and tent stakes. Weaponry is not the issue, but potential contamination. Microorganisms

The cascade of Earland Falls drains Roberts Lake, an impressive 265 feet (81 m) above. PHOTO BY PETER POTTERFIELD.

carried here from other continents on a Vibram sole could wreak environmental havoc on this remote island country. So declare yourself on arrival and brace for a good going over. It's well worth the trouble. One of the best reasons for doing the Routeburn is that it's a great excuse to come down to this engaging island country where a sense of light-hearted fun and self-indulgence prevails right through to the wilderness.

LOGISTICS & STRATEGY

International hikers arrive in New Zealand via Auckland, the capitol and largest city in this island nation of reserved but affable Kiwis. Affectionately known as The Big Smoke, this cosmopolitan city on the North Island is a worldly and entertaining place, well suited for a day or two of easy living while working through the major-league jet lag acquired on the way.

ABOVE: *A foot bridge crosses the green waters of the Routeburn, where the Maori once searched for prized nephrite jade.* PHOTO BY PETER POTTERFIELD.

OPPOSITE: *The track descends from the Humboldt Mountains down to Routeburn Flats as it travels toward its conclusion at the Dart River.* PHOTO BY PETER POTTERFIELD.

The Routeburn Track is on the wilder and more sparsely populated South Island, home to Mount Cook, the highest peak in the country, as well as the most famous of all New Zealand backcountry routes, the Milford Track. A two-hour flight from Auckland takes you to Queenstown, a small but humming city nestled by the shore of Lake Wakatipu, in the very shadow of a range of mountains called the Remarkables ("the Remarx" to the locals). Remember those fairy-tale mountains you saw in *Lord of the Rings*? Those were the Remarx.

Queenstown is the hub for outdoor activity on the South Island, where quirky pastimes like jet boating and bungee jumping were invented, but where the mountains still hold sway for recreational dominance. Think of the place as the Jackson Hole or Chamonix of New Zealand, a city so perfectly in tune with its role and its setting *Condé Nast Traveler* rates it among the top ten cites in the world. Whether

you're looking for a gas canister for the stove, a guide service, or a helicopter lift into the Darran Range, you'll find it all within a block or two. Queenstown's popularity with foreign visitors means there's food and lodging across the range of possibilities.

The Routeburn Track is one of nine New Zealand hiking routes collectively deemed the Great Walks by the country's Department of Conservation. Six are found on the South Island, and three are best staged from around Queenstown. The Routeburn Track is one of these, although where you start depends on the style in which you want to do this long, high traverse.

Like most of the major hiking routes in New Zealand, the Routeburn Track boasts a series of huts placed at strategic intervals. These simple but comfortable structures are equipped with gas stoves for cooking (some have coal-fired stoves for heat) and bunkrooms for sleeping. The huts make carrying tents or stoves unnecessary, so the Routeburn becomes an opportunity for go-light hiking. There's another benefit: When coming from North America, Europe, or some other distant place, there is that much less backcountry gear to bring. For those who simply must sleep in a tent to feel like a wilderness traveler, no worries, that's permitted—although just where you can pitch your tent is carefully regulated by the Department of Conservation.

In New Zealand, a civilized country, some of the premier tramping routes have yet another option, the guided hike, in which a concessionaire offers trailhead transportation, guides, meals, and enhanced accommodations. The low-key guides, who know the route well, do the cooking and interpret flora and fauna. On some routes, such as the Routeburn Track, guided clients stay in more comfortable lodges equipped with hot showers. The hiking itself is much the same as going alone: You can walk by yourself, if that's your preference, or stick closer to the guides for commentary on wildlife and terrain, and exposure to wry Kiwi humor. When coming from afar, the guided-hike option makes sense. Because packs and sleeping bags are provided, clients need bring only personal gear such as boots and clothing. The guides are knowledgeable, the lodgings extremely comfortable, and the meals appetizing.

For entirely different reasons, the guided option served me well in 2002 when I pushed my luck too far while indulging my preference for off-season hiking. I attempted the route much too early, before Halloween. After two days, we arrived at a snowbound Harris Saddle, the high point of the route, only to find avalanche conditions blocked the way. (The danger was obvious: Even if the potential slides were unlikely to be big enough to bury you, they would still push you off the cliff and kill you even so.) Had I been on my own, there would have been no option save turning around and going down. But since I was on a guided hike the situation became a mere delay. Glenn, the guide, simply got on the radio and summoned a helicopter from Queenstown. In short order a Hughes 500 appeared under the low-lying cloud and ferried the five of us a few hundred yards past the avalanche slope, where we continued on. New Zealand is full of fun surprises.

The Routeburn can be traveled in either direction. If hiking on your own, departure for a south-to-north hike is best staged from the small, mellow village of Te Anau, a three-hour drive or bus ride from Queenstown. From Te Anau, trailhead transportation runs on a regular daily schedule, and most hotels and lodgings happily store your luggage. For those who decide on the guided hike, the trip stages in Queenstown, and starts with a van ride to the trailhead, with a stop for tea in Te Anau.

Because the Routeburn is essentially a high traverse connecting two valleys by a high pass, there are no real variations or route options once on the track, with the exception of a couple of short side trips. You can, however, make the route longer, a good thing. Add approximately 18 miles (29 km) and two days to the trek by doing the Greenstone Track first. This route, essentially a long walk down the valley of the Greenstone River, starts on the west shore of Lake Wakatipu and joins the Routeburn Track at Lake Howden. I highly recommend this variation. While the Greenstone is not as alpine or as aggressively scenic as the Routeburn itself, it allows for more time in the national parks, and for a psychological acclimatization that enhances the Routeburn experience. Both guided and non-guided hikes of the combined routes are best staged from Queenstown.

HAZARDS

Weather in the mountains of the South Island can be cold and wet any time of year, so come prepared—cheating on your storm gear for the upper Hollyford Face can mean a fast trip to hypothermia. Besides unpredictable weather, and the usual perils of hiking, there are few significant or unusual dangers on the track, or anywhere in New Zealand. In fact, with no snakes or man-eating predators, the Routeburn is as benign and forgiving as any backcountry route in this book.

SEASON

The usual season is mid-November to mid-March, and that's when most people chose to do it. But the Routeburn can be tramped most any time of year—as long as snow has not closed the route through Harris Saddle—so adding a month to either end of the traditional season is not foolhardy. I hiked the route before Halloween during a particularly cold austral spring and got stopped, but most years the route is passable by then.

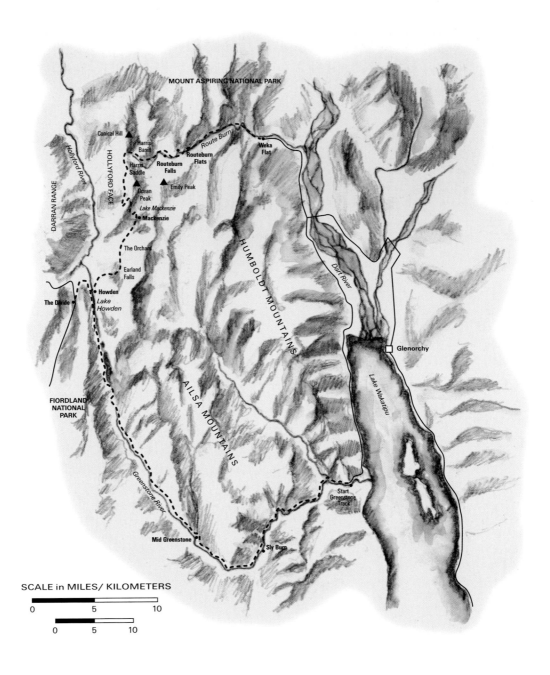

SCALE in MILES/ KILOMETERS

0   5   10

0   5   10

ROUTE

The trailhead for the Routeburn Track is located at "the Divide" on New Zealand 94 (the Milford Sound Highway), approximately four hours from Queenstown and one hour from Te Anau. A parking lot and restroom facility beside the highway mark the start of the wide, rocky track as it ascends through a silver-beech rain forest heavily hung with moss and fern. The track gains elevation from the start, reaching within an hour the turnoff for Key Summit, an hour-long side trip up to the view from a 3,000-foot (900 m) plateau. The route then descends to Lake Howden (and the Department of Conservation hut) at 2,250 feet (680 m), and the junction with the Greenstone Track, before climbing again for two hours to the base of spectacular 250-foot (75 m) Earland Falls at 3,200 feet (970 m). The trail continues traversing along the flank of the Ailsa Mountains above the Hollyford River, with the first views to the Darran Range. The trail passes through a picturesque grove of ribbonwood trees known as the Orchard and, a little later, another magical forest of silver beech before arriving in the hanging valley that holds Lake Mackenzie (and the lodges) at 2,700 feet (820 m), 8 miles (13 km) from the trailhead. In clear weather, 6,000-foot (1,830 m) Emily Peak reflects in Lake Mackenzie, which is surrounded by huge granite boulders and thick stands of emerald green dragon-leaf shrubs.

Day two, and the Routeburn leaves the side valley of Lake Mackenzie via steep switchbacks through a wildflower garden to Ocean Peak Corner, an unforgettable landmark where the route begins a long, ascending traverse up the Hollyford Face. Views open up to Key Summit and the Darran Range all the way to Lake McKerow, even a glimpse way down the Hollyford Valley to Martin's Bay on the Tasman Sea. A long, gradually ascending traverse leads up toward Harris Saddle. This exposed section can be glorious on a fine day but treacherous on a snowy, stormy one. Two hours or so on the Hollyford Face ends with a short, steep section leading to the emergency shelter at Harris Saddle (4,200 feet, 1,280 m), a welcome place in bad weather. From the small summit hut, a strenuous but popular side trip leads to Conical Hill, at nearly 5,000 feet (1,520 m) the high point on the route but a problematic summit given the fickle nature of New Zealand weather. From Harris Saddle, the Routeburn continues beyond Lake Harris before descending into the headwaters of the Routeburn Valley and into Mount Aspiring National Park. The track passes through a series of high and wild basins of tussock grass and snow daisies, ringed by waterfalls pouring off nearby mountains. This area below Harris Saddle can be a highlight of the trip regardless of conditions. From the high basins, the track quickly drops down to Routeburn Falls, a complex series of dramatic waterfalls. Just below the falls are the hikers' lodges, at 3,300 feet (1,000 m), 10 miles (16 km) from Lake Mackenzie.

On the final day of the Routeburn the trail drops steeply down from the falls through a pleasant, even stately mixed beech forest, crossing the path of a huge landslide that closed the track for months in 1994. The track reaches the wide expanse of Routeburn Flats, and another Department of Conservation hut, within two hours. From the flats, the Routeburn finishes with a flourish. The track enters a gorge that features surging whitewater and beautiful clear pools of jade green water. Ferns hang in lush bunches from the sidewalls as the trail meanders down beside the river until the flow vanishes into a chaos of rock and deadfall known as The Sump. The final 4 miles (6 km) of the track follow an ever-widening valley floor as the Routeburn flows toward the Dart River. The trail crosses the Routeburn River a final time on a long suspension bridge before reaching the car park at the Dart River trailhead, 10 miles (16 km) from the lodge at Routeburn Falls, and 28 miles (45 km) from the Divide. Wait here for the bus back to Te Anan or your car; guided parties are picked up in a private van.

Information

Huts and Permits

DEPARTMENT OF CONSERVATION
Great Walks in New Zealand
www.doc.govt.nz/Explore/002~Tracks-and-Walks/Great-Walks/index.asp

QUEENSTOWN DISTRICT DOC
37 Shotover St.
Queenstown, New Zealand
64-3-442-7933, 64-3-442-7932 (fax)

Serene Lake Mackenzie nestles in the Ailsa Mountains, where the calls of bellbird and tomtit emanate from the weird dragon leaf shrubs. PHOTO BY PETER POTTERFIELD.

Guide Services

ROUTEBURN WALK LTD.
P.O. Box 568
Queenstown, New Zealand
64-3-442-8200
www.routeburn.co.nz
www.ultimatehikes.co.nz/Routeburn_Track

New Zealand Tourism

www.purenz.com
www.travelplanner.co.nz

Seven

ANTARCTIC REGION

SHACKLETON CROSSING
South Georgia Island

South Atlantic Ocean

DISTANCE: 28 miles (45 km), King Haakon Bay to Stromness
TIME: 3–5 days for the crossing, 20 days for the sea voyage
PHYSICAL CHALLENGE: 1 2 **3** 4 5
PSYCHOLOGICAL CHALLENGE: 1 2 3 **4** 5
STAGING: Ushuaia, Tierra del Fuego, Argentina

At age ten, I first read Alfred Lansing's *Endurance,* the first modern narrative recounting Ernest Shackleton's epic voyage. The agonizing, uplifting truths of that story resonated with me like nothing else: The men of the ship *Endurance* became for all practical purposes dead men as they struggled to survive after their ship was trapped, then crushed by ice in the Weddell Sea. The *Endurance* finally sank in 1915, her men left adrift on a frozen sea for 18 months. Eventually, the party was marooned on a bleak, uninhabited island. To find help, Shackleton and five of his men set out on a heroic 16-day voyage of more than 800 miles (1,300 km) in a 22-foot (7 m) open boat. Thanks to brilliant navigation by Frank Worsley, Shackleton and the others at last reached South Georgia Island, a 100-mile-long (30 km) chain of unexplored, glacier-draped mountains rising over 9,000 feet (2,750 m) from the sea. But they landed on the wrong side, so three of the party had to cross the completely unmapped ranges of South Georgia's interior to reach help at a Norwegian whaling station on the opposite coast.

That historic, 28-mile (45 km) crossing has become a new but already classic adventure, an outrageously exotic one, of alpine travel. With modern equipment and by now at least some knowledge of the terrain, repeating Shackleton's route across South Georgia has become one of the most sought-after of modern day wilderness trips. Much of the appeal is its location in a place of unparalleled beauty and solitude, far from the madding crowd of mainstream adventure travelers. The crossing is no more physically challenging than many other four-day winter ski or snowshoe adventures, but it takes some real doing just to get there.

Because South Georgia Island is located in Antarctic waters, this is not the sort of outing one can do on the spur of the moment, or on one's own. But it can be done. Adventure travel companies have for decades offered birdwatchers, photographers, and other extreme travelers excursions to various destinations in Antarctica. South Georgia, with its King Penguin rookeries and abundant wildlife, long has been a routine stop on the journey "to the ice." But with the recent outpouring of books, documentaries, and feature

PRECEDING PAGE: *Trident Ridge, South Georgia Island.* PHOTO BY PETER POTTERFIELD.

LEFT: *The wildlife on South Georgia Island, including these King penguins, has no fear of human visitors.* PHOTO BY PETER POTTERFIELD.

OPPOSITE: *Just getting to South Georgia can be treacherous. Here, the Russian trawler Grigiory Mikheev carefully enters Drygalski Fjord.* PHOTO BY PETER POTTERFIELD.

films about Shackleton's incredible journey of survival, some companies have created new itineraries to allow for a crossing of the remote island.

The trip's growing popularity is easy to figure: You get to see penguins, whales, seals, albatrosses, icebergs, and other sights of the Antarctic, yet take time out in the middle of the trip for an exhilarating five-day alpine traverse of a pristine mountain landscape. The historic nature of the trip is a hugely appealing element. Many of those who attempt the crossing are long-term Shackleton admirers, drawn here almost helplessly, ecstatic to be able to walk a mile in his shoes. All crossings are made with the mother ship on standby, ready to retrieve the party in the event of trouble, a necessary precaution but one that makes the adventure reasonable despite its extreme remoteness.

I'll never forget the day I arrived at Stromness, the whaling station where Shackleton himself eventually reached safety, after completing his route. It was a moving moment, a surprisingly emotional one. One member of our party, a New Zealand Shackleton scholar, was moved to tears. There was little back-slapping, and few high fives. There was quiet celebration, but not of our own achievement—we were mere recreationists in search of adventure—but of Shackleton's. His incredible journey was made not for sport, but because his life and the lives of 27 crewmen depended on his arriving here safely. Shack did it because he had to, we did it for fun, and, oh, did we know the difference.

The whaling stations on the island are by now rusting ruins, but add historical interest. At the largest one, Grytviken, a British sailor named Tim Carr has almost single-handedly restored the church and several other buildings. When our ship called there, I took the time to have a look around and found myself alone among the abandoned buildings. Out past the church in which Shackleton's funeral was held, and out past the former dormitories and the rusting remains of the whaling factory, I saw what I was looking for: a small plot on the far side of the settlement surrounded by a white fence. This is the local cemetery, the place where those whalers unfortunate enough to die so far from home were put to rest.

Among the dozen or so gravestones is one that's higher and more ornate than the others. The upright granite block

marks the site of Shackleton's grave, and carved into the polished stone are these words:

> I HOLD THAT A MAN SHOULD STRIVE TO THE UTTERMOST FOR HIS LIFE'S SET PRIZE.

The lines are from Robert Browning, who was a favorite of Shackleton's, and they seem appropriately spare yet reflective of the drive that Shackleton brought to his explorations, one that mirrors a drive that even today brings adventuring souls to this wild and lonely place.

LOGISTICS & STRATEGY

To undertake a Shackleton Crossing as a private party would necessitate hiring one's own vessel to distant South Georgia Island, an enterprise prohibitively expensive for most of us. So those who want to attempt this historic crossing sign up for one of the few guided trips organized by a handful of Antarctic adventure-travel companies. Chartering ships suitable for the stormy Southern Ocean, these companies also provide professional mountaineering guides to lead the way on the crossing attempts.

Much of the Antarctic adventure-cruising industry uses Ushuaia, Argentina, as its base. Afternoon flights to Ushuaia from Buenos Aires make it possible to fly direct from North America without an overnight stop in Buenos Aires. You will need to transfer from the international terminal at Ezeiza to the domestic airport at Aeroparque, about an hour by cab or bus. Tiera del Fuego's Ushuaia is a pleasant if rough small city with a spectacular setting, squeezed between the mountains and the Beagle Channel. Like a lot of end-of-the-line towns, Ushuaia has an end-of-the-earth feel. It is a place accustomed to hosting a large number of international visitors as they come and go to and from Antarctica. Comfortable hotels and exceptional restaurants are easily found, as well as opportunities to buy any outdoor gear you might have forgotten. You definitely don't want to miss your boat to the Southern Ocean, so a good strategy is to plan on arriving the day before your ship departs and use that extra time to explore Ushuaia, maybe take a hike in the nearby mountains to shake off the jet lag.

Big icebreakers, formerly of the Soviet navy, are the flagships of Antarctic cruising, but the voyage to South Georgia is usually made on much smaller ships. A dozen of these former Soviet "research" ships—some would say spy ships—have been converted in recent years for cruising between the southern tip of South America and Antarctica. Just over 200 feet (60 m) in length, these Finnish-built trawlers have ice-hardened hulls well suited to the stormy conditions in the Southern Ocean, and their Russian crews have long experience in this extreme environment. Typically, Russian crews operate the vessel while European "hotel staff" take care of

Working up toward the crest of Trident Ridge, the high point on the Shackleton Crossing. PHOTO BY PETER POTTERFIELD.

the passenger side of things, such as the dining room, the bar, accommodations, and laundry.

The vessels are comfortable, but not luxurious, and accommodate about 30 passengers. Most of the tour companies offering trips to South Georgia are experienced and reliable, but you should check them out thoroughly. The best advice is to pay attention to the quality of the ship, the crew, the experience of the mountaineering guides, the on-board physician—as well as the food and the accommodations. For two weeks, your enjoyment and safety will depend absolutely on the people who run the ship and guide the crossing.

About three weeks is typical for a Shack Crossing party, allowing for the voyage from Ushuaia to South Georgia and back again and approximately five to six days on the island. All the food and gear required on the crossing is carried by each party member in a pack, or in a small plastic sled pulled behind, and carrying food and fuel for much more than that becomes impractical. The voyage from Ushuaia to South Georgia requires four to six days each way, depending on sea conditions, which typically are startlingly rough. I've seen seasoned Himalayan climbers reduced to quivering fear by the scary storms of the Southern Ocean.

On arrival at South Georgia, the ship drops off the crossing party. While the crossing party attempts to follow Shackleton's route across the island, those who remain on board (often birdwatchers and photographers) continue to tour the island. The crossing party stays in radio contact with the ship and arranges a final rendezvous for the pick-up when its members reach the end of the route, or become stranded somewhere else.

Shackleton landed in King Haakon Bay at the end of his heroic voyage in 1916, and that's where modern crossing parties are dropped off. This dangerous bay on the island's stormy south side is full of rocks and shoals that present grave hazard to the ship. My experience was fairly typical. The crew carefully guided the ship into the bay and quickly off-loaded the crossing party via Zodiac boat before steaming immediately to the safety of open water. Crossing parties usually begin at the site of Shackleton's Peggoty Camp (so named because the shipwrecked men lived under their overturned boat, as did the Dickens character). The crossing party must then travel a mile or so down the beach to a point where they can start up toward Shackleton Gap. From there the route climbs to Trident Ridge, then down to the Crean Glacier, then along the length of the Crean up to the rock feature Shackleton called the Great Nunatak. From there the route traverses the huge Fortuna Glacier down to Fortuna Bay. From the shore of the bay, it's only a half day's travel to Stromness, the whaling station where Shackleton and his men eventually reached safety.

From King Haakon Bay to Stromness, the Shackleton Crossing covers approximately 28 miles (45 km) of pristine

Pinned down for two nights by foul weather, the crossing party shares a meal on the upper Crean Glacier. PHOTO BY PETER POTTERFIELD.

and ineffably beautiful alpine terrain. Most of the travel is on snow slopes and glaciers, but there is a short section of coastal plain on the final walk in to Stromness. As alpine traverses go, the "Shack Crossing," as it has become known, is not serious in terms of technical difficulty. The high points of the trip—the passes in Trident Ridge—are less than 4,000 feet (1,200 m). The route can be covered wearing snowshoes, or on Nordic or alpine touring skis with skins. (I never took my skins off, as there is no downhill skiing on the route unless one seeks it out.) Glacier travel is required, so the party will rope up in places, although the actual risk of going in a crevasse is low. The chief requirement for those who wish to do the crossing is a good level of fitness and snow camping experience. The chief difficulty is weather, and that can be a major problem.

The violent weather is what makes this outing a potentially dangerous one. South Georgia Island sees some of the lowest atmospheric pressure in the world, and as a consequence, some of the worst weather. All the wind and water in the Pacific are squeezed between Cape Horn and the Antarctic Peninsula to create a Venturi effect that blasts South Georgia. Seas so high they crash over the bridge of the ship are not at all uncommon, nor are 70-mile-per-hour (110 kph) winds and gale-driven snowstorms. Weather can definitely foil a crossing attempt, and indeed, at least two parties that recently tried never made it off the beach at King Haakon Bay.

While crossing parties camp in mountaineering tents, the real shelter comes in the form of the ship. That's why the Shackelton Crossing is only attempted by parties whose ships remain nearby (rather than sailing off to the Antarctic Peninsula, say, to return later). The ship must stay close because it is the crossing party's lifeline. In the short history of modern Shack Crossing attempts, at least three parties have been retrieved from some stormy South Georgia beach

RIGHT: *Waiting out bad weather can become an essential skill for the crossing party.* PHOTO BY PETER POTTERFIELD.

OPPOSITE: *Shackleton and his men reached safety at the whaling station at Stromness. This ruin, which retains an aura of death, marks the end of the trek.* PHOTO BY PETER POTTERFIELD.

Members of the crossing party at Fortuna Bay, just half a day away from the conclusion of the route at Stromness. PHOTO BY PETER POTTERFIELD.

well short of Stromness. Given a fit party with competent guides, the weather is the single factor that will determine success or failure of any crossing attempt.

Part of the fun of attempting the Shack Crossing is what comes when you're back on board: a tour of South Georgia Island. There is much to see here, notably the King Penguin rookeries at Gold Harbor and Salisbury Plain, places where several hundred thousand animals, including penguins and elephant and fur seals, live in total and noisy harmony (or disharmony) with no help, or interference, from man. The ship will make several stops a day to visit penguin rookeries, historical sites (such as the abandoned whaling stations), and dramatic geographic features (such as Drygalski Fjord). While the ship was underway, I never tired of watching the big Wandering Albatrosses soar and dive behind the stern, or the icebergs float by.

HAZARDS

While the usual dangers of alpine travel are present on this outing, the sheer remoteness of South Georgia Island is the principle hazard. There is no government, no agency, no helicopter—no resource at all one can turn to in times of trouble. The handful of British marines stationed on the island reminded our party, "If you get into trouble, there's nothing we can do for you." The region is so remote that there is no hope of outside rescue in the event of injury or medical emergency. For that reason, it is imperative you be a competent wilderness traveler before starting out, that you go with skilled guides, and that the ship on which you go has a crew experienced in the waters around South Georgia.

SEASON

The Antarctic summer is short, mid-November to early February, but at the end of the season the big glaciers on South Georgia begin to break up and present problems. Most attempts at the Shackleton Crossing are made in December.

ROUTE

Most parties will land on the beach at King Haakon Bay and immediately set out on the 28-mile (45 km) crossing, as weather at King Haakon seems to be consistently bad. From the beach the route ascends toward a low saddle, called Shackleton Gap, that separates King Haakon Bay from Possession Bay, a potential bail-out point for parties caught in stormy weather. The route doesn't quite reach Shackleton Gap, however, instead turning southeast to work up the Murray Snowfield. The Murray Snowfield rises to a high point, approximately 3,500 feet (1,070 m), at Trident Ridge—this is the famous ridge described by Shackleton as being like the fingers on a hand: rocky pinnacles with passes in between. Most parties camp on the Murray Snowfield before crossing Trident Ridge, about 8 miles (12.8 km) from King Haakon Bay.

Shackleton writes that he and his men crossed Trident Ridge via the col on the far left; my party crossed uneventfully over the col third from the left, the lowest of the four, and by far the easiest. At the pass, there's a stunning view up the length of the Crean Glacier, with Antarctic Bay and the Southern Ocean beyond. We plunged down approximately 1,000 feet (300 m) to the Crean Glacier, and fought our way up the glacier along Antarctic Bay in ferocious down-slope winds of more than 50 miles per hour (80 kph). Some in our party were blown right off their feet before we managed to climb out of the big winds spilling into Antarctic Bay by pro-